DIMITY CONVICTIONS

DIMITY CONVICTIONS

The American Woman

in the

Nineteenth Century

BARBARA WELTER

OHIO UNIVERSITY PRESS: ATHENS: 1976

What soft cherubic creatures
These gentlewomen are.
One would as soon assault a plush
Or violate a star.

Such dimity convictions,
A horror so refined
Of freckled human nature,
Of deity ashamed—

It's such a common glory
A fisherman's degree.
Redemption, brittle lady,
Be so ashamed of thee.

Emily Dickinson

To Merle Curti

ACKNOWLEDGEMENTS

A number of these essays originally appeared as follows: "The Cult of True Womanhood" (*American Quarterly*, 1966); "Anti-Intellectualism and the American Woman" (*Mid-America*, 1967); "Coming of Age in America: The American Girl in the 19th Century" (*Journal of Marriage and the Family*, 1969); "The Merchant's Daughter: A Tale from Life" (*New England Quarterly*, 1970); "Female Complaints" (Journal of the History of Medicine, 1970); "The Feminization of American Religion" (*Insights and Parallels*, ed., William O'Neill: Burgess, 1973).

CONTENTS

1   COMING OF AGE IN AMERICA: *The American Girl in the Nineteenth Century*   3

2   THE CULT OF TRUE WOMANHOOD: *1800-1860*   21

3   THE MERCHANT'S DAUGHTER: *A Tale from Life*   42

4   FEMALE COMPLAINTS: *Medical Views of American Women*   57

5   ANTI-INTELLECTUALISM AND THE AMERICAN WOMAN   71

6   THE FEMINIZATION OF AMERICAN RELIGION: *1800-1860*   83

7   DEFENDERS OF THE FAITH: *Women Novelists of Religious Controversy in the Nineteenth Century*   103

8   MURDER MOST GENTEEL: *The Mystery Novels of Anna Katharine Green*   130

9   MYSTICAL FEMINIST: *Margaret Fuller, a Woman of the Nineteenth Century*   145

    Notes and References   199

DIMITY CONVICTIONS

1

COMING OF AGE IN AMERICA
The American Girl in the Nineteenth Century

Daisy Miller, the archetype of American adolescent girls, was
defined as "an inscrutable combination of audacity and innocence." Her emergence as a popular national type and her cautionary tale reflected an enthusiasm for the American maiden
which amounted at times to "a girl fetish." The girl was exalted
as the symbol of the nation while the American matron sat on the
shelf and the American male built his bridges and his empires.
Part of this "girl worship" was the American love of youth and the
child-centered home, but the cult expressed certain unique patterns, typically female and typically nineteenth century.[1]

Adolescence in the nineteenth-century was, for most young
women, a relatively brief and stormy period, marked on the one
hand by her first menstruation at fourteen or fifteen, and on the
other by her marriage at eighteen to twenty. Whatever the physiological boundaries of adolescence, these years marked the
psychological perimeter for most middle-class American girls.
The twentieth birthday was invested with great significance,
a "now I have put away the things of a child" landmark, as
the young woman self-consciously abandoned the lighthearted-
ness of girlhood and prepared for the weighty cares of domesticity and maternity. This essay discusses the young girl's discovery
of her identity through the agencies of the family, church, school,
and the mentors of her society such as periodical and popular
literature, medical texts and etiquette manuals. It also suggests
the way this identity crystallization fits into prevailing cultural
configurations of nineteenth-century American society.[2] The
principal sources used are manuscript diaries, published or unpub-
lished autobiographical accounts, and the mentor literature of the
period.[3]

3

The role of dutiful daughter was clearly defined and urged upon the American girl from her earliest years. She was expected to help her mother in tasks recognized as "female," and mothers were advised to subtly direct their daughters toward those skills which would be most useful to them in maturity. These tasks were supposed to inculcate equally well-recognized feminine "virtues." The nineteenth century was confident that it knew the differences between the sexes and that these differences were total and innate. Women were inherently more religious, modest, passive, submissive and domestic than men, and were happier doing tasks, learning lessons, and playing games that harmonized with their nature. As the century unfolded the sharp differences in external upbringing of women and men, especially in such areas as education and sports, diminished. Coeducational high schools and colleges, as well as female seminaries and colleges offered education in the same subjects and, theoretically, at the same level to young men and women. Girls who, in the pre-Civil War period, were not supposed to skate or sled but only to slide decorously on the ice, by 1900 took the lead in such coeducational sports as croquet and bicycling. But the beliefs about the internal differences between the sexes persisted, making it even more difficult for the girl during the transitional adolescent period to prepare herself for a specific female role.

The daughter was, because of these differences of nature and capacity, expected to be, above all else, obedient. Obedience and self-control were the two virtues on which society relied to protect young girls from those forces which it could not legislate, like falling in love. In one dramatic story the girl allows her demented father to dangle her over a cliff, rather than challenge his authority. The god-on-earth who must not be disobeyed was, however, subject to the prior claims of the heavenly father. If man, stronger but more prone to sin than woman, should try to interfere with the performance of her religious obligations, then it was not only her right but her duty to resist him. This was part of the regenerative function which woman assumed practically from babyhood; the popular literature of the period is sticky with tales of the redemptive child, usually female.

The famous scene in *Elsie Dinsmore* where Elsie's agnostic father orders her to play the piano on the sabbath illustrates this function: with tears streaming down her "little white face" at having to disobey "darling papa" Elsie remains mute at the piano bench until she falls in a faint. In the illness that follows, her father is, literally, brought to his knees, asking forgiveness from his daughter, and from God, in that order. In the version of redemption which was particularly popular in New England, "The Merchant's Daughter" reclaims her family from the vices of materialism and fashionable living which are the hazards of prosperity. When her father's business fails, he is despondent and her mother collapses; the truehearted young girl packs up the family and moves them all to a handy cottage, which she sweeps with a smile. The character of everyone improves vastly under straitened circumstances; *her* character, of course, is already perfect. The happy ending finds the father back on the road to prosperity, while the daughter's virtue has won her a worthy and potentially wealthy young man.

The redemptive role extended to her brothers as well. It was the duty of a sister to make home so pleasant for young men that they would not be tempted to look elsewhere for diversion. Later she would be expected to help her fiancé overcome any moral imperfections she might discover. Letters between young lovers are full of helpful hints for improvement from her side, and grateful recognition of her aid from his. Young men, of course, subscribed to the belief in woman's moral superiority and the double standard. A story by Louisa Mae Alcott, "Silver Pitchers," illustrated the way in which "the three Sweet P's, Polly, Portia, and Priscilla," rescued a brother from the gaming tables, a father from the temptations of the wine decanter, and a fiancé from rowdy companions, through moral suasion and rejection until the straying males were deemed worthy to enter again the presence of innocence.

Since woman's innocence was so fragile a state that a breath of scandal could mar it irreparably, a man had to be in a state of grace to approach the young girl's shrine. There is a good deal of this symbolism attached to the whole ritual of courtship. Man must be worthy of woman as the would-be communicant must be worthy of receiving the sacrament, even to the extent of doing some public penance. The girl treasured her innocence of spirit and physical virginity as the "pearl of great price" which was her greatest asset. Of course the knowledge that marriage, the normal end of this adolescent period, would result in the removal of the treasure from its vault, created certain tensions. For this reason the young girl was counselled never to speculate on what marriage meant, but to use her energies to prepare for it.

In the seduction stories the end of virtue begins when the girl disobeys her parents and arranges an assignation or reads a *billet doux* without their knowledge. This might seem a small thing, but it is the whole point of nineteenth-century mentor literature that nothing is small when dealing with absolutes; the mere creating of a tiny crevice in the tight wall of security around a girl's chastity is enough to let in hordes of dangerous fantasies and acts. When dealing with something as fundamental as female purity, hyperbole is necessary to provide sufficient deterrent strength. Not only is a girl's soul ruined, but madness and/or death inevitably follow, or so it is written in *Godey's Lady's Book*. A girl did not marry "for love but to love" as Charlotte Brontë said, and female delicacy precluded her feeling any tenderness until the intentions of the man had been fully established.

The assumption is twofold: the American female was supposed to be so infinitely lovable and provocative that a healthy male could barely control himself when in the same room with her, and the same girl, as she "comes out" of the cocoon of her family's protectiveness, is so palpitating with undirected affection, so filled to the brim with tender feelings, that she fixes her love on the first person she sees. She awakes from the midsummer night's dream of adolescence, and it is the responsibility of her family and society to see that her eyes fall on a suitable match and not some clown with the head of an ass. They do their part by such restrictive measures as segregated (by sex and/or class) schools, dancing classes, travel, and other external controls. She is required to exert the inner control of obedience. The combination forms a kind of societal chastity belt which is not unlocked until the marriage partner has arrived, and adolescence is formally over.

An interesting family pattern emerges in the lives of woman suffragists. The girl is usually the firstborn, often without any male children in the family, or at least not for several years. The father assumes direction of his daughter's education and character, while the mother is relegated to the role of invalid or nurse-housekeeper for younger children. The girl and her father develop an extraordinarily close relationship, as a part of which she feels that she must compensate him for the son she is sure he wished her to be. In later life these women, who achieved much more than most of their contemporaries, look back on their father with some ambivalence, and see their mother's role as that of a silent martyr. They both blame and credit their fathers with their own desire for achievement, which, in nineteenth century values, was not a desirable quality in a woman. Many of these women choose weak husbands, whose careers they eclipse, and they themselves are preoccupied, in their reforms or their writings, with finding a suitable definition of woman's nature and role.[4]

Most women, as distinct from these women of achievement, were much closer to their mothers during the adolescent period, since they worked with her in the house when they were not in school. In diaries there is evidence that the young girl was not "understood" by her mother, lacked sympathy or real affection from her, and could not wait to get out from under her thumb. There is also frequent evidence of devotion and admiration for "dearest mama."

After marriage, most girls became close and even admiring daughters to their mothers, now both equal members of the higher order of knowledge and power (and pain) conferred by the status of wifehood and motherhood. Perhaps significantly, those women who do not leave the family to get married, or who articulate in their diaries their fears of leaving home, are most often the ones who are attached to their fathers or whose mothers are either dead or invalids, giving up to them the direction of the household. The young girl, however much she is warned against ambition, might eschew fame and wealth as unsuitable for females, but she was quite explicit in her desire for status and power, which almost inevitably had to arrive through marriage.

The relationship between sisters was usually close; they almost invariably slept in the same room, even in the same bed, and since many families in the nineteenth century spanned a whole generation or had sets of half-brothers and sisters from second marriages, the adolescent girl often had an older married sister in whose home she visited. It was common for her to "help out" when a sister had a baby, or during the illness of a child. Although mothers and daughters suffered from what one behavior manual called "a regrettable lack of frankness on intimate matters," this was less true between sisters, and a knowledge of life as wife and mother was apt to be more explicit from her sisters than from her parent.

Even if they were less than enchanted with their parents' or siblings' marriages, almost every girl expected to marry. There are, however, innumerable diary entries declaring that the writer is convinced she will never take the fatal step. Occasionally this is because of delicate health, but often there is an expressed belief that since she would only marry an exceptional man, she is doomed to spinsterhood, for no such paragon would ever look at her. In these adolescent years the diaries are explicit about the craving for love, and the attempts to find it in the family and at school. A category of autobiography—"my blighted life" (a young woman makes one big mistake and tells the tale)— almost inevitably begins with a statement of the lack of love in her home, which she sees as the specific cause of her tragic error.

Status, power and love through marriage was reflected in a number of subtle ways. A married woman was allowed to discuss certain topics and look at certain works of art—the "Greek Slave," for example—that an unmarried woman could not. Emily Dickinson wrote:

> I'm "wife"—I've finished that—
> That other state—
> I'm Czar—I'm "Woman" now—
> It's safer so—[5]

Marriage was a demonstrable step up in the hierarchy of society, one of the few ways in which a woman could make such a move. Marriage could provide for a woman the improved economic and social benefits which men received through education, speculation, the professions, business, and marriage. Most American girls believed that this new state automatically brought happiness, because they believed that to marry for anything but the purest love was unworthy of their sex and nation. This freedom of choice was more apparent than real; most American girls married within their own class, religion, and geographic background. But popular fiction specialized in the heterogeneous marriage: the white hunter and the Indian maiden (this turned out badly); the fisherman's daughter and the merchant prince (the fisherman's daughter often turned out to be gently born and mysteriously abandoned); the Northern bluestocking and the plantation owner (even when done by Henry James, the auguries for successful marriage were ominous).

Such fiction reflects the variety and the self-consciousness of American citizens seeking their own niche in a diverse, but still mobile, society. Marriage was the unit by which the niche was carved out; the country was socially a vast Noah's Ark, in which the male and female roles were carefully apportioned and differed according to economic, class, and ethnic background. The lower-class girl often had more freedom than the upper-class young lady, a condition which markedly increased after the Civil War when the distinction among the classes became more obvious. There was even discussion that the European tradition of the chaperone should be revived, to protect that important national resource, the marriageable daughter. Protestant girls in similar economic and social backgrounds were not ordinarily so constrained as Catholic or Jewish girls.

The difference among the classes and backgrounds of American girls was less noticed by contemporaries than the differences between American and European girls. A popular subject for the magazines was the contrast between the French woman, whose life only started with marriage after a repressed girlhood, and the American female, whose carefree girlhood ended abruptly in staid and drab matronhood. The American girl rarely troubled herself over this prospect. She might, as one Philadelphia belle did, close her diary with the words: "And now these pages must come to a close, for the romance ends when the heroine marries." But if the French woman's freedom meant in any way the right to take liberties with the marriage vow, the American girl wanted no part of it. The "married flirt" was a late-blooming phenomenon of the nineteenth century, flourishing mostly at European resorts, and regarded with horror and disapproval by the mentors of American society and by the puritanical young women themselves. American girls, no matter how lighthearted their international image, were for the most part intensely moralistic about all the institutions they inherited from their God-fearing parents, whether marriage, the church, or democracy, and almost completely without any desire to fundamentally alter these institutions, even if they grumbled at them.

Indeed the American girl did not know what happiness was unless she saw it in middle-class life as wife and mother. In almost every case where a diary asserts "I am a happy woman" the statement follows a vignette of idyllic and conventional home life—

children asleep, firelight shining on new furniture (for which the cost is often recorded), husband reading, and the wife recording the fleeting moment to preserve it. The American girl was conditioned to equate this picture with happiness. Contrary to her press, the fabled American girl, in her "Diana-like mixture of freedom and modesty" most often shows the desire to pass into the next stage, to be a woman, a wife and mother.

The adolescent girl therefore spent much time preparing for a "good" marriage. Theoretically her family and society handled most of the grubby detail, but a girl was expected to prepare herself with certain skills and virtues to be a "good" wife. Since fortunes were believed the prerogative of the nineteenth-century American male, the female believed she would share in them through her marriage. She expected that a life of self-sacrifice and right thinking would bring her, by some kind of divine justice, a "good," i.e., successful and kind husband. It was the same logic which rewarded the "manly little fellow" of the Horatio Alger stories with riches, the result of his virtue, not his business acumen.

A part of this preparation for maturity, the girl had to find her way through two crises: death and sex. The one subject was actively discussed in Victorian society; the other permeated it by implication. Obviously both subjects engaged the young man in his search for identity, but he followed a different path in resolving them. All young people were cautioned to be prepared for sudden death. Since girls were supposed to be much more delicate than boys—a theory not substantiated by the actuarial tables—their musings on an early death were likely to be more frequent. Partly this was a religious concern, a desire to be always ready to meet her Maker, but it was also a response to a real situation. Young women did die: of consumption, in childbirth, of various diseases, even, apparently, from disappointment in love. Catalogs of female seminaries featured black-bordered pages in which they announced the death of a classmate, "torn from her grieving family in the full bloom of her youth," and admonished the surviving students, "Be ye then also ready." Faith in their own immortality seems such an integral part of today's adolescents that it is hard to posit generations of young people who accepted as a premise the imminence of their own demise. But the diaries dutifully note on every birthday that the writer is conscious it may be her last.

The death of a young girl was so celebrated as a triumph of beauty and innocence that a whole ritual grew up around it. The poetry of doomed young maidens, like Lucretia and Margaret Davidson, two teenagers who died of tuberculosis, enjoyed a certain vogue. It was believed that a progressive spiritualization occurred, edifying to those who remained behind, and sanctifying those who went ahead: "only the good die young." The death of Beth in *Little Women* has brought tears to the eyes of several generations, and might be viewed as a literary effusion except that the real Marmee's diary is full of even more heart-rending details. Louisa Mae actually edited the dialogue. Mothers were cautioned against precocity in their children, whether mental or religious, because it was believed that unusual achievements might signify consumptive tendencies. The diaries of young girls caught up in this progressive decline make sobering reading. First she expects to get well; then she doubts that she will but cannot quite believe it; there is frequently the remark that she does not regard herself as good enough to die so young. Then, with the docility which marked the behavior of well-brought-up young women, she accepts the whole process.

The dying maiden is so highly regarded as the quintessence of female virtue, a being literally too good for this world, that one suspects the age and the young women themselves of a certain necrophilia. The medical profession shared in the gloomy forebodings. Adolescence was the most "interesting" and "critical" period in a woman's life, except for her first childbearing. The doctors were concerned with the feeble health of America's girls, and they blamed part of it on the mothers who wanted their daughters married too young. A typical illness of female adolescence was "chlorosis," or the green sickness, a kind of anemia in which the young woman turned pale green, exhibited extreme lassitude, and frequently a desire to consume substances such as chalk and slate. It was believed to be caused by overstrain of the nervous and physical systems, brought on by such events as being cooped up in the house caring for an invalid relative, being sent away to school, or being thwarted in love.

Medical literature pictured adolescence as a psychological crisis for the young woman; she became more romantic and maternal with the coming of the menses. Tomboy tendencies disappeared, visions "of love in a cottage" took their place; thoughts turned from intense female friendships, love of siblings and pets, to a member of the opposite sex. Doctors differed on whether girls should take a week off from school or work every month because of the "periodicity" of their female functions. Edward Clarke wrote with great passion that most diseases of American woman-hood were caused by women failing to recognize their need for rest from mental activity during this "critical" period. "The stream of vital and constructive force evolved within her was turned steadily to the brain and away from the ovaries and their accessories." The result was female disease and often death for the girl who for-got her specific female nature.[6]

Dio Lewis developed a series of exercises to build up the Ameri-can girl whom he saw deteriorating "into the smallest race of peo-ple in the land," while the American male waxed as one of the tallest. Margaret Fuller, and other reformers, urged that the Amer-ican girl develop her body and mind so that she turned into a real woman, fit to be "mothers of a mighty race." Now, Miss Fuller concluded, "there are no American women, only overgrown chil-dren."[7]

The preoccupation with death often produced a scene in early childhood which a number of autobiographies recall in vivid de-tail and which is sometimes the earliest specific memory: the girl is led by a parent, usually her father, into the room where a small brother or sister has just died and is told to kiss the child's cold lips. A surprising number of these accounts mention how guilty the girl felt about this death, and how conscious of her own change in status within the family. Girls on the verge of marriage fre-quently speculated about the possibility of dying in childbirth, something they accepted as one of the hazards of married life, but which they seemed to welcome almost joyfully, at the same time that they feared it. The young girl quite naturally longed for a chance to show that she was a true woman, that she knew how to suffer well. To risk life yearly in childbirth was proof of woman's moral superiority, and a yearly reenforcement of her claims in the eyes of her husband. No matter what the psychological roots, there is no doubt that the nineteenth century appreciated heroes and heroics, and short of martyrdom, a crown available to only a chos-en few, the risk of childbearing was practically the only opportun-ity for the young girl to show her heroic qualities.

The other important crisis of the young girl—sex—was directly related to the fear of childbirth. In that act the two fears mingled, perhaps explaining its preeminence as a heroic goal for the adolescent woman. Whether or not one accepts the psychoanalytic interpretation of adolescence, the diaries of the nineteenth-century girls exhibit a high degree of anxiety and guilt. Some explicit fears are: fear that she did not love God enough or loved some mortal too much, making an "idol" of him, and therefore leaving herself open to retaliation by a jealous God; fear of storms; fear of ghosts (girls relished table rappings and specters in graveyards); fear of losing her looks and growing old (this starts about the age of eighteen); fear of not marrying, a fear of leaving childhood. This last fear expresses the reluctance of a girl to put up her hair, lower her skirts, and assume the female role. Often when such concern is expressed, although not always by any means, the writer does not marry and never does leave home.[8] Womanhood, as the girl was told, was fraught with suffering; woman was a being with "so much to suffer, so much to fear," and accepting the female identity involved accepting this liability.

And yet, with all the emphasis on suffering, the nineteenth-century girl did not regard sex in marriage as unmitigated misery. Victorian prudery has been accepted too much at its face value. It is easy to mistake reticence for hypocrisy in the bedroom, parlor, or counting house; and the Victorians, in their zeal to be "civilized" (or as they sometimes unfortunately expressed it, "genteel") overlay their most significant actions with as much rhetoric as gilt on dressers and bibelots on mantelpieces. The nineteenth-century American girl, no matter how carefully nurtured, no matter how imbued with the idea that her ignorance was equated with her innocence, knew more than she let on. By the time of the Civil War her role was institutionalized and she played it well, as did the rest of the cast of characters in any Victorian household: the paterfamilias, the faithful retainer, the rakish bachelor. The girl's magnificent innocence was painted on. She did not discuss Traviata with her fiancé, but she attended the opera, and had an accurate idea of what it was all about.[9]

The American girl might fear the physical aspect of marriage; but she was conditioned to expect happiness in marriage, and she was quite explicitly informed that physical pleasure was a part of that happiness. It might not occur, frequently it did not, but the girl usually entered marriage expecting to be made happy in ways she had not known before. Whether or not nineteenth-century women often attained sexual fulfillment is difficult for the historian to ascertain, but they most certainly achieved a great deal of psychic satisfaction from their new knowledge of and initiation into sex, as well as the satisfaction of knowing the pleasure they were giving, presumably a desirable female achievement in itself. Diary entries written in the weeks after marriage are often ecstatic and mention that married life "is all and more than I expected."

More often than one would expect, letters between husbands and wives in the nineteenth century refer to their lives together in physical terms; one Southern matron of impeccable ancestry complained bitterly about a health resort which forbade intercourse as part of its therapy. The correspondence of Sophia and Nathaniel Hawthorne was edited by Sophia after her husband's death to remove the evidence of conjugal bliss on any but the most exalted plane. This did not imply that Sophia was ashamed of their affection, nor did it make her any less receptive as a marriage partner, but it was an example of the Victorian mentality which insisted on the utmost privacy as well as the utmost sanctity for the marriage bed. It was an age when much of life was becoming highly publicized and socialized, there was a corresponding emphasis on the home as a citadel and sanctuary, a refuge from the materialism and sharp practices of business. One historian has suggested that the protracted invalidism of prominent English Victorians was simply their way of withdrawing from their hyperactive society in order to get something done. And the same logic might apply to the retreat into the home.

The American girl was supposed to be chaste before marriage, which meant that she assumed a certain reserve—some called it coldness—of manner. Although this was criticized by foreign travellers, the American mentors were quick to explain that the seeming coldness was only prudence, and that once married, the American girl was warm and loving. They favorably referred to the number of large families in the country as proof of their contention. After all, none of these ladies who wrote etiquette books had read Freud, and so they were blissfully unaware that anyone might contradict their logic; perfect purity before marriage was the best training for perfect happiness in marriage. One might point out that a girl conditioned to believe she would be rewarded by physical happiness as a result of physical self-control before marriage might very well be psychologically ready to relax and enjoy the experience.

While most girls prepared for their eventual female role as wives and mothers, there were a few deviates within the society. There were women who confessed that they had always wanted to be boys and who, in a few cases, looked upon war as an excellent opportunity to don man's clothing and perform male functions.[10] Some of the woman's rights reformers challenged the limitations of the female role and function; most accepted the definition of woman's nature. In fact, so far as the American girl was concerned, the woman's rights movement was a kind of revitalization crusade, as Anthony Wallace uses the term. They sought a regenerative process by which the true woman, the Puritan maiden of an earlier simpler time, reemerged, rather than the puppet and doll into which the American girl was deteriorating. They expected that this new model of the sturdy pioneer woman would be able to cope with the rigors of the coming-out season, the woman's college, or the office, without losing those qualities which were indigenous to the American female in the good old days.

As society became more self-conscious towards the end of the century, American girls played an increasingly important role in defining their parents' place in the hierarchy. It was necessary to develop not only a manual of ritual for the dinners, calling cards, and balls of "the 400," but also to develop a "morality of fashion." This assured the anxious populace that the American girl remained internally the same as she had always been, no matter how elaborate the society which enveloped her. Increased wealth and style provided only a larger arena for her traditional good works and civilizing functions.

The woman's colleges, as interpreted by the periodicals which wrote about them, were, on the whole, a good influence, since they prepared a woman for a useful, active life, without trying to make a bluestocking of her. She would be, with additional education, a better helpmeet to the American man. The same argument supported the entrance of women into the working force. The mill girls at Lowell were widely reported to be among the truest women in New England, which meant, of course, as true women as existed in the world. Their adolescent purity was maintained by rigorous supervision of hours, required church attendance, and a schedule of self-improvement lectures. The "business girl" of the post-Civil

War period was expected to possess the same qualities as every other good woman, although she might be exposed to graver temptations.

In the columns of advice in such publications as *The Ladies' Home Journal*, the working girl was advised to live at home, or, if that were not possible, to go to church regularly. Even when giving directions on what to do if her employer fell in love with her, the advice was unchanged: pack up your things and immediately go home to mother and tell her all about it. Although for the girl of an earlier period such a situation would have been impossible, the ethic with which she was to handle it remained exactly the same. Working outside the home provided excellent training for those virtues of thrift, industry, and self-control which turned a girl into a woman.

The American girl was told that self-improvement was her task and that she could change her condition for the better, whether economic, social, physical, or religious. To this end the young girl made endless lists: questions to ask herself at the end of every day; books she had read or ought to read; resolutions for the future; examination of conscience for the past; and schedules in which each hour shone with some elevating purpose. The diaries have long paragraphs in which the young woman regrets the way she has not lived up to her own lists and has not succeeded in this self-improvement. She sometimes analyzes her own personality and character, finding herself too diffident, awkward in public; sometimes she compares her social attitude unfavorably with that of a sister or friend. Economic and social mobility for American girls depended on personal charm and they were very much aware of it. They were also aware that they were expected to aid their husband in his rise in the world. One young woman attended a boarding school for a year after her marriage—her husband visited her two nights a week in the parlor—in order to be a better helpmeet for him.

Although she piously affected to believe and was informed in pulpit and periodical that beauty of soul was infinitely more likely to bring her a better husband than beauty of body, the young girl spent considerable time and effort on her personal appearance. Recipe books are crowded with potions that bleach excess hair, whiten chapped hands, and remove wrinkles. One girl recalled her mother's bursting into tears when she discovered three tiny freckles on her daughter's face, so highly did she esteem beauty as a prerequisite for the "good" marriage.

The girl was aware that money, social position, refinements in manner, accomplishments, and looks were marketable assets which gave her more or less leverage as a commodity. These efforts at self-improvement were her contribution to accomplishing the good life which the nineteenth century held out as a reasonable goal to its citizens. The rest of her destiny was in the hands of others, and she not only should not, but could not, assume the responsibility herself. Really, as one writer pointed out, she was luckier than any other member of society. All she need do was "obey her mother and be a good girl. . . . If she avoided clandestine meetings with young gentlemen and all foolish love affairs," and safeguarded her health, ". . . she may be quite sure that her bark will float gaily on to the comfortable port of a happy marriage and a successful future."[11]

The nineteenth-century man must have felt some envy; such a guaranteed formula for success was infinitely less strenuous, if more subtle, than arranging a railroad merger or a steel trust. The major events of a girl's life were to be products of arrangement and fate, not of intellect and will, and she was expected to passively await them, as she awaited the arrival of her love. Whether in society, college, or business she was still symbolically the lady in the tower, weaving her tapestry and gazing into the mirror for reflections of her own life. Science and industry rationalized man's life somewhat; only the young woman remained, as all mankind once had felt itself to be, helpless in the hands of capricious destiny or omniscient divinity.

Besides the family, the major institution with which the young girl had contact in her search for identity, and which contributed to that identity, was the church. The nineteenth century required women to be religious, and increasingly the church became a female institution as men put their energies elsewhere. Young girls often went through an intensely religious phase, initiated by or culminating in a conversion experience. This religious crisis often arrived at the same time as the menses and was described by the girl in sensual terms. The girl felt waves of undulating ecstasy, culminating in a shriek of anguish torn from her against her will. Other physical manifestations included "the holy laugh," "the gift of tongues" and the pulsations of "the blessing." This religious experience, once expected in some form by all Christians, by the time of the Civil War was largely the result of the revival meetings, and a girl could live a life in which her religion played an important part, without going through a physical experience.

Nonetheless "becoming a Christian" was, for most girls in the nineteenth century, their most important experience before marriage, . . . It taught them something of the depths and heights which they could reach, and took them outside themselves, showing them a range of emotion not found in their own lives or in their family life. The days of a young girl were likely to be so standardized and monotonous that the religious experience loomed even larger because of the contrast. Statements of boredom with the routine of their existence are found in most diaries. One young woman, discussing what her conversion had meant to her, began with the statement: "I had grown so infinitely tired of me."

Just as the religious experience provided a testing ground for new feelings, so did the crush or intense "woman friendship." Most of the time this affection was transferred to a heterosexual relationship, when society allowed it to develop. It served the purpose of preconditioning the girl, showing her in some way what love was.[12]

Melodramatic literature, so dear to the hearts of young girls, so frowned upon by their preceptors, accomplished some of the same purposes. It informed the gentle reader: this is how a woman loves a man; those are the kind of caresses he bestows upon her; this is the way she responds; this is what married love is like. The young girl almost never saw anything like this fiction in the reality of marriage, her parents', relatives', or her own. But popular literature was a blueprint for a kind of life of which the young girl could dream, even though she knew, with her rather shrewd appraisal of her own prospects, that in reality she would not live it. It provided for her some of the same vistas that the gold fields of California did for the American male; he might never reach them, but he liked to know they were there.

The institution of the state made relatively little impact on the nineteenth-century girl since she played no official role in it, and her informal position was tied in with religious and family values. External events, unless they could be depicted in human terms, rarely found their way into young girls' diaries. The Civil War was an exception. Girls who came to adolescence during those years were involved in the country's policy and external events in a way none of their sisters shared. For a number of young women the fact that they had to assume roles and qualities not ordinarily associated with their sex changed their view about themselves permanently.

Girls in both North and South exhibit complete faith that their side will conquer and are convinced that God and divine justice are their guarantee of victory. The shock and disbelief of the Southern girl after Appomattox are coupled with her questioning how God could allow such a disaster to occur. In several Southern diaries the girl mentions that until the war she had always assumed her father was invincible, but she saw him frustrated by superior force or poverty. Both sides, especially the Confederacy, required that the young girl go without material possessions and yet for both sides the war was a time of increased excitement and heightened awareness of young men. Especially in the South a kind of female society developed, similar to the eighteenth-century whaling towns like Nantucket, where women assumed all the various roles in the community.

If for the Southern girl the Civil War ultimately shook her faith in progress and optimism, it only reinforced those qualities for the Northern girl. This belief in the innate goodness of men had been a component of the eighteenth century founders of the country, but was being replaced in the philosophy of most nineteenth-century businessmen by the need to look sharply and suspiciously at their fellow man. Young women still had the luxury of optimism and belief in virtue, purchased for them by their loving fathers and husbands. In the era of pragmatism and the slum, the young girl's simple, trusting nature was one of the few relics of the Enlightenment and the City on the Hill.

The belief in innate virtue had certain drawbacks. The American girl, so confiding and pliable, was pruned, in the rhetoric of the period, to attach herself to some sturdy oak of a man, whose goodness and strength would protect her from the winds of adversity. However there was always the chance that she might attach herself to some noxious specimen, despite the watchful guardianship of her family and society. One of two things would happen: either she would be led by him into a downward path of degradation (to which she would take even more rapidly than he, because when women "went bad" they fell faster and farther than

men), or she would be so blasted by the shock to her delicate
system that she would curl up and die. Either extreme reaction was
accepted as a natural, although regrettable, result of a system
which no one really wanted to change. The hyperbole again was
necessary to defend the absolute.

The innocence of the American girl was understood to resemble
the innocence of the United States in a world of depraved and
greedy countries. The girl, without guile, wanted no shadows or
mysteries, open covenants openly arrived at. She was fearless and
accustomed to having her own way. There was ". . . nothing between her and the thing she wanted since she learned to walk. To
steadily approach the tree and to gather the peach has been her
manifest destiny."[13] The ambiguities of moonlit walks in the
Coliseum escaped her as the ambivalence of expansion escaped
the nation. That which was good for her was assumed to be without
harm, to be as innocent as she was. Europeans, less pure in the
body politic and moral, misunderstood the lack of convention and
fearlessness of the nation and the girl. Both were, in their posture
before the rest of the world, free from materialism, idealists in the
best sense of the word. Europeans persisted in seeing America as
another nationalistic country with colonial ambitions, and the
American girl as a tease who did not deliver what her behavior
promised.

The United States believed itself the best country in the world,
and its young women the finest in the world. "To stand before
kings" had thrilled even the democratic Franklin and in the age of
titled marriage, American blood actually mingled, if not with that
of kings, at least of dukes and princelings. It was in many ways a
final sad identification of the American girl with the American
spirit. The high hopes of the Revolutionary period, that the United
States would set forth an example of democracy and enlightened
rule to the rest of the world, were overshadowed by the fact that
America's influence, when it became great, was largely based on
her wealth and power. The American girl, who had been bred to
show the superiority of freedom linked to moral purity, gained
renown not as the true woman or Puritan maiden, but as the
heiress. The dilemma of democracy had always been to retain
both freedom and power; the dilemma of the American girl, to be both
bold and innocent, was equally perplexing and equally unsolved.

2

THE CULT OF TRUE WOMANHOOD
1820-1860

The nineteenth-century American man was a busy builder of bridges and railroads, at work long hours in a materialistic society. The religious values of his forebears were neglected in practice if not in intent, and he occasionally felt some guilt that he had turned this new land, this temple of the chosen people, into one vast countinghouse. But he could salve his conscience by reflecting that he had left behind a hostage, not only to fortune, but to all the values which he held so dear and treated so lightly. Woman, in the cult of True Womanhood[1] presented by the women's magazines, gift annuals and religious literature of the nineteenth century, was the hostage in the home.[2] In a society where values changed frequently, where fortunes rose and fell with frightening rapidity, where social and economic mobility provided instability as well as hope, one thing at least remained the same—a true woman was a true woman, wherever she was found. If anyone, male or female, dared to tamper with the complex of virtues which made up True Womanhood, he was damned immediately as an enemy of God, of civilization and of the Republic. It was a fearful obligation, a solemn responsibility, the nineteenth-century American woman had —to uphold the pillars of the temple with her frail white hand.

The attributes of True Womanhood, by which a woman judged herself and was judged by her husband, her neighbors and society, could be divided into four cardinal virtues—piety, purity, submissiveness and domesticity. Put them all together and they spelled mother, daughter, sister, wife—woman. Without them, no matter whether there was fame, achievement or wealth, all was ashes. With them she was promised happiness and power.

Religion or piety was the core of woman's virtue, the source of her strength. Young men looking for a mate were cautioned to search first for piety, for if that were there, all else would follow.[3] Religion belonged to woman by divine right, a gift of God and nature. This "peculiar susceptibility" to religion was given her for a reason: "the vestal flame of piety, lighted up by Heaven in the breast of woman" would throw its beams into the naughty world of men.[4] So far would its candle power reach that the "Universe might be Enlightened, Improved, and Harmonized by WOMAN!!"[5] She would be another, better Eve, working in cooperation with the Redeemer, bringing the world back "from its revolt and sin."[6] The world would be reclaimed for God through her suffering, for "God increased the cares and sorrows of woman that she might be sooner constrained to accept the terms of salvation."[7] A popular poem by Mrs. Frances Osgood, "The Triumph of the Spiritual Over the Sensual," expressed just this sentiment, woman's purifying passionless love bringing an erring man back to Christ.[8]

Dr. Charles Meigs, explaining to a graduating class of medical students why women were naturally religious, said that "hers is a pious mind. Her confiding nature leads her more readily than men to accept the proffered grace of the Gospel."[9] Caleb Atwater, Esq., writing in *The Ladies' Repository*, saw the hand of the Lord in female piety: "Religion is exactly what a woman needs, for it gives her that dignity that best suits her dependence."[10] And Mrs. John Sandford, who had no very high opinion of her sex, agreed thoroughly: "Religion is just what woman needs. Without it she is ever restless or unhappy. . . ."[11] Mrs. Sandford and the others did not speak only of that restlessness of the human heart, which St. Augustine notes, that can only find its peace in God. They spoke rather of religion as a kind of tranquilizer for the many undefined longings which swept even the most pious young girl, and about which it was better to pray than to think.

One reason religion was valued was that it did not take a woman away from her "proper sphere," her home. Unlike participation in other societies or movements, church work would not make her less domestic or submissive, less a True Woman. In religious vineyards, said the *Young Ladies' Literary and Missionary Report*, "you may labor without the apprehension of detracting from the charms of feminine delicacy." Mrs. S. L. Dagg, writing from her chapter of the Society in Tuscaloosa, Alabama, was equally reassuring: "As no sensible woman will suffer her intellectual pursuits to clash with her domestic duties" she should concentrate on religious work "which promotes these very duties."[12]

The women's seminaries aimed at aiding women to be religious, as well as accomplished. Mt. Holyoke's catalogue promised to make female education "a handmaid to the Gospel and an efficient auxiliary in the great task of renovating the world."[13] The Young Ladies' Seminary at Bordentown, New Jersey, declared its most important function to be "the forming of a sound and virtuous character."[14] In Keene, New Hampshire, the Seminary tried to instill a "consistent and useful character" in its students, to enable them in this life to be "a good friend, wife and mother" but more important, to qualify them for "the enjoyment of Celestial Happiness in the life to come."[15] And Joseph M' D. Mathews, Principal of Oakland Female Seminary in Hillsborough, Ohio, believed that "female education should be preeminently religious."[16]

If religion was so vital to a woman, irreligion was almost too awful to contemplate. Women were warned not to let their literary or intellectual pursuits take them away from God. Sarah Josepha Hale spoke darkly of those who, like Margaret Fuller, threw away the "One True Book" for others, open to error. Mrs. Hale used the unfortunate Miss Fuller as fateful proof that "the greater the intellectual force, the greater and more fatal the errors into which women fall who wander from the Rock of Salvation, Christ the Saviour. . . ."[17]

One gentleman, writing on "Female Irreligion" reminded his readers that "Man may make himself a brute, and does so very often, but can woman brutify herself to his level—the lowest level of human nature—without exerting special wonder?" Fanny Wright, because she was godless, "was no woman, mother though she be." A few years ago, he recalls, such women would have been whipped. In any case, "woman never looks lovelier than in her reverence for religion" and, conversely, "female irreligion is the most revolting feature in human character."[18]

Purity was as essential as piety to a young woman, its absence as unnatural and unfeminine. Without it she was, in fact, no woman at all, but a member of some lower order. A "fallen woman" was a "fallen angel," unworthy of the celestial company of her sex. To contemplate the loss of purity brought tears; to be guilty of such a crime, in the women's magazines at least, brought madness or death. Even the language of the flowers had bitter words for it: a dried white rose symbolized "Death Preferable to Loss of Innocence."[19] The marriage night was the single great event of a woman's life, when she bestowed her greatest treasure upon her husband, and from that time on was completely dependent upon him, an empty vessel,[20] without legal or emotional existence of her own.[21]

Therefore all True Women were urged, in the strongest possible terms, to maintain their virtue, although men, being by nature more sensual than they, would try to assault it. Thomas Branagan admitted in *The Excellency of the Female Character Vindicated* that his sex would sin and sin again, they could not help it, but woman, stronger and purer, must not give in and let man "take liberties incompatible with her delicacy." "If you do," Branagan addressed his gentle reader, "You will be left in silent sadness to bewail your credulity, imbecility, duplicity, and premature prostitution."[22]

Mrs. Eliza Farrar, in *The Young Lady's Friend*, gave practical logistics to avoid trouble: "Sit not with another in a place that is too narrow; read not out of the same book; let not your eagerness to see anything induce you to place your head close to another person's."[23]

If such good advice was ignored the consequences were terrible and inexorable. In *Girlhood and Womanhood: Or Sketches of My Schoolmates*, by Mrs. A. J. Graves (a kind of mid-nineteenth-century *The Group*), the bad ends of a boarding school class of girls are scrupulously recorded. The worst end of all is reserved for "Amelia Dorrington: The Lost One." Amelia died in the almshouse "the wretched victim of depravity and intemperance" and all because her mother had let her be "high-spirited not prudent." These girlish high spirits had been misinterpreted by a young man, with disastrous results. Amelia's "thoughtless levity" was "followed by a total loss of virtuous principle" and Mrs. Graves editorializes that "the coldest reserve is more admirable in a woman a man wishes to make his wife, than the least approach to undue familiarity."[24]

A popular and often-reprinted story by Fanny Forester told the sad tale of "Lucy Dutton." Lucy "with the seal of innocence upon her heart, and a rose-leaf on her cheek" came out of her vine-covered cottage and ran into a city slicker. "And Lucy was beautiful and trusting, and thoughtless: and he was gay, selfish and profligate. Needs the story to be told? . . . Nay, censor, Lucy was a child—consider how young, how very untaught—oh! her innocence was no match for the sophistry of a gay, city youth! Spring came and shame was stamped upon the cottage at the foot of the hill." The baby died; Lucy went mad at the funeral and finally died herself. "Poor, poor Lucy Dutton! The grave is a blessed couch and pillow to the wretched. Rest thee there, poor Lucy!"[25] The frequency with which derangement follows loss of virtue suggests the exquisite sensibility of woman, and the possibility that, in the women's magazines at least, her intellect was geared to her hymen, not her brain.

If, however, a woman managed to withstand man's assaults on her virtue, she demonstrated her superiority and her power over him. Eliza Farnham, trying to prove this female superiority, concluded smugly that "the purity of women is the everlasting barrier against which the tides of man's sensual nature surge."[26]

A story in *The Lady's Amaranth* illustrates this dominance. It is set, improbably, in Sicily, where two lovers, Bianca and Tebaldo, have been separated because her family insisted she marry a rich old man. By some strange circumstance the two are in a shipwreck and cast on a desert island, the only survivors. Even here, however, the rigid standards of True Womanhood prevail. Tebaldo unfortunately forgets himself slightly, so that Bianca must warn him: "We may not indeed gratify our fondness by caresses, but it is still something to bestow our kindest language, and looks and prayers, and all lawful and honest attentions on each other." Something, perhaps, but not enough, and Bianca must further remonstrate: "It is true that another man is my husband, but you are my guardian angel." When even that does not work she says in a voice of sweet reason, passive and proper to the end, that she wishes he wouldn't but "still, if you insist, I will become what you wish; but I beseech you to consider, ere that decision, that debasement which I must suffer in your esteem." This appeal to his own double standards holds the beast in him at bay. They are rescued, discover that the old husband is dead, and after "mourning a decent season" Bianca finally gives in, legally.[27]

Men could be counted on to be grateful when women thus saved them from themselves. William Alcott, guiding young men in their relations with the opposite sex, told them that "Nothing is better calculated to preserve a young man from contamination of low pleasures and pursuits than frequent intercourse with the more refined and virtuous of the other sex." And he added, one assumes in equal innocence, that youths should "observe and learn to admire, that purity and ignorance of evil which is the characteristic of well-educated young ladies, and which, when we are near them, raises us above those sordid and sensual considerations which hold such sway over men in their intercourse with each other."[28]

The Rev. Jonathan F. Stearns was also impressed by female chastity in the face of male passion, and warned woman never to compromise the source of her power: "Let her lay aside delicacy, and her influence over our sex is gone."[29]

Women themselves accepted, with pride but suitable modesty, this priceless virtue. *The Ladies' Wreath*, in "Woman the Creature of God and the Manufacturer of Society" saw purity as her greatest gift and chief means of discharging her duty to save the world: "Purity is the highest beauty—the true pole-star which is to guide humanity aright in its long, varied, and perilous voyage."[30]

Sometimes, however, a woman did not see the dangers to her treasure. In that case, they must be pointed out to her, usually by a male. In the nineteenth century any form of social change was tantamount to an attack on woman's virtue, if only it was correctly understood. For example, dress reform seemed innocuous enough and the bloomers worn by the lady of that name and her followers were certainly modest attire. Such was the reasoning only of the ignorant. In another issue of *The Ladies' Wreath* a young lady is represented in dialogue with her "Professor." The girl expresses admiration for the bloomer costume —it gives freedom of motion, is healthful and attractive. The "Professor" sets her straight. Trousers, he explains, are "only one of the many manifestations of that wild spirit of socialism and agrarian radicalism which is at present so rife in our land." The young lady recants immediately: "If this dress has any connexion with Fourierism or Socialism, or fanaticism in any shape whatever, I have no disposition to wear it at all . . . no true woman would so far compromise her delicacy as to espouse, however unwittingly, such a cause."[31]

America could boast that her daughters were particularly innocent. In a poem on "The American Girl" the author wrote proudly:

> Her eye of light is the diamond bright,
> Her innocence the pearl,
> And these are ever the bridal gems
> That are worn by the American girl.[32]

Lydia Maria Child, giving advice to mothers, aimed at preserving that spirit of innocence. She regretted that "want of confidence between mothers and daughters on delicate subjects" and suggested a woman tell her daughter a few facts when she reached the age of twelve to "set her mind at rest." Then Mrs. Child confidently hoped that a young lady's "instinctive modesty" would "prevent her from dwelling on the information until she was called upon to use it."[33] In the same vein, a book of advice to the newly-married was titled *Whisper to a Bride*.[34] As far as intimate information was concerned, there was no need to whisper, since the book contained none at all.

A masculine summary of this virtue was expressed in a poem "Female Charms";

> I would have her as pure as the snow on the mount—
> As true as the smile that to infamy's given—
> As pure as the wave of the crystalline fount,
> Yet as warm in the heart as the sunlight of heaven.
> With a mind cultivated, not boastingly wise,
> I could gaze on such beauty, with exquisite bliss;
> With her heart on her lips and her soul in her eyes—
> What more could I wish in dear woman than this.[35]

Man might, in fact, ask no more than this in woman, but she was beginning to ask more of herself, and in the asking was threatening the third powerful and necessary virtue, submission. Purity, considered as a moral imperative, set up a dilemma which was hard to resolve. Woman must preserve her virtue until marriage and marriage was necessary for her happiness. Yet marriage was, literally, an end to innocence. She was told not to question this dilemma, but simply to accept it.

Submission was perhaps the most feminine virtue expected of women. Men were supposed to be religious, although they rarely had time for it, and supposed to be pure, although it came awfully hard to them, but men were the movers, the doers, the

actors. Women were the passive, submissive responders. The
order of dialogue was, of course, fixed in Heaven. Man was
"woman's superior by God's appointment, if not in intellectual
dowry, at least by official decree." Therefore, as Charles Elliott
argued in *The Ladies' Repository*, she should submit to him "for
the sake of good order at least."[36] In *The Ladies Companion* a
young wife was quoted approvingly as saying that she did not
think woman should "feel and act for herself" because "When,
next to God, her husband is not the tribunal to which her heart
and intellect appeals—the golden bowl of affection is broken."[37]
Women were warned that if they tampered with this quality they
tampered with the order of the Universe.

The Young Lady's Book summarized the necessity of the passive
virtues in its readers' lives: "It is, however, certain, that in whatever situation of life a woman is placed from her cradle to her
grave, a spirit of obedience and submission, pliability of temper,
and humility of mind, are required from her."[38]

Woman understood her position if she was the right kind of
woman, a true woman. "She feels herself weak and timid. She
needs a protector," declared George Burnap, in his lectures on
The Sphere and Duties of Woman. "She is in a measure dependent. She asks for wisdom, constancy, firmness, perseverance, and she is willing to repay it all by the surrender of the
full treasure of her affections. Woman despises in man every
thing like herself except a tender heart. It is enough that she is
effeminate and weak; she does not want another like herself."[39]
Or put even more strongly by Mrs. Sandford: "A really sensible
woman feels her dependence. She does what she can, but she is
conscious of inferiority, and therefore grateful for support."[40]

Mrs. Sigourney, however, assured young ladies that although
they were separate, they were equal. This difference of the sexes
did not imply inferiority, for it was part of that same order of
Nature established by Him "who bids the oak brave the fury of
the tempest, and the alpine flower lean its cheek on the bosom
of eternal snows."[41] Dr. Meigs had a different analogy to make
the same point, contrasting the anatomy of the Apollo of the
Belvedere (illustrating the male principle) with the Venus de
Medici (illustrating the female principle). "Woman," said the
physician, with a kind of clinical gallantry, "has a head almost
too small for intellect but just big enough for love."[42]

This love itself was to be passive and responsive. "Love, in the heart of a woman," wrote Mrs. Farrar, "should partake largely of the nature of gratitude. She should love, because she is already loved by one deserving her regard."[43]

Woman was to work in silence, unseen, like Wordsworth's Lucy. Yet, "working like nature, in secret" her love goes forth to the world "to regulate its pulsation, and send forth from its heart, in pure and temperate flow, the life-giving current."[44] She was to work only for pure affection, without thought of money or ambition. A poem, "Woman and Fame," by Felicia Hemans, widely quoted in many of the gift books, concludes with a spirited renunciation of the gift of fame:

> Away! to me, a woman, bring
> Sweet flowers from affection's spring.[45]

"True feminine genius," said Grace Greenwood (Sara Jane Clarke) "is ever timid, doubtful, and clingingly dependent; a perpetual childhood." And she advised literary ladies in an essay on "The Intellectual Woman"—"Don't trample on the flowers while longing for the stars."[46] A wife who submerged her own talents to work for her husband was extolled as an example of a true woman. In *Women of Worth: A Book for Girls*, Mrs. Ann Flaxman, an artist of promise herself, was praised because she "devoted herself to sustain her husband's genius and aid him in his arduous career."[47]

Caroline Gilman's advice to the bride aimed at establishing this proper order from the beginning of a marriage: "Oh, young and lovely bride, watch well the first moments when your will conflicts with his to whom God and society have given the control. Reverence his *wishes* even when you do not his *opinions*."[48]

Mrs. Gilman's perfect wife in *Recollections of a Southern Matron* realizes that "the three golden threads with which domestic happiness is woven" are "to repress a harsh answer, to confess a fault, and to stop (right or wrong) in the midst of self-defense, in gentle submission." Woman could do this, hard though it was, because in her heart she knew she was right and so could afford to be forgiving, even a trifle condescending. "Men are not unreasonable," averred Mrs. Gilman. "Their difficulties lie in not understanding the moral and physical nature of our sex. They

often wound through ignorance, and are surprised at having
offended." Wives were advised to do their best to reform men,
but if they couldn't, to give up gracefully. "If any habit of his
annoyed me, I spoke of it once or twice, calmly, then bore it
quietly."⁴⁹

A wife should occupy herself "only with domestic affairs—
wait till your husband confides to you those of a high importance
—and do not give your advice until he asks for it," advised the
Lady's Token. At all times she should behave in a manner becoming a woman, who had "no arms other than gentleness."
Thus "if he is abusive, never retort."⁵⁰ *A Young Lady's Guide
to the Harmonious Development of a Christian Character* suggested
that females should "become as little children" and "avoid a controversial spirit."⁵¹ *The Mother's Assistant and Young Lady's
Friend* listed "Always Conciliate" as its first commandment in
"Rules for Conjugal and Domestic Happiness." Small wonder that
these same rules ended with the succinct maxim: "Do not expect
too much."⁵²

As mother, as well as wife, woman was required to submit to
fortune. In *Letters to Mothers* Mrs. Sigourney sighed: "To bear
the evils and sorrows which may be appointed us, with a patient
mind, should be the continual effort of our sex. . . . It seems,
indeed, to be expected of us; since the passive and enduring
virtues are more immediately within our province." Of these
trials "the hardest was to bear the loss of children with submission" but the indomitable Mrs. Sigourney found strength to
murmur to the bereaved mother: "The Lord loveth a cheerful
giver."⁵³ *The Ladies' Parlor Companion* agreed thoroughly in "A
Submissive Mother," in which a mother who had already buried
two children and was nursing a dying baby saw her sole remaining child "probably scalded to death. Handing over the infant to die in the arms of a friend, she bowed in sweet submission
to the double stroke." But the child "through the goodness of
God survived, and the mother learned to say 'Thy will be
done.' "⁵⁴

Woman then, in all her roles, accepted submission as her lot.
It was a lot she had not chosen or deserved. As *Godey's* said,
"the lesson of submission is forced upon woman." Without comment or criticism the writer affirms that "To suffer and to be
silent under suffering seems the great command she has to

obey."[55] George Burnap referred to a woman's life as "a series of suppressed emotions."[56] She was, as Emerson said, "more vulnerable, more infirm, more mortal than man."[57] The death of a beautiful woman, cherished in fiction, represented woman as the innocent victim, suffering without sin, too pure and good for this world but too weak and passive to resist its evil forces.[58] The best refuge for such a delicate creature was the warmth and safety of her home.

The true woman's place was unquestionably by her own fireside—as daughter, sister, but most of all as wife and mother. Therefore domesticity was among the virtues most prized by the women's magazines. "As society is constituted," wrote Mrs. S. E. Farley, on the "Domestic and Social Claims on Woman," "the true dignity and beauty of the female character seem to consist in a right understanding and faithful and cheerful performance of social and family duties."[59] Sacred Scripture reenforced social pressure: "St. Paul knew what was best for women when he advised them to be domestic," said Mrs. Sandford. "There is composure at home; there is something sedative in the duties which home involves. It affords security not only from the world, but from delusions and errors of every kind."[60]

From her home woman performed her great task of bringing men back to God. *The Young Ladies' Class Book* was sure that "the domestic fireside is the great guardian of society against the excesses of human passions."[61] *The Lady at Home* expressed its convictions in its very title and concluded that "even if we cannot reform the world in a moment, we can begin the work by reforming ourselves and our households—It is woman's mission. Let her not look away from her own little family circle for the means of producing moral and social reforms, but begin at home."[62]

Home was supposed to be a cheerful place, so that brothers, husbands and sons would not go elsewhere in search of a good time. Woman was expected to dispense comfort and cheer. In writing the biography of Margaret Mercer (every inch a true woman) her biographer (male) notes: "She never forgot that it is the peculiar province of woman to minister to the comfort, and promote the happiness, first, of those most nearly allied to her, and then of those, who by the Providence of God are placed in a state of dependence upon her."[63] Many other essays in the women's journals showed woman as comforter: "Woman, Man's Best Friend," "Woman, the Greatest Social Benefit," "Woman, A Being to Come Home To," "The Wife: Source of Comfort and the Spring of Joy."[64]

One of the most important functions of woman as comforter was her role as nurse. Her own health was probably, although regrettably, delicate.[65] Many homes had "little sufferers," those pale children who wasted away to saintly deaths. And there were enough other illnesses of youth and age, major and minor, to give the nineteenth-century American woman nursing experience. The sickroom called for the exercise of her higher qualities of patience, mercy and gentleness as well as for her housewifely arts. She could thus fulfill her dual feminine function—beauty and usefulness.

The cookbooks of the period offer formulas for gout cordials, ointment for sore nipples, hiccough and cough remedies, opening pills and refreshing drinks for fever, along with recipes for pound cake, jumbles, stewed calves head and currant wine.[66] *The Ladies' New Book of Cookery* believed that "food prepared by the kind hand of a wife, mother, sister, friend" tasted better and had a "restorative power which money cannot purchase."[67]

A chapter of *The Young Lady's Friend* was devoted to woman's privilege as "ministering spirit at the couch of the sick." Mrs. Farrar advised a soft voice, gentle and clean hands, and a cheerful smile. She also cautioned against an excess of female delicacy. That was all right for a young lady in the parlor, but not for bedside manners. Leeches, for example, were to be regarded as "a curious piece of mechanism . . . their ornamental stripes should recommend them even to the eye, and their valuable services to our feelings." And she went on calmly to discuss their use. Nor were women to shrink from medical terminology, since "If you cultivate right views of the wonderful structure of the body, you will be as willing to speak to a physician of the bowels as the brains of your patient."[68]

Nursing the sick, particularly sick males, not only made a woman feel useful and accomplished, but increased her influence. In a piece of heavyhanded humor in *Godey's* a man confessed that some women were only happy when their husbands were ailing that they might have the joy of nursing him to recovery "thus gratifying their medical vanity and their love of power by making him more dependent upon them."[69] In a similar vein a husband sometimes suspected his wife "almost wishes me dead—for the pleasure of being utterly inconsolable."[70]

In the home women were not only the highest adornment of civilization, but they were supposed to keep busy at morally uplifting tasks. Fortunately most of housework, if looked at in true womanly fashion, could be regarded as uplifting. Mrs. Sigourney extolled its virtues: "The science of housekeeping affords exercise for the judgment and energy, ready recollection, and patient self-possession, that are the characteristics of a superior mind."[71] According to Mrs. Farrar, making beds was good exercise, the repetitiveness of routine tasks inculcated patience and perseverance, and proper management of the home was a surprisingly complex art: "There is more to be learned about pouring out tea and coffee, than most young ladies are willing to believe."[72] Godey's went so far as to suggest coyly, in "Learning vs. Housewifery" that the two were complementary, not opposed: chemistry could be utilized in cooking, geometry in dividing cloth, and phrenology in discovering talent in children.[73]

Women were to master every variety of needlework, for, as Mrs. Sigourney pointed out, "Needle-work, in all its forms of use, elegance, and ornament, has ever been the appropriate occupation of woman."[74] Embroidery improved taste; knitting promoted serenity and economy.[75] Other forms of artsy-craftsy activity for her leisure moments included painting on glass or velvet, Poonah work, tussy-mussy frames for her own needlepoint or water colors, stands for hyacinths, hair bracelets or baskets of feathers.[76]

She was expected to have a special affinity for flowers. To the editors of *The Lady's Token* "A Woman never appears more truly in her sphere, than when she divides her time between her domestic avocations and the culture of flowers."[77] She could write letters, an activity particularly feminine since it had to do with the outpourings of the heart,[78] or practice her drawingroom skills of singing and playing an instrument. She might even read.

Here she faced a bewildering array of advice. The female was dangerously addicted to novels, according to the literature of the period. She should avoid them, since they interfered with "serious piety." If she simply couldn't help herself and read them anyway, she should choose edifying ones from lists of morally acceptable authors. She should study history since it "showed the depravity of the human heart and the evil nature of sin." On the whole, "religious biography was best."[79]

The women's magazines themselves could be read without any loss of concern for the home. *Godey's* promised the husband that he would find his wife "no less assiduous for his reception, or less sincere in welcoming his return" as a result of reading their magazine.[80] *The Lily of the Valley* won its right to be admitted to the boudoir by confessing that it was "like its namesake humble and unostentatious, but it is yet pure, and, we trust, free from moral imperfections."[81]

No matter what later authorities claimed, the nineteenth century knew that girls *could* be ruined by a book. The seduction stories regard "exciting and dangerous books" as contributory causes of disaster. The man without honorable intentions always provides the innocent maiden with such books as a prelude to his assault on her virtue.[82] Books which attacked or seemed to attack woman's accepted place in society were regarded as equally dangerous. A reviewer of Harriet Martineau's *Society in America* wanted it kept out of the hands of American women. They were so susceptible to persuasion, with their "gentle yielding natures" that they might listen to "the bold ravings of the hard-featured of their own sex." The frightening result: "such reading will unsettle them for their true station and pursuits, and they will throw the world back again into confusion."[83]

The debate over women's education posed the question of whether a "finished" education detracted from the practice of housewifely arts. Again it proved to be a case of semantics, for a true woman's education was never "finished" until she was instructed in the gentle science of homemaking.[84] Helen Irving, writing on "Literary Women," made it very clear that if women invoked the muse, it was as a genie of the household lamp. "If the necessities of her position require these duties at her hands, she will perform them nonetheless cheerfully, that she knows herself capable of higher things." The literary woman must conform to the same standards as any other woman: "That her home shall be made a loving place of rest and joy and comfort for those who are dear to her, will be the first wish of every true woman's heart."[85] Mrs. Ann

Stephens told women who wrote to make sure they did not sacrifice one domestic duty. "As for genius, make it a domestic plant. Let its roots strike deep in your house. . . ."[86]

The fear of "blue stockings" (the eighteenth-century male's term of derision for educated or literary women) need not persist for nineteenth-century American men. The magazines presented spurious dialogues in which bachelors were convinced of their fallacy in fearing educated wives. One such dialogue took place between a young man and his female cousin. Ernest deprecates learned ladies ("A *Woman* is far more lovable than a *philosopher*") but Alice refutes him with the beautiful example of their Aunt Barbara who "although she *has* perpetrated the heinous crime of writing some half dozen folios" is still a model of "the spirit of feminine gentleness." His memory prodded, Ernest concedes that, by George, there was a woman: "When I last had a cold she not only made me a bottle of cough syrup, but when I complained of nothing new to read, set to work and wrote some twenty stanzas on consumption."[87]

The magazines were filled with domestic tragedies in which spoiled young girls learned that when there was a hungry man to feed French and china painting were not helpful. According to these stories many a marriage is jeopardized because the wife has not learned to keep house. Harriet Beecher Stowe wrote a sprightly piece of personal experience for *Godey's*, ridiculing her own bad housekeeping as a bride. She used the same theme in a story "The Only Daughter," in which the pampered beauty learns the facts of domestic life from a rather difficult source, her mother-in-law. Mrs. Hamilton tells Caroline in the sweetest way possible to shape up in the kitchen, reserving her rebuke for her son: "You are her husband—her guide—her protector—now see what you can do," she admonishes him. "Give her credit for every effort: treat her faults with tenderness; encourage and praise whenever you can, and depend upon it, you will see another woman in her." He is properly masterful, she properly domestic and in a few months Caroline is making lumpless gravy and keeping up with the darning. Domestic tranquillity has been restored and the young wife moralizes: "Bring up a girl to feel that she has a responsible part to bear in promoting the happiness of the family, and you make a reflecting being of her at once, and remove that lightness and frivolity of character which makes her shrink from graver studies."[88] These stories end with the heroine drying her hands on her apron and vowing that *her* daughter will be properly educated, in piecrust as well as Poonah work.

The female seminaries were quick to defend themselves against any suspicion of interfering with the role which nature's God had assigned to women. They hoped to enlarge and deepen that role, but not to change its setting. At the Young Ladies' Seminary and Collegiate Institute in Monroe City, Michigan, the catalogue admitted few of its graduates would be likely "to fill the learned professions." Still, they were called to "other scenes of usefulness and honor." The average woman is to be "the presiding genius of love" in the home, where she is to "give a correct and elevated literary taste to her children, and to assume that influential station that she ought to possess as the companion of an educated man."[80]

At Miss Pierce's famous school in Litchfield, the students were taught that they had "attained the perfection of their characters when they could combine their elegant accomplishments with a turn for solid domestic virtues."[90] Mt. Holyoke paid pious tribute to domestic skills: "Let a young lady despise this branch of the duties of woman, and she despises the appointments of her existence." God, nature and the Bible "enjoin these duties on the sex, and she cannot violate them with impunity." Thus warned, the young lady would have to seek knowledge of these duties elsewhere, since it was not in the curriculum at Mt. Holyoke. "We would not take this privilege from the mother."[91]

One reason for knowing her way around a kitchen was that America was "a land of precarious fortunes," as Lydia Maria Child pointed out in her book *The Frugal Housewife: Dedicated to Those Who Are Not Ashamed of Economy*. Mrs. Child's chapter "How To Endure Poverty" prescribed a combination of piety and knowledge—the kind of knowledge found in a true woman's education, "a thorough religious *useful* education."[92] The woman who had servants today, might tomorrow, because of a depression or panic, be forced to do her own work. If that happened she knew how to act, for she was to be the same cheerful consoler of her husband in their cottage as in their mansion.

An essay by Washington Irving, much quoted in the gift annuals, discussed the value of a wife in case of business reverses: "I have observed that a married man falling into misfortune is more apt to achieve his situation in the world than a single one . . . it is beautifully ordained by Providence that woman, who is the ornament of man in his happier hours, should be his stay and solace when smitten with sudden calamity."[93]

A story titled simply but eloquently "The Wife" dealt with the quiet heroism of Ellen Graham during her husband's plunge from fortune to poverty. Ned Graham said of her: "Words are too poor to tell you what I owe to that noble woman. In our darkest seasons of adversity, she has been an angel of consolation—utterly forgetful of self and anxious only to comfort and sustain me." Of course she had a little help from "faithful Dinah who absolutely refused to leave her beloved mistress," but even so Ellen did no more than would be expected of any true woman.[94]

Most of this advice was directed to woman as wife. Marriage was the proper state for the exercise of the domestic virtues. "True Love and a Happy Home," an essay in *The Young Ladies' Oasis*, might have been carved on every girl's hope chest.[95] But although marriage was best, it was not absolutely necessary. The women's magazines tried to remove the stigma from being an "Old Maid." They advised no marriage at all rather than an unhappy one contracted out of selfish motives.[96] Their stories showed maiden ladies as unselfish ministers to the sick, teachers of the young, or moral preceptors with their pens, beloved of the entire village. Usually the life of single blessedness resulted from the premature death of a fiancé, or was chosen through fidelity to some high mission. For example, in "Two Sisters," Mary devotes herself to Ellen and her abandoned children, giving up her own chance for marriage. "Her devotion to her sister's happiness has met its reward in the consciousness of having fulfilled a sacred duty."[97] Very rarely, a "woman of genius" was absolved from the necessity of marriage, being so extraordinary that she did not need the security or status of being a wife.[98] Most often, however, if girls proved "difficult," marriage and a family were regarded as a cure.[99] The "sedative quality" of a home could be counted on to subdue even the most restless spirits.

George Burnap saw marriage as "that sphere for which woman was originally intended, and to which she is so exactly fitted to adorn and bless, as the wife, the mistress of a home, the solace, the aid, and the counsellor of that ONE, for whose sake alone the world is of any consequence to her."[100] Samuel Miller preached a sermon on women: "How interesting and important are the duties devolved on females as WIVES . . . the counsellor and friend of the husband; who makes it her daily study to lighten his cares, to soothe his sorrows, and to augment his joys; who, like a guardian angel, watches over his interests, warns him against dangers, comforts him under trials; and by her pious, assiduous, and attractive deportment, constantly endeavors to render him more virtuous, more useful, more honourable, and more happy."[101] A woman's whole interest should be focused on her husband, paying him "those numberless attentions to which the French give the title of *petits soins* and which the woman who loves knows so well how to pay . . . she should consider nothing as trivial which could win a smile of approbation from him."[102]

Marriage was seen not only in terms of service but as an increase in authority for woman. Burnap concluded that marriage improves the female character "not only because it puts her under the best possible tuition, that of the affections, and affords scope to her active energies, but because it gives her higher aims, and a more dignified position."[103] *The Lady's Amaranth* saw it as a balance of power: "The man bears rule over his wife's person and conduct. She bears rule over his inclinations: he governs by law; she by persuasion. . . . The empire of the woman is an empire of softness . . . her commands are caresses, her menaces are tears."[104]

Woman should marry, but not for money. She should choose only the high road of true love and not truckle to the values of a materialistic society. A story "Marrying for Money" (subtlety was not the strong point of the ladies' magazines) depicts Gertrude, the heroine, rueing the day she made her crass choice: "It is a terrible thing to live without love. . . . A woman who dares marry for aught but the purest affection, calls down the just judgments of heaven upon her head."[105]

The corollary to marriage, with or without true love, was motherhood, which added another dimension to her usefulness and her prestige. It also anchored her even more firmly to the home. "My Friend," wrote Mrs. Sigourney, "If in becoming a mother, you have reached the climax of your happiness, you have also taken a higher place in the scale of being . . . you have gained an increase of power."[106] The Rev. J. N. Danforth pleaded in *The Ladies' Casket*, "Oh, mother, acquit thyself well in thy humble sphere, for thou mayest affect the world."[107] A true woman naturally loved her children; to suggest otherwise was monstrous.[108]

America depended upon her mothers to raise up a whole generation of Christian statesmen who could say "all that I am I owe to my angel mother."[109] The mothers must do the inculcating of virtue since the fathers, alas, were too busy chasing the dollar. Or as *The Ladies' Companion* put it more effusively, the father "weary with the heat and burden of life's summer day, or trampling with unwilling foot the decaying leaves of life's autumn, has forgotten the sympathies of life's joyous springtime. . . . The acquisition of wealth, the advancement of his children in worldly honor—these are his self-imposed tasks." It was his wife who formed "the infant mind as yet untainted by contact with evil . . . like wax beneath the plastic hand of the mother."[110]

The Ladies' Wreath offered a fifty-dollar prize to the woman who submitted the most convincing essay on "How May An American Woman Best Show Her Patriotism." The winner was Miss Elizabeth Wetherell who provided herself with a husband in her answer. The wife in the essay of course asked her husband's opinion. He tried a few jokes first—"Call her eldest son George Washington," "Don't speak French, speak American"—but then got down to telling her in sober prize-winning truth what women could do for their country. Voting was no asset, since that would result only in "a vast increase of confusion and expense without in the smallest degree affecting the result." Besides, continued this oracle, "looking down at their child," if "we were to go a step further and let the children vote, their first act would be to vote their mothers at home." There is no comment on this devastating male logic and he continues: "Most women would follow the lead of their fathers and husbands," and the few who would "fly off on a tangent from the circle of home influence would cancel each other out."

The wife responds dutifully: "I see all that. I never understood so well before." Encouraged by her quick womanly perception, the master of the house resolves the question—an American woman best shows her patriotism by staying at home, where she brings her influence to bear "upon the right side for the country's weal." That woman will instinctively choose the side of right he has no doubt. Besides her "natural refinement and closeness to God" she has the "blessed advantage of a quiet life" while man is exposed to conflict and evil. She stays home with "her Bible and a well-balanced mind" and raises her sons to be good Americans. The judges rejoiced in this conclusion and paid the prize money cheerfully, remarking "they deemed it cheap at the price."[111]

If any woman asked for greater scope for her gifts the magazines were sharply critical. Such women were tampering with society, undermining civilization. Mary Wollstonecraft, Frances Wright and Harriet Martineau were condemned in the strongest possible language—they were read out of the sex. "They are only semi-women, mental hermaphrodites." The Rev. Harrington knew the women of America could not possibly approve of such perversions and went to some wives and mothers to ask if they did want a "wider sphere of interest" as these nonwomen claimed. The answer was reassuring. " 'NO!' they cried simultaneously, 'Let the men take care of politics, *we will take care of the children!*' " Again female discontent resulted only from a lack of understanding: women were not subservient, they were rather "chosen vessels." Looked at in this light the conclusion was inescapable: "Noble, sublime is the task of the American mother."[112]

"Women's Rights" meant one thing to reformers, but quite another to the True Woman. She knew her rights,

> The right to love whom others scorn,
> The right to comfort and to mourn,
> The right to shed new joy on earth,
> The right to feel the soul's high worth . . .
> Such women's rights, and God will bless
> And crown their champions with success.[113]

The American woman had her choice—she could define her rights in the way of the women's magazines and insure them by the practice of the requisite virtues, or she could go outside the home, seeking other rewards than love. It was a decision on which, she was told, everything in her world depended. "Yours it is to determine," the Rev. Mr. Stearns solemnly warned from the pulpit, "whether the beautiful order of society . . . shall continue as it has been" or whether "society shall break up and become a chaos of disjointed and unsightly elements."[114] If she chose to listen to other voices than those of her proper mentors, sought other rooms than those of her home, she lost both her happiness and her power —"that almost magic power, which, in her proper sphere, she now wields over the destinies of the world."[115]

But even while the women's magazines and related literature encouraged this ideal of the perfect woman, forces were at work in the nineteenth century which impelled woman herself to change, to play a more creative role in society. The movements for social reform, westward migration, missionary activity, utopian communities, industrialism, the Civil War—all called forth responses from woman which differed from those she was trained to believe were hers by nature and divine decree. The very perfection of True Womanhood, moreover, carried within itself the seeds of its own destruction. For if woman was so very little less than the angels, she should surely take a more active part in running the world, especially since men were making such a hash of things.

Real women often felt they did not live up to the ideal of True Womanhood: some of them blamed themselves, some challenged the standard, some tried to keep the virtues and enlarge the scope of womanhood.[116] Somehow through this mixture of challenge and acceptance, of change and continuity, the True Woman evolved into the New Woman—a transformation as startling in its way as the abolition of slavery or the coming of the machine age. And yet the stereotype, the "mystique" if you will, of what woman was and ought to be persisted, bringing guilt and confusion in the midst of opportunity.[117]

The women's magazines and related literature had feared this very dislocation of values and blurring of roles. By careful manipulation and interpretation they sought to convince woman that she had the best of both worlds—power and virtue—and that a stable order of society depended upon her maintaining her traditional place in it. To that end she was identified with everything that was beautiful and holy.

"Who Can Find a Valiant Woman?" was asked frequently from the pulpit and the editorial pages. There was only one place to look for her—at home. Clearly and confidently these authorities proclaimed the True Woman of the nineteenth century to be the Valiant Woman of the Bible, in whom the heart of her husband rejoiced and whose price was above rubies.

3

THE MERCHANT'S DAUGHTER:
A Tale From Life

A popular cautionary tale in the nineteenth century praised the Merchant's Daughter who, faced with her father's ruin, was forced to make her own way in the world. She stood up to outrageous fortune with fortitude, convinced that her character as well as that of her parents would be improved by the change in circumstances. True Womanhood provided a posture and rhetoric for economic disaster, as it did for most contingencies of life, and they were as well-known and inflexible as any folk rite.[1]

The Merchant's Daughter Tale is an example of the ambivalence with which the New England conscience viewed the man of commerce: scorning his pursuit of money while regarding prosperity as a mark of Divine favor. The New England woman, as daughter or wife, was supposed to be the best countervailing force to this dangerous materialism. America in the 1840s was a "Land of Precarious Fortunes" in which women might well find themselves confronted with the sudden need to earn a living. Caroline Healey's actions after her father lost his money in the depression of 1842 constituted a real-life paradigm of the Merchant's Daughter Tale, and an example of literary conventions applied to life. Her story suggests several other patterns in the culture of a New England girl of the mid-nineteenth century: her definition of woman's nature and role; the opportunities open to a new female member of the deserving poor; woman's relationship to a changing church and to certain reform movements; and the way in which an individual could select elements in these movements which appealed to his own personality and needs.[2]

Caroline would be affiliated with many reforms in her long life, especially those which concerned women. Her passion was for self-justification, and woman as victim and martyr was a congenial image with which she could identify. From her position on the fringes of so many groups she personalized and made more simple (and frequently more vulgar) their philosophy and goals.

Caroline Healey's life before the panic which cost her father his fortune was a kind of cultural conditioning for her actions during that crisis. Coming of age in New England meant, for her, inheriting the family traditions of Calvin and descent from the martyr John Rogers. It meant attending the Unitarian West Church in Boston, and hearing Theodore Parker's Sermons and Margaret Fuller's Conversations. She was no stranger to decided or unpopular views. "I have never known what it was to be *without* an opinion of my own," she wrote in 1840, and implicit in this statement was her eternal sense of grievance toward those who refused to acknowledge her rectitude. In her autobiography she proudly noted that human approbation had never dictated her actions; her conduct was never governed "by anything but my own sense of right."[3]

Mark Healey, her father, was an importer whose ships were part of the prosperous bustle at Central Wharf. Although wealthy he probably did not have the economic stature his daughter remembered, for she had a tendency to aggrandizement especially where he was concerned. A self-made man, Healey's name never adorned the committees of church, charitable, or political organizations served by those whose wealth was older.[4] Caroline's relations with him were close and complex, "like no other I have ever seen," she wrote to her fiancé. Her mother had been very ill at her birth and remained a semi-invalid while bearing seven more children. Caroline, who typically claimed to have recovered from her delicate infancy completely by her own will, with no help from her mother, was brought up by a father who had "desired a son" and "determined I should supply the place of one." Like many men whose education had been neglected, Mark Healey had "in consequent, extravagant views on the advantages of education," which he forcefed to his daughter. This family pattern was common among nineteenth-century feminists.[5]

Healey was no stereotype of a money-grubbing merchant. The escaped slave Ellen Crafts hid in his home, and he was among the Boston businessmen who raised money to hire the Music Hall for Theodore Parker. In her autobiography Caroline regretted that her father's obituaries (he died in November, 1879) stressed his mercantile career: "He had a great love of nature, of budding flowers

and leaves, of young animals and children."[6] But this assessment
came much later; in the 1840s she fixed much of the blame for her
unhappy childhood on the once-adored father.[7]

By her own admission she possessed qualities which virtually
guaranteed a miserable youth. She was awkward, plump, near-
sighted, "without gayety—habitually sad—and avoiding all my own
age." Her schoolmates called her "The Disappointed" because
nothing and no one turned out as she required. Her father was her
first and greatest disappointment. Until the age of ten she could
not "imagine that anything would be more perfect than my father's
character." Then her illusion vanished when he refused "to accede
to many of the philosophical positions which I assumed."[8]

These positions, as she pointed out in a long autobiographical
letter to Theodore Parker, were the result of much painful thought
and introspection. At the age of nine she had been a confirmed
doubter; "Did you ever hear of a skeptic child? I was such a child."
She was "morbidly conscientious," scrupulous to a fault, requiring
more of herself than even "Christianity required from me." She
determined to find a rationale for what she believed. Her starting
points, the fruits of her father's secular education, were "a love of
the beautiful and mechanics." From these she was moved "to seek
infinite beauty and law." She accepted the Platonic concept of an
ideal universe and the existence of some absolute moral law which
made man want to do good and avoid evil. "I connected Moral
Force with my idea of the Absolute Intellect, and became convinced
of my accountability and immortality." *Cogito ergo credo*, the intellectual answer to the eighteenth-century rationalists and their version of the evangelical conversion experience. In Caroline's case an
obvious echo of Parker and Emerson, couched in the style of the
popular novels where an intellectually gifted woman works her way
through learned tomes and finally makes an intuitive leap to faith
and Divine Love. It is then her mission to convert the still-skeptic
male.[9]

Parker referred to her letter as "the expression of a soul that
loves truth and is itself full of piety and love"; he invited further
correspondence and meetings. Besides Parker's influence, Caroline's religious views were formed by her admiration for Joseph
Tuckerman, who founded the ministry-at-large among the urban
poor. Tuckerman stressed compassion and the charity of Christ,
doing good rather than being good. Charles Dall, the idealistic
young man whom Caroline married, was one of these "laborers in
the vineyard," and she told him often during their courtship that

his special ministry was the greatest bond between them. Working as she did among these people, "going frequently into very doubtful houses and on very unwelcome errands," Caroline regarded herself as consecrated to this special work of relief and rehabilitation. Tuckerman she called "one of the two most potent factors in my religious life."[10]

The other was the gentle Dr. Charles Lowell, father of the poet, and pastor of the West Church. Dr. Lowell had refused to participate in any of the controversies which divided Protestants. God, for him, was simply "Father" and "Best Friend," and his worship "had much more to do with the affections than with the understanding." True religion consisted of "humility, meekness, charity, piety. There is no controversy about them." These ideas were typical of the trends towards a less harsh—some said more feminine—church.[11]

Characteristically Caroline translated Parker and Lowell into a "Jesus-Loves-Me" simplicity. In two books written after she had augmented her beliefs with a study of the Septuagint in the original, she posited Christ as a man who led "a simple, pure, and natural life," not bent "under the weight of the Godhead." The problem of miracles, which she had argued with Parker, was resolved by re-stating Emerson's belief that "Man's life is a miracle." A more personal statement of her religious beliefs is found in a series of children's books which she wrote in the 1860s and which she admitted were "chiefly autobiographical." These books were a triumph, almost an orgy, of wish-fulfillment. The heroine, "dear little Patty Gray," is Caroline herself, but given a happy childhood by her loving, understanding parents. They realize, as her own parents had failed to, that Patty's own "very tender little conscience" will cause her sufficient agonies if she does wrong; no outside force is needed. On the other hand, "if her little heart told her she was doing right, all the world might blame her, and Patty could still hold up her head stiffly, and go merrily on her way."

Her father taught her to pray to a gentle God who "will send a sweet, loving peace into her heart, which will make her happy, whatever else fails; and so taught, little Patty was merry all day long."

A crisis arises in one of the books when Patty is weeping because she has not been good enough. Mama tells her she won't be good until she is happy:

"Mama, was Jesus happy?"
"The very happiest person that ever was," said Mama brightly.[12]

These religious views made Caroline, according to her own statement, a Transcendentalist. She offered her rather hazy definition of the term in answer to her pupil's question, "Miss Healey, do you know whether transcendentalism means anything deep?"

> "I can tell you what it means, Minerva," said I, "but I am afraid you will not understand. It means faith in evidence *transcending* the evidence of the senses—faith in God speaking within. . . ."[13]

In later lectures Caroline linked the Transcendentalist movement with most of the liberal reforms of the century, especially with those concerning women. She went so far as to claim Anne Hutchinson as the first Transcendentalist, and Margaret Fuller as the last and greatest.[14]

Caroline claimed that "the greatest blessing" of her life was to have been "almost as a child to Margaret Fuller." She praised Miss Fuller for her generosity to single women, and her remarkable way of making the young feel they too could do great things. However Caroline's private record of Margaret's conversations is more revealing than that which she published.[15]

Caroline was not only the youngest member of the groups which listened to Miss Fuller's improvisations, but undoubtedly one of the most self-absorbed. Still, with her passion for setting the record straight, she wrote down what she remembered. If it reads badly it may be partly because Margaret always lost something in translation. Caroline's clairvoyance, "that sad oppressive gift, which it was God's will that I should have," told her that Margaret found her presence distasteful. Elizabeth Peabody wrote her a note asking her not to speak unless spoken to. But Caroline, having "paid my money" would not be put down. After one unhappy performance Miss Peabody remarked, "If you had only seen Emerson look at you last night I am sure you would never have said some things you did." Caroline was undaunted. "Emerson had a right to think my questions silly . . . he had *no* right to feel as he did toward me, in consequence."

Caroline had some insight into this select circle, even though she stood outside it. She noted that Parker and Margaret were never close because both demanded "a sort of personal submission before newcomers could be admitted to a cordial understanding." Margaret wanted a mesmerized audience, not dialogue with equals.

Caroline was awed by no one, not even "Sages" or "Delphic Oracles." She cherished her "instinct of self possession" and refused to be "so enamored of any, as to lose my own centre." This, of course, is only good Transcendental doctrine. Much as Caroline longed to be loved by Margaret and her friends, she was content to remain aloof in this world since "I felt more sure of being understood by them in another."[16]

The comparisons between Margaret Fuller and Caroline Healey are many; indeed one suspects that Caroline deliberately structured her writings so as to make their lives seem even more alike. Both had nondescript mothers, and fathers who were the dominant forces in their lives. Both had strong wills and egos and possessed the New England drive for self-culture almost to the point of mania. But where Margaret had the "magnetism" which attracted even as it repelled, Caroline could exact only grudging tribute for her diligence and good works. Both women admitted to strong passions. Margaret found one happy if unconventional interlude before her tragic early death. Caroline's emotional life, although more conventional, was increasingly bitter and frustrated, and she lingered to an eccentric old age.

Margaret Fuller's ideas on women formed part of Caroline's own concept of womanhood. Woman was all sympathy, wisdom and genius, the higher and better part of creation. She had not developed as she should, held back by the same restrictive society that prevented man's full potential from being realized. Transcendentalism by stressing the divine in every human being was perforce a kind of woman's rights movement, since it did not except women from its hopes for mankind.

Theodore Parker's ideas on women coincided with Miss Fuller's. He was convinced that "theology would have been in a vastly better state than it is now" had women been consulted; certainly "no woman would have preached the damnation of babies newborn." Parker suggested a "Father-Mother God" as an expression of the Allness of the Almighty. Woman's nature was superior "in affairs of emotion—moral, affectional, religious." Woman's mission was "to correct man's tastes, mend his morals, excite his affections, inspire his religious faculties." This mission, like charity, should begin at home, but, again like charity, could go anywhere. "Who would think of making Jenny Lind nothing but a housekeeper?"[17]

Cyrus Bartol, curate at the West Church from 1836 and pastor after Dr. Lowell's retirement, also influenced Caroline's ideas on women. His wife Elizabeth, with whom Caroline was closely associated in her Sunday School work, was for the younger woman a model of behavior, especially for a minister's helpmeet. Frederick Hedge eulogized Mrs. Bartol's life as "within its allotted sphere . . . complete . . . A saint in simplicity and meekness, innocent of personal vanity and worldly ambition, she struggled for none of the prizes of life: they came to her unsought."[18]

Caroline dedicated one of her books "To the Ministers and People of the West Church, and especially to Cyrus A. Bartol, whose Life is Fit to Be a Woman's Inspiration." Bartol eventually wrote on woman's nature. He concluded that although man has more brain, "he also has more body and beard. Woman has more fineness, if less strength. She is more angelic, and he more animal."[19]

Another West Church influence on Caroline's ideas was that of Charles Loring, the leading layman in the church and Mark Healey's solicitor. Loring was noted for "his peculiar chivalric bearing towards women," and only the pressure of other work kept him from completing his proposed treatise on woman's "rightful claims to property and labor." These two subjects would be Caroline's most ardent crusades. Loring liked to quote "last at the cross and first at the grave" to illustrate woman's special nature which made her seek "enterprises requiring humility and self-sacrifice, with no other reward than the consciousness of duty faithfully attempted."[20]

Caroline's views on female nature combined elements from all these sources, stressing, as one might expect, woman's nobility and suffering. She early dismissed the so-called woman's rights movement, "There is no modern reform that we take so little interest in. . . ." The really important task "of our country and our age . . . is to organize the rights of man. One of the holiest of his rights is to find woman in her proper place. . . ." Providence did not intend women to meddle in politics, "We feel that this is utterly incompatible with the more precious and positive duties of the nursery and the fireside."

She assumed all the conventions regarding woman's superior piety and purity, as well as her proper sphere. Writing to her fiancé, she recounted an offensive remark that had been addressed to her. "I do not believe that a woman who is perfectly delicate and proper will ever meet anything but respect. Somewhere, then, I have failed." She recommended that he read Fredrika Bremer's

Our Neighbors, because "it will show you more of a woman's heart and head than any book I know." Miss Bremer's book opens with these words:

> But in every time, and every nation, the hearth of home is in the care of woman. And if ever a nation shall deserve to present to the world a new and higher force of home-life, it must be that people in which woman is treated with the highest regard and true chivalry—where she is permitted to become all that nature intended her to be.[21]

Marriage and children were women's destined and sacred lot. Even Margaret Fuller, according to Caroline, was truly happy "when she laid her head upon the heart of her husband; and, through him, sweet Mother Nature finally appeased the hunger which no classic lore, no aesthetic culture, no contact with the wide world of social welcome, or resounding fame, had power to sate." But Caroline had seen unhappy marriages, had known "what it is to live with others, without being understood by them." She herself would prefer "the sin of infanticide" rather than the "sin of those who rear a child in the midst of dissension. . . ." Moreover, marriage was an end to separate identity and any woman feared "this yielding up of herself to another."[22]

Although Caroline judged herself rigidly according to the conventions of True Womanhood, she judged her fallen sisters by gentler standards. In this attitude, too, she reflected the views of her mentors. Joseph Tuckerman devoted much of his ministry to helping the virtuous country lass who, in the city, was "seduced, despoiled, destroyed, by profligate and base young men, who yet call themselves *gentlemen!*" Theodore Parker and Margaret Fuller both wrote with compassion about the suffering of the prostitute, more sinned against than sinning, whose guilt lay on the shoulders of society. It was assumed that women sinned either from economic necessity or from an excess of womanly generosity rather than from love of vice. Since transcendentalism stressed the validity of emotion and valued so much the heart-felt response, the sin of a too-loving woman would not be entirely black. In this treatment of the "fallen women," these reformers replaced the ethic of Puritanism which regarded carnal sins as the most scarlet and deepest damned, with an ethic closer to Dante's, where the icy sins of the intellect were punished more severely than those of the flesh.[23]

Caroline's essay, "The Sister," begged the virtuous woman to remember that only chance and providence kept her from those temptations "which beset the friendless and the loveless, the ignorant and the poor." Many women remain virtuous only because they are "surrounded by a natural or acquired coldness of temperament" and are completely without "opportunity." There are "*states of mind* more guilty than some single deeds. . . ." A later book, *Women's Rights Under the Law*, was dedicated to "the Friends of the Forsaken Women Throughout the World . . . because the lives of such women are the legitimate result of the spirit of the laws."[24]

Besides believing prostitution another burden laid on suffering women by inhumane society, Caroline was fascinated by the seduction story, that popular form of woman's magazine fiction. Like most girls of her era, she had avidly read *Charlotte Temple* and *The Coquette*. However Caroline carried her curiosity further than the average gentle reader; she compiled a book on the historical originals, *The Romance of the Association, or, One Last Glimpse of Charlotte Temple and Eliza Wharton: A Curiosity of Literature and Life*. Here Caroline refused to accept the classic plot and lesson which the anguish of conscience and death in childbirth of the heroine was supposed to provide. Instead she has nature improving art and insists that Elizabeth Whitman, the real life Eliza, had been legally married to someone of "foreign birth, rank and distinction, younger than herself." Although he "loved her to the point of marrying her," he was a typical male "not brave enough to encounter the indignation of his own family." Another example of man's cowardice and perfidy and woman's virtue duly noted.[25]

Woman's role was to counsel misguided man. Caroline would advise her "dearest Charlie" on every subject from his digestion to the degree of *ex tempore* permissible in his sermons. She would even, after their marriage, write a note rebuking him for having missed his son's first smile because he was closeted with his books. Combined with her sense of woman's mission was Caroline's certitude that her own opinion was unassailable, since she was "sanctified." This tenet must have been hard to live with when literally adhered to; with Caroline's personality it was often disastrous. Her husband would eventually prefer long absences in India to her ministrations. Her sisters resisted every attempt to improve their minds and characters, and, most unregenerate of all, her father persisted in his heresies.

Mark Healey was determined to turn his "devotional" child into a "literary" one. After a coming-out party where five hundred "perfect white scentless camellias" were distributed to the guests, he wanted to send her abroad to finish her education. She refused: "I knew that if I had any danger—it was that of loving the intellectual too well and pursuing it too far." Learning for its own sake was a distraction from the work of her ministry to the poor. She continued her classical studies only to prepare her beloved brother for college; the child died shortly before her father's failure.

Her father insisted she teach the younger children and serve as his secretary. She refused to give up her Sunday school teaching —at one time she taught five classes—her parish visiting or her religious reading. Her health broke under these activities and the strain "of trying to gain the love of those who would not appreciate me." Although she suffered, she was patient "because I knew it was my duty." Her role would be that of the Child Redeemer, another type favored in popular literature.[26]

At last there seemed to be some progress. Her father began to support her authority with the younger children; he even listened as she pointed out "the weaknesses in Hume and Hobbes." Then his business failed, and despite her protestations that loss of material possessions meant nothing to her, "his old faithlessness returned."[27]

A letter from one of Caroline's former teachers, Miss Eliza Hastings, written during flush times, closed with the prophetic words:

> You are entering life, my dear young friend, with every facility for improvement, usefulness, and happiness, and may these tokens of God's kindness be ever continued; but the lot of man is almost as variable as the atmosphere, and that person is most favored, that can with resignation and profit, meet the changes that occur.

Miss Hastings' advice would have been equally useful had Caroline's health failed, another contingency which found True Womanhood prepared. However the vicissitude of monetary loss was one which Caroline was particularly fortified to meet. In all the nineteenth-century literature on fickle fortune there is the hint of just punishment. After all, the rich man entering heaven has proverbially the problems of the camel getting through the eye of a needle. Caroline referred to that parable in an early sketch of idyllic home life, "The Sabbath." The father strokes "the golden locks of the fair daughter" as she reads the Bible to the younger children. Caroline apostrophizes: "The father, the successful merchant, the lucky speculator, the much caring, much enduring man of business, sighs as he hears how hardly the rich man shall enter into the kingdom of heaven. . . ."[28]

Caroline, "the good daughter," took the somewhat smug although sanctioned attitude that her father's failure is not *her* fault; she is the guiltless woman, making the best of his disaster. She behaved exactly as her religious beliefs and her statements on woman's nature conditioned her to act. Her "independence" is an approved response to a given stimulus, not an initiated action.

She thought primarily of teaching, either in a school or as a governess, and she approached her own friends and those of her family with a polite letter stating her recent misfortune and the necessity of earning a living. Her respondants were so uniform in their answers that one suspects certain prominent citizens worked out a "Merchant's Daughter Form Letter" to send to all worthy, suddenly impoverished young women.

Naturally she turned first to Theodore Parker. Her recent misfortune meant nothing to her except that the "necessity of self-exertion" precluded her "metaphysical interests." Still she hoped by her own adjustment to give her father "a glimpse of the silver lining" in this dark cloud.

Parker would eventually give a "Sermon on Merchants" addressed to "the most powerful and commanding" class in America, warning them against the temptation of "an extravagant desire for wealth. . . ." In another eloquent sermon, "The Moral Dangers Incident to Prosperity," Parker remarked on "how much we need the continual check of failure and disappointment. When the body is over-fed, leanness devours the soul." Both these sermons were delivered in embryo in his response to Caroline. He reacted almost with pleasure to news of her misfortune for he told himself that "this will be an advantage to her" because "she has the *intellect* and the *heart* and the soul to make a [blessing] of affliction *now*, or of prosperity *heretofore*." Her father's losses were for the best because "a perfect system of goodness governs the world"; a "Higher presence" converts "the apparent *accidents* of life into greater goods." Unlike some weaker mortals, *she* "will make this disappointment into a gain."[29]

Another logical recipient of her letter was Mrs. George Lee, author of the best-selling *Three Experiments in Living* and its sequel *Elinor Fulton*. Mrs. Lee's books were particularly appropriate because they dealt with the dangers of high living and the blessings of forced adversity. The three "experiments" of her title were the three financial styles of the Fulton family: Living Within the Means; Living Up to the Means; and Living Beyond the Means. Dr. Frank Fulton's practice and the family's happiness are sacrificed to Jane Fulton's extravagance and ambition. Frank, driven to speculation and finally to bankruptcy, goes west, leaving his family to manage as best they can.

In the sequel the beautiful virtuous daughter Elinor, with her "uncompromising sense of duty" singlehandedly brings the family back from economic disaster and, even more important, from spiritual bankruptcy. Thanks to her the family regains its moral integrity and a modest prosperity. Elinor's reward is marriage to an admirable man whom she truly loves.

Mrs. Lee, who made her reputation getting fictional heroines out of similar predicaments, suggested that Caroline check the New York papers advertising for governesses in the south. Her closing counsel could have been written by Elinor Fulton herself: "The enterprise and talents God has given you are the best security for your success."[30]

Another person whom Caroline approached was Horace Mann, Secretary of the Massachusetts Board of Education. Mann was a friend of Parker's, and since Caroline knew his wife slightly, she presumed to ask his advice. Mann's ideas on women were similar to Parker's. Female nature "is male nature, once more refined . . . *his* spirit was taken from the cruder straw below; *hers* from the more incorrupt and purer ether above. . . ." He was much in favor of enlarging woman's economic sphere, particularly as teachers, a profession which fitted her "peculiar principles of organization." However far woman might reach, the "center and beginning" of her "work of love" must, of course, remain "*at home*."

One of the advantages of teaching was that it did not pay well. Thus it had "the power of converting material wealth into spiritual well-being, and of giving to its possessors lordship and sovereignty alike over the temptations of adversity, and still more dangerous seducements of prosperity. . . ." Women as teachers would help save youth from the materialism of the age, and fulfill the moral of the Merchant's Daughter Tale. Mann sent Caroline a copy of his report containing some of these sentiments, along with his regrets that he knew of no situations. He added, she should remember that it was "one of the compensations of Providence, that such misfortunes tend strongly to develop and improve characters."[31]

George B. Emerson, cousin of Ralph Waldo Emerson, was the principal of one of the most fashionable seminaries in Massachusetts. Lacking a place for Caroline on his faculty, he could only suggest an assistantship at the New Bedford Academy, teaching drawing, French, and algebra for $500 a year. He did not recommend that she take this job, although he was in favor of her decision to teach. In the definitive work on the school and the schoolmaster on which Emerson collaborated with Alonzo Potter, he praised female teachers since their presence led to "the improvement of manners and morals in schools," and had a "peculiar power of awakening the sympathies of children, and inspiring them with a desire to excel." The same work also warned that a teacher should have "a strong predilection" for teaching and not engage in it "from compulsion and as a last resort, but as the most desirable and honorable of employments."[32]

A friend and fellow school-board member of her cousin, Samuel Foster Haven in Worcester, added his rhetorical voice: "To a strong heart like yours" temporal loss "cannot be other than a gain." The Reverend Alonzo Hill could only offer a position paying $286 a year, but nonetheless he was almost happy about the national debacle. He had observed so many " . . . noble instances of cheerful resignation, of ready adaptation to altered circumstances and unfailing trust in God" that "I can hardly regret the tornado that has swept over this country."[33]

George Choate, father of Joseph Hodges Choate, the lawyer, was chairman of Salem's school committee and active in educational reform. He knew of no openings, but told Caroline that although her plans might be vague, her happiness at least "was secure whatever may be the outward circumstances of your condition." He admired those "excellent principles with which your mind is richly stored," and congratulated her on her "noble resolves" to "achieve independence, by the exercise of your talents in so honorable and useful a pursuit. I have not the least doubt that you will find a solution—mutually profitable—to yourself and others."[34]

There were many more similar responses: from Philadelphia, where the panic was particularly severe, came the admonition that she was "valued above all for this noble effort at *independence*, saving I trust a heartfelt *dependence* on God." A source in New York told of a governess who had saved $3000 in three or four years in the south, where the people were pleasant even though "it was sickly in Summer, and she was much tormented by misquetoes." From Pomeroy, Ohio, arrived the hard-luck story of her correspondent, but from his own trials he drew the strength to encourage her, that one day these dark hours would seem "the brightest of your life, because you will feel they tended most of all, to strengthen and develop your character."[35]

When the flurry of correspondence subsided, Caroline accepted a position at Miss Lydia English's Seminary in Georgetown, District of Columbia, a select establishment whose students were often the daughters of southern plantation owners and politicians. Andrew Johnson's daughter was an alumna. The school was housed in a large and pleasant building, surrounded by a courtyard, where jessamine and orange trees blossomed.[36]

To Caroline it was another exotic world. Later she would compare it to the boarding school in *Villette*, and would see herself as a kind of exile and missionary, confronting an alien culture. She came to feel that her enforced absence from her family and her beloved Boston served the highest of purposes. Mrs. Gray (who, on occasion, represented Caroline the adult as Patty was Caroline the model child), remembered:

> If I was ever to be of any use in the world, I must learn to look at things truly, and find out that love is as precious as justice, charity dearer than bigotry, and that all good, and all grace, and all wisdom are to be found wherever God pleases to have them. To learn this I was sent away.[37]

Like any expatriate she saw many things more clearly once she was removed in distance. She renewed her acquaintance with Charles Dall, whom she would marry. She had her first real experience with slavery, and became an Abolitionist. But most of all she demonstrated her ability to rise above material loss and convert it, as the rhetoric of her correspondents had stressed, into spiritual gain. The reenforcement of all she had been taught to believe and expect convinced her that only one thing remained to vindicate her long struggle—the happy ending which literature provided for the Merchant's Daughter. Life was less kind.

Her marriage was marked by her husband's increasing ill-health and erratic behavior, and her increasing irascibility and preoccupation with woman's wrongs.[38] Finally he went off to be a missionary, returning at ever longer intervals, and leaving Caroline to continue her lonely and difficult life. Mark Healey's fortunes improved. It might be ironic proof that "the sins of the fathers are to be laid upon the children" but, in nineteenth-century terms, the ending was wrong. It was as if sweet Jessica's marriage failed while Shylock, still haggling over his ducats and pound of flesh, lived happily ever after.

4

FEMALE COMPLAINTS
Medical Views of American Women (1790-1865)

Travellers to America during the first half of the nineteenth century usually praised the delicate beauty and high spirits of the
American girl, but they regretted that she was abnormally pale,
collapsed under maternal responsibilities, and was likely to be a
faded invalid by thirty.[1] The doctors who prescribed for America's
ailing women shared these concerns. They shared also certain
views of woman's proper nature and role. The diseases they
treated and the treatment they chose were partly the result of the
definition of woman and of her sphere.[2]

Medical treatises on female complaints were written in a spirit
of moral regeneration and patriotic fervor. Woman was supposed
to be, if she were a true woman, pious, pure, submissive, and
domestic. She was destined to bring comfort and beauty into
man's life and to combat his more sensual nature and the materialism of business. The American woman was manifestly destined
to be the mother of a mighty race. If the republic were faltering
in its purpose, achieving less than its high promise, the fault
might lie with its seed-bearers—the too-frail wives and mothers of
its struggling statesmen and entrepreneurs.

Society itself was sick, argued some reformers, and was the specific cause of many diseases of which women were the suffering victims. Nineteenth-century medicine participated in some
areas of societal reform and was, in this sense, truly a social
science. It also served as a conservative influence, supporting the
traditional definition of woman's nature and role by the weight
of its evidence, against attempts to enlarge or change them. Physicians joined other arbiters of the country's moral and physical
well-being in a crusade to improve the health of this most interesting creature, adding the special quality of their rhetoric to that

57

of the clergy, the women's magazines, and the various reform movements. Dr. John Quackenbush addressed the students of the Albany Medical College in 1857 in woman's behalf: ". . .her gentleness, her feebleness, her peculiar trials, her dependence upon man for her support, her comfort and her happiness in life, entitle her to the warmest feelings of our heart, and make her the happy recipient of our love."[3]

Other physicians agreed that men addressing themselves to the "sacred fields" of obstetrics, midwifery, and the diseases of women and children, should do so with a spirit of reverence for their patients. "What do we owe her?" Dr. Charles Meigs asked a graduating class at the Jefferson Medical College. Only "life, peace, liberty, social order . . . Christianity is propagated by her domestic influence—Were it not for her we were this day clothed in sheep skins, and should lie down in dens and caves."[4]

Woman differed constitutionally from man; she was "more virtuous and less passionate."[5] Each woman was worthy of the respect a man would give to his own mother; and, therefore, the young doctors were exhorted in the strongest possible language to maintain the most rigorous standards of propriety and gentlemanly behavior. Whenever possible, a third person should be in the room during an examination, patient should remain lightly clothed, and the light should be dim. "Gentlemanly attentions" were as requisite at the bedside as in the parlor.[6] One professor urged as due "to this self-sacrificing being, that we, who know so well how to value her excellence, should labor assiduously to determine her sufferings, and assuage the sorrows incident to her sex."[7]

Conscious of their own inferiority in moral worth, the young male physician accepted other physical and mental distinctions of the sexes. Obviously woman's stature was smaller, the bones of her cranium "thinner, smaller, and more pliant; and the space destined to be filled with the brain is smaller."[8] From this it was easily deduced that woman was inferior to man in her ability to reason logically, however superior in spiritual matters. Dr. W. B. Beach summarized a discussion of woman's cerebral construction: "The intellectual powers of the female are, as a general rule, less than those of the male."[9] Woman's skin was softer, the organs "more mutable" than man's. She was "a passive vessel, waiting to be filled," as opposed to his active life principle.[10] Perhaps her outstanding physiological difference was the development of a nervous system "much more acute and more finely balanced than the male."[11] The nerves themselves were smaller and more delicately made, so that woman had naturally greater sensibility "and hence the increased susceptibility of impression from physical and moral causes. . . ."[12] These impressions, made so quickly, might pass away just as quickly, for women, although they bruised more easily, did not scar as did men.[13] As a result of this exquisite moral vulnerability woman bore ". . . the greater crosses . . . She dies a willing martyr for religion, for country—for her children."[14]

Woman did all this, not for fame or for money, but for love. It was her motivating force, sustaining her through the sufferings of childbirth and the strains of maternity. One doctor saw her lot as, "quite simply . . . First, to love; second, to love but one; third, to love always."[15] This stress upon woman's nonintellectual nature, the primacy of her heart over her head, affected the treatment of several diseases peculiar to, or suffered largely by, her sex. Many physicians felt that all her ailments stemmed "either directly or indirectly, from the womb, the organ of love and maternity."[16] The "qualities of the heart are oftener attended to by the womb than the abilities of the head," as one lecturer in obstetrics told his class, so it was not surprising that the largest class of female complaints was termed hysteria, from the Greek word for womb.[17]

Most treatises on female complaints included a section on hysteria, and it was a commonplace that the disease was virtually confined to young women. Instances of hysterical asthma and paralysis were discussed long before Freud opened his door to the hysterical ladies of Vienna. Certain manifestations of the disease were particularly common, such as the fear of suffocation and constriction of the esophagus. Other women had great fear of going outside the home or into crowds. Some feared death, predicted the day of death, or had suicidal tendencies. Cases were recorded of women breaking pins into pieces with "a wild distracted look on their faces," and of "long continued inveterate scolding, until she falls down in a swoon." In the absence of specific diagnoses for some mental illnesses, the woman was pronounced hysterical who had sudden changes "from grave to gay," or indulged in "much weeping without knowing why." One volume of homeopathy has an herb to treat each hysterical symptom, running the gamut from aconite to zinc, with asafoetida, ipecec, nux mosch, sepia, valeriana, and belladonna in between.[18]

An English physician, Walter Johnson, in his essay on "Regular and Irregular Hysteria," believed the incidence of the disease to be "in some measure the barometer of national prosperity." It flourished during periods of national crisis, such as the French Revolution or the Irish Rebellion. But Johnson's chief insight into the nature of hysteria was to "look into the patient's mind" and "extract from the patient's bosom the secret, perhaps jealously guarded, of why the hysteria . . . exists." It was necessary to get the patient outside herself, perhaps by suggesting a contemplation of flowers or a collection of rocks. The "self-involution" which was the essence "of the hysterical mind" could thus be reversed. Johnson regarded this task as made simpler by the essentially simple nature of woman. He quoted with approval and accepted the validity of the other Dr. Johnson's famous dictum: "Woman is happier than man, because she can hem a pocket handkerchief."[19]

American physicians of the soul or the body, including such famous practitioners as Cotton Mather and Benjamin Rush, believed both in the psychosomatic nature of much of female illness and in the mode of treating it.[20] But there was a significant difference between the male physician and the reforming female on the desirability of love forming, as Lord Byron believed, "woman's whole existence," and on the dubious pleasures of handkerchief-hemming. A male physician might pose the question: What causes hysteria, sick headaches, et cetera? And answer fondly: "Not being loved enough."[21] But women reformers took issue with this diagnosis, even when advanced by Dr. Johnson and Lord Byron.

Harriot Hunt, who practiced medicine in Boston, wrote that she "often found physical maladies growing out of concealed sorrows." Her patients exhibited the outward signs of those societal conventions which denied them knowledge of their interior life. "Mind had been uncultivated—intelligence smothered—aspirations quenched. The result was physical suffering." Very often she treated not the disease—hysteria, chlorosis, dyspepsia—but the soul of the women who consulted her. She describes her remarks to one sufferer: "Be frank—utter yourself in confidence and trust, so we shall be one in exploring your case—for you are a chronic invalid—years you have suffered and suffered in silence—you have hugged your chains."

The woman responded: "I know no language in which to utter myself," possibly the most succinct summary of woman's emotional problems that the nineteenth century has provided us. Dr. Hunt tried to stimulate and reach her patient by reading aloud a few verses from *Proverbial Philosophy*. Then she asked softly, "What of your childhood?" Tears filled the woman's eyes. "I never had a childhood," and she began a recital of her unhappy home life, her struggle to escape, the tensions of her own marriage, and all the other accumulated wounds which had brought her seeking health. Dr. Hunt prescribed: "Abandon all medicine; commence a diary, go back into the chambers of the past, catch up your mother's lessons." She described a course of wholesome diet, cold baths, and serious reading, all aimed at making the woman consciously remember those traumas which she had rejected. Instant insight resulted, and the patient realized that she had "banished Mother from her mind" because her "life has been fashionable, and so at variance with *her* counsels." The physical symptoms, needless to say, disappeared shortly.[22]

Woman's sensibilities, always acute, were at their height during adolescence, when she divested herself "of the light and airy habiliments of girlhood" and assumed "the more staid and dignified mantle of womanhood."[23] During this "brilliant period of life" the girl's character changed, and she became more tender-hearted, more sensitive, and "appeared to attach herself to everything about her." Desires arose, without as yet a "definite object" and "vague emotions, of an instinct that seeks some object —it knows not what."[24] Physicians noted "how tremulous" her nervous system became, necessitating particular vigilance on the part of her family to maintain her health and mental balance.[25] It was particularly important to realize how easily "perfect purity" could be destroyed by thoughtlessness. Short dresses on young girls were attacked by one physician as "pernicious" since the girls "frequently observe men gazing at their limbs, they overhear remarks relative thereto, inquiries are made among each other to know what all this means, sensual ideas are soon developed, and pure morality is forever destroyed."[26] Normal girls were to be allowed their dreams of "love in a cottage, maternity, and endless bliss. . ." so long as the specifics were not dwelled upon. There was, of course, the fear that this girlish enthusiasm might be misdirected into religious fanaticism where "mystic love takes the place of a grosser passion."[27]

This transitional period was terminated by the "brilliant and stormy crisis" when the menses began. Menstruation marked the end of childhood and signified the ability to marry. Physicians were annoyed at all the mothers who insisted on hurrying nature in order to push their daughters into the brilliant marriages which they had determined upon.[28] On no account, warned the doctors, should a girl be allowed to marry before the beginning of menstruation, a process which generally took place at fourteen or fifteen. Like everything else connected with this interesting creature, the American girl, menstruation was fraught with problems and mismanaged badly by society. Those who "lived luxuriantly in cities" were even thought to start their periods earlier than those who lived in the country.[29]

Some synonyms for menstruation during the nineteenth century give an idea of the way in which it was regarded: catamenia, menses, courses, terms, periods, the reds, being unwell, indisposed, has her troubles. Nervous girls menstruated sooner than phlegmatic types and had more difficulty. If a girl of fifteen were suffering from flushes, languor, and a "feeling of heaviness," the menses could be brought on by a spare diet, moderate exercise, and warm baths. In really difficult cases, where the girl was robust and florid without any tendency to consumption, the physician might resort to bleeding. For those girls who seemed "cold, apathetic, and indifferent," some doctors cautiously prescribed a course of books, balls, and theatres which might "prove useful in exciting their sensibility, and thus inviting the menstrual exhalations."

Intellectual labors should be avoided during this time, because "by establishing a high cerebral excitement" they provided "an unequal distribution of the vital forces," causing "an afflux towards the brain of the blood which ought to flow toward the genital apparatus." Dr. Edward Clarke's influential and widely read book, *Sex in Education: or, A Fair Chance for Our Girls*, made this point at great length and with many lugubrious case studies. Dr. Clarke attempted to prove that the "grievous maladies which torture a woman's earthly existence—among them leucorrhoea, amenorrhoea, dysmenorrhea, chronic and acute ovaritis, prolapsus uterus, hysteria, neuralgia . . ." were the results of overexertion during the monthly period. In pursuing her intellectual or vocational tasks, "the stream of vital and constructive force evolved within her was turned steadily toward the brain, and away from the ovaries and their accessories." Thus he told the cautionary tale of the unfortunate "Miss M": "Believing that woman can do what man can, for she held that faith, she strove with noble but ignorant bravery to compass man's intellectual attainment in a man's way, and died in the effort.[30] Such opinions express in physiological terms what other critics of feminist reforms couched in moral or psychological language. If woman "unsexed herself" by claiming a role or opportunity not accorded her, she lost her chance to play her one great part, to bear healthy children for American men. "The greatest end and object of woman's existence is, evidently, to perpetuate the species," claimed Dr. Morrill, and most of his profession and his age agreed with him.[31] The assumption that there was not enough "vital energy" to go around, if woman devoted herself to her intellectual as well as her maternal development, is part of that same definition of woman as a being born to and for love. The nineteenth-century belief in the immutable and absolute qualities of nature extended in particular to those aspects of human nature which propped up society. When Darwinism, biological or social, became acceptable, it was rarely applied to those most sacred and therefore most unchangeable institutions: God, Democracy, and Mother.

The onset of menstruation might coincide with chlorosis, or "greensickness." One doctor noted the "tender interest" and "touching compassion" aroused by the "paleness, suffering, and languor" of the young chlorotic girl. "Like some delicate plant, deprived of the beneficent rays of the sun, she is a flower which withers and droops away, even before its blossoming."[35]

The disease was brought on by circumstances "which depress the mind, and keep the feelings in a state of painful suspense" such as unrequited affection, separation from family and friends, or the care of aged or infirm persons. It was marked by menstrual difficulties, anaemia, and, of course, the green-tinged complexion which gave it its name.[36] The cure was often to remove the cause—the "continuous irritation, or tension, or depression, or exaltation" to which the girl was subjected, or to wait and hope that maturity would provide the requited affection and stable life which constituted woman's health and happiness.[37]

The morbid fancies of chlorosis or "lovesickness" might express themselves in a particularly malevolent form. Female masturbation, although not so widely practiced as among young boys, was nonetheless a matter of grave concern to nineteenth-century physicians. It was thoroughly denounced as an "execrable and fatal evil" which destroyed woman's beauty, impaired her health, and conducted her "almost always to a premature grave."[38] Other certain consequences of practicing "individual transgression" or "solitary indulgence" were idiocy, St. Vitus dance, epilepsy, and the drying up of "animal juices."[39] Predictably, when a female reformer like Mary Gove Nichols discussed the problem, she blamed society and the restrictions on woman's education and training. "If girls are taught to reason," Mrs. Gove argued, "they will not spend their days reading fiction, and their nights in morbid dreams of love."[37]

Masturbation might lead to worse evils, particularly to nymphomania, which one authority defined as "an exaggerated voluptuous sensation, accompanied by venereal desire, which is irresistible and insatiable."[38] The gratification of this morbid desire at its "highest but not its only level" consisted in "the reveries and dreams of amorous imagination and fancy by day or by night."[39] The best preventatives for masturbation and nymphomania were a regime of plain living and high thinking. A strict vegetable and fruit diet should be followed, with all "animal foods" avoided. Feather beds should be replaced with straw mattresses, and licentious books, overheated rooms, and exciting entertainment or conversation should be avoided. Professor Beach was convinced that "High-living excites venery, and leads directly to sensuality."[40] If all else failed, it was sometimes necessary "in desperate cases" to use an apparatus, "a sort of wire work, whose meshes are so close as to prevent the passage of a finger.[41]

One cheerful note was sounded in the midst of these dire warnings of erotic excess. William Alcott, "The Old Physician," took a more sanguine view. Indeed he felt that "the husband . . . in these days, who finds himself united, for life, to a woman whose only defect or weakness is a slight nymphomania, may think himself quite fortunate."[42]

This stress on the morbidly sensual was often blamed on the artificiality and precocity demanded by fashion. Dr. Bedford, writing as a New York physician of long standing, complained of the early inflammation of passions in urban society:

Look at our metropolis, New York, with its enterprise, its commercial
prosperity, its immense wealth, its princely edifices . . . city life, with
its rounds of excitement, its prurient books, and no less prurient dance,
has forced into premature action the nervous system of the young girl.
. . .[43]

Chapter headings in another New York physician's polemic
against fashion developed the same theme: "Pathology of a Lady
of Fashion," "What Are the Causes of Early Decay in American
Women?" and "Toilette of the New York Ladies: What Are the
Actual Causes of Cold Feet?" The low-cut dress, however chic,
was "as injurious to the health of the body as to the purity of the
soul."[44] Case histories abounded of young women in the bloom of
youth fallen victim to the "flushed cheek and hectic eye" which
every reader of fiction recognized as the symptoms of galloping
consumption. Had their mothers been more prudent and less enslaved by "fashion," their daughters would not have danced in
thin-soled slippers, nor exposed their arms and shoulders in overheated ballrooms, and would have had a happier fate. The moral as
well as the physiological dangers of these activities were usually
noted, together with a plea for wholesome exercise, simple diet,
and early hours of rising and retiring. American doctors reserved
their highest pitch of fury for the fashion of tight lacing, which
they believed caused female ailments, from a collapsed lung to
prolapsed uterus.[45] When Freud used the phrase to symbolize
woman's restricted life and frustrated sexual drives, he was no
more censorious than these nineteenth-century physicians denouncing the physical reality.

Many doctors who wanted women to remain in the home nonetheless found fault with domesticity. Women led "too much confined and sedentary a life, under the false impression of making
them delicate and genteel."[46] In what was regarded as an age of
progress, woman was largely responsible for her own suffering,
because of "her ignorance of herself,"[47] an ignorance which surrounded her with "unnatural social habits," and thus "rendered
her extremely susceptible to uterine disease."[48] Constipation,
"the ruin of many constitutions, families, and incomes . . ."
was a result of improper food, and constant stimulation of the
body, without sufficient exercise.[49] Moreover, woman was "more
restrained by the severity of decorum, and is frequently compelled
to delay compliance with natural necessities.[50]

The sick headache was a commonplace of fiction and life, the refuge of the unhappy or fearful woman, and the usual accompaniment of the other diseases to which she was susceptible. It was, like menstrual complaints and digestive disorders, regarded by physicians as indicative both of her high degree of nervous sensitivity and as an example of society gone wrong. Practically every cookbook or family health manual had several headache remedies. Among the most ingenious was: "Take a tea-spoonful of powdered charcoal in molasses every morning, and wash it down with a little tea; or drink half a glass of raw rum or gin, and drink freely of maywood tea."[51] Beset by headaches, excitable to the point of hysterics, threatened by consumption, chlorosis, or worse, the American girl needed marriage and motherhood as stabilizing forces in her personality and to her physique. The unmarried woman was incomplete. One phrenologist wrote: "Properly to know man in the person of her husband, develops the feminine and thereby augments every female charm and perfection; because it calls out and fulfils her whole nature." Once married, a woman needed to bear a child to be true to her nature's "great duty and destiny."[52]

However, it was the duty of the husband to see that the exercise of his marital rights did not overburden woman's delicate frame and spirit. Dr. Woodward opposed frequent sexual intercourse on principle. "He who indulges frequently, even with his lawful wife, *cannot but* associate her in his own mind with this debased feeling to which she administers."[53] Men were so gross as to insist on their wives' compliance during the time when she was pregnant or nursing. "At these periods she almost always loathes it—proof enough that it was wrong. Besides, it withdraws that vital energy required by her precious charge." He reminded husbands "whose demands are frequent" that they paid the price of "the increased irritability, and fretfulness, and crossness of your wives the next day. . . ."[54]

Men were advised to be "self-denying" and not to make their early married life into "little better than a season of prostitution."[55] Animals at least were wise enough to restrict coition to "purposes of generation," but man, in marriage, resorted to it frequently "as the most common indulgence of his lower appetites." The "continued and extreme excitement in the sexual system" was bad for both sexes, but "it produced the most disastrous effects upon women for obvious physiological reasons." Young doctors were told to be relentless in insisting on "entire abstinence" from the sexual act while treating various female complaints; a private interview should be arranged with the husband to break the news.[56] The basic principle to be followed in marriage was *"never indulge in the propensity while it can well be avoided,* for the same reason that we should never eat till we are hungry. . . ."[57] This conservation of energy was based on the assumption that woman's higher spiritual nature rebelled at the demands of man's lower sensual one. When she was so unfortunate as to experience a "nervous orgasm," she was warned that her chances of aborting or producing a deformed child were substantially increased.[58]

Mrs. Nichols refused to accept the "apathy of the sexual instinct" as innate in women. Predictably she blamed it on "the enslaved and unhealthy condition in which she lives." The Medical College at Albany, hinted Mrs. Nichols darkly, had pathological proof of what happens to women because of man's excesses, in the form of uterine tumors weighing up to twenty-four pounds. These wives were martyrs to "the Laws of Marriage—pious, virtuous, reputable, ignorant women."[59] "Legality and duty" were only disguises for man's indulgence of his baser nature. The consensus of the authorities was that "a female who unfortunately contracts a matrimonial alliance with a merely animal man is much to be pitied."[60]

Since the marital rights were to be indulged in so seldom—once in a lunar month and only for purposes of procreation, the condition of pregnancy was treated as the most important state of a woman's life. Several doctors stressed the point that pregnancy was not a disease, but was rather a period of increased health.[61] The diagnosis of pregnancy was a matter of concern to the young doctor. The notorious mistake in maligning the character of Lady Flora Hastings was a horrible example to avoid. Dr. Gunning Bedford spent several pages detailing the troubles of a virtuous young woman, who fled England and came to America to escape the calumnies of those who claimed she was going to have a child. Her father followed her in time to hear her death bed protestations of innocence; in the postmortem which followed, a large uterine tumor vindicated her honor. The father seized it, saying: "This is my trophy, and I will return with it to England, and it shall confound the traducers of my child."[62] Notwithstanding such dramatic vignettes, most doctors advised their students that "No matter what a woman's *character* is—form your own opinions —from your own knowledge."[63]

The young woman approached pregnancy in a state of fear and trembling. One young wife, the daughter of a doctor and married to a doctor, wrote in her diary: "I have arranged all my worldly goods and now am prepared in case I die . . . I am waiting hourly for my baby—my blood runs cold when I think of it."[64] John Quackenbush exhorted his students to do their best for woman during "the anxieties, the troubles, and the accidents which sometimes precede the hour when she becomes a mother . . . the dangers which frequently hover around and darken that hour, and make it the time of woman's great necessity."[65] According to another professor of obstetrics, "Men cannot suffer the same pains as women. What do you call the pains of parturition? There is no name for it but *Agony*."[66]

As the woman approached her confinement—referred to as "sickness" or "illness" by most of them, no matter what she was assured by her doctors—she was subjected to frightening old-wives stories. "Rules for Mothers," quoted in several of the medical books, make a point of counselling the young wife to ignore these foolish tales, to "guard against any sudden gust of passion" and to cultivate, "solicit and attain, as far as possible, tranquility and equanimity of mind." She was urged to remember how rarely death occurred "during, or after a well-conducted labor," and spend her time constructively being "passive and obedient, feeling assured that her friends and physician understand and feel for her situation to pass, and will faithfully release her of all that can safely be spared her." Naturally she should shun unpleasant sights and severe study and conserve her physical and moral strength for her "great hour of trial."[67]

Obstetricians and midwives were warned of milk fever and puerperal mania and given instructions about such "preternatural cases" as breech presentations. Most doctors preferred to avoid instrument births—"Dame Nature is the best Midwife"— and one physician went so far as to declare "on the strength of historical testimony . . . as well as sound logic, that women are naturally as able as other animals to reproduce their species without extrinsic aid. . . ."[68] She was not, however, encouraged to practice "natural" childbirth when it came to getting up from the childbed and going back to the fields. That was, indeed, the way the savages gave birth and therefore, in those days before anthropological perspective had become popular, reason enough for civilized nations to behave differently. An American woman needed at least eight to ten days of complete bedrest after she had given birth,[69] even after her time had been eased by the discovery of anaesthesia. The reaction to this invention was almost universally positive. Most doctors concurred with Professor Bedford who hailed ether as "among the most sterling offerings of the human mind."[70]

The American doctor of the mid-nineteenth century not only tried to apply his understanding of woman's nature to his care of her, but also had women apply this same concept of womanhood to his own profession. The subheading of the multifaceted "Woman Question" entitled: "Should Women Be Doctors?" was a subject of controversy in many of the medical schools and books. Such eminent healers as Florence Nightingale and Oliver Wendell Holmes took a negative position, but by 1850 a few women were going to medical school and setting up practice. One of them, Ann Preston, defended her choice of a vocation by saying that her sex, who shrank instinctively from what was coarse, "fain would raise the moral tone" of the medical profession, and "teach reverence and purity to the grossness of the world. . . ." Naturally, if she attempted this exalted mission, she must "ever wear about her the spotless role of delicacy as her own protecting investment."[71]

The same logic which stated that women were morally superior to men made it almost a moral imperative for her to go where vice and corruption seemed to exist. The suffragist who believed her sex more pure was almost required to enter politics, since men were making such a dirty game of it. In the medical profession, where the nature and role of women preconditioned the diagnosis and treatment of her ailments, it was just as much a female duty to preserve that perfect modesty and seek that sympathy of heart and mind which only another woman could provide.

The men who formulated the theories of female disease, and the woman patient who came, in some few cases, to be the physician as well, took their obligation to God and to the republic very seriously. It was their privilege and their duty to improve the health of America's mothers and wives, and, in so doing, to improve the health of the body politic. If the age desired "Men to match our Mountains," America's physicians were dedicated to providing women to match our men. In the "sweet land of liberty," liberty must be a goddess. But the official title of many physicians—'Professor of the Diseases of Women and Children'—revealed the basic preconception of the profession that, as one woman reformer claimed, "Now there is no woman, only an overgrown child."

5

ANTI-INTELLECTUALISM AND THE AMERICAN WOMAN
1800-1860

Nineteenth-century American man often preferred common sense or intuition to reason, as modes of achieving wisdom and truth.[1] But if mankind, generically, was anti-intellectual, woman was so in a particular way—one in which her very essence was involved. Indeed, the more she used her heart rather than her mind the more feminine she was. Anti-intellectualism was implicit in the cult which exalted women as creatures who did not use logic or reason, having a surer, purer road to the truth—the high road of the heart. Womanhood as defined by contemporary science, religion, literature, and many of the leading citizens of the period, symbolized the romantic desire of a romantic age to replace the deductive by the impulsive, the rational by the supra-rational. Woman's nature, so defined, transcended the grossness of the flesh and the grubbiness of the market place, in which man was so frequently mired by his passions and his greed. Another role assigned her was the Earth-Mother, whose life-giving body and powers were beyond the power of mere man using mere mind to comprehend. When man spoke of something bigger than all of us, mysterious, sublime, and unresponsive to logic, the sea, the weather, the fates, he spoke of "her." Thus whether she drew man to a higher spiritual plane or bound him to earth by her life-force, female nature and functions were untouched by human intellect.[2]

Most authorities on anatomy and gynecology agreed that woman's cerebral system was less well-developed, her nervous system better developed than man's. William P. Dewees, Adjunct Professor of Midwifery at the University of Pennsylvania, averred that "The bones of her cranium are thinner, smaller, and more pliant, and the space destined to be filled by the brain is smaller."[3] Hugh L. Hodge, his colleague, Professor of Obstetrics and Diseases

71

of Women and Children, stated that "Woman's nervous system is more highly-organized, her responses to stimuli more instinctive and intuitive than man's."[4] Her skin was softer, causing her to bruise and scar more easily than man, and all her tissues, including the grey matter of the brain, were more delicate. The passive organs associated with gestation, not the active ones of movement, were developed in her; she was, physically and symbolically, a vessel waiting to be filled.[5] One physician classified feminine beauty into three categories: Beauty of the Locomotive System, Beauty of the Nutritive System, and Beauty of the Thinking System. Of this third type he said severely it was "less proper to woman, less feminine" than a highly-developed "nutritive system, . . . since it is not the intellectual system, but the vital one which is, and ought to be most developed in woman."[6]

The pseudo-science of phrenology echoed these findings. Predictably women had larger bumps of Benevolence, Veneration, Approbativeness, Conscientiousness, Adhesiveness, Secretiveness, Ideality, Individuality, and Philoprogenitiveness, while Amativeness, Combativeness, Destructiveness, Self-Esteem, Firmness, Acquisitiveness, Constructiveness, Causality, and Comparison were stronger in the male. In translation from the jargon used on the phrenology charts, "Veneration" meant obedience and submission to authority; "Approbativeness" stood for the desire for approval; "Adhesiveness" (a little bump appropriately nestled near "Union for Life") signified monogamy and loyalty in misfortune; "Ideality" was idealism and imaginativeness; and "Philoprogenitiveness" identified the love of children.[7] Professor Lorenzo Fowler summarized the phrenological differences between the sexes: "The male has stronger intellect, will, and propensities, together with greater force and energy of character; while the female has the stronger moral sentiments and domestic feelings."[8]

These laws of science and pseudo-science were God's laws as well, since according to most interpreters of the Bible woman was supposed to have a natural and simple piety, the unquestioning obedient religion of a docile child. Woman was not prone to passion's temptation, according to the argument from the pulpit, nor did she toil in a world of sharp business practices. This "seclusion of the scenes in which her lot has been cast," as the minister of the Amity Street Baptist Church advised the Maternal Association, which might be seen "as a prison to the vaulting and ambitious spirit," seemed instead to the unambitious woman to provide "scenes favorable to innocence and peace, to religious meditation and to prayerful consistency."[9]

A. B. Muzzey, addressing the "Young Maidens of our Favored Union," found in religion "qualities with which the capacities and power of woman singularly harmonize." Religion is based on deep feeling and faith which "with her is natural, the growth of her moral being; in man it is usually acquired as the result of thought." Religion also requires "what have sometimes been termed the passive virtues, fortitude, submission, patience, resignation. The acquisition of these qualities is to man, a most arduous task. . . . In woman, they find a congenial spirit, a heart open, and waiting for their reception."[10]

A natural religion avoided speculation, doubt and controversy and was exempt from the musings of a restless intellect. Woman did not question her God; she served Him. In *A Lady's Gift*, subtitled "Woman As She Ought to Be," the Christian Mother is quoted on the religious education of daughters:

> All religious controversy . . . is carefully guarded against with daughters, for it was her opinion that it encourages doubts and perplexities upon points which are not essential to our eternal welfare, and gives rise to feelings which are incompatible with it . . . she thought it sufficient for one of her sex to recollect that God, and his laws, have remained unchanged since the formation of the universe.[11]

Although woman was naturally good, her moral superiority rested on her complete innocence. Innocence meant, in turn, the absence of carnal knowledge and, frequently, of knowledge at all. Eve had made a fatal error and eaten from the Tree of Knowledge; her daughters wisely safeguarded themselves from that dangerous fruit as well as from her fall from grace. The seduction stories so popular in the ladies' magazines showed woman in all her natural goodness and innocence betrayed by her own ignorance and man's greed.

"Maria, a Sketch from Life," a typical example of the genre in *Godey's Lady's Book*, told the familiar tale of a young girl, favored by birth and fortune, "the only daughter of affectionate parents by whom her every wish was anticipated and every delight bestowed. . . . Amiable as she was good, everyone loved her. . . . Then she was happy—*then she was innocent*—but alas! the scene changed."

Enter the villain, Captain Sydenham; "What breast could have harbored feelings of evil toward her? What being could have cherished thoughts deadly to the purity and holiness of that spirit which pervaded her fragile frame? *Sydenham was that man.*" Three years later Maria, seduced and abandoned, dies in the gutter, but it was not her fault: "Knowing no guile herself, and dreaming not of guile in others . . . too truly she believed—too truly was a victim."[12]

Woman could not protect her innocence herself; for that she required man's strong arm. Man had the essential reasoning power to convince her to do wrong. It was the secret of his dominance over her, and the test of his chivalry that he chose not to exercise this power but to do the decent thing and marry her. Woman's dependence on man was both "the true secret of her moral influence" and the "proof of her inferiority," according to a piece of premarital advice, "Hints to Young Ladies." Woman's inferiority indicated her duty: "She must be in subjection to her husband."[13] Mrs. John Sandford, writing in a similar vein, believed woman's submission more than justified by her deficiences. "It is in discernment, rather than in capacity, that the inferiority of woman exists. She chose wrong at first, and liability to error seems entailed upon her."[14]

Marriage exemplified that order of society in which woman's choices were, in theory, at least, subject to the approval of her husband, in order to prevent a repetition of Eve's mistake. *The Ladies' Wreath* published a story with the explicit title: "Florence Lee or the Model Wife." Dramatis personae include, besides Florence, who is a True Woman, Isabelle who, woefully, is not, and Ned, for whose affection both vie. Isabelle makes the mistake of arguing with her beloved about woman's place in society: "Let me tell you, sir, that woman has a living, thinking, feeling soul, and that she has as lofty aims and as daring visions as the wildest schemes of your sex . . . God created man the superior in many respects, I acknowledge—but He made woman to be a help-meet for him. . . ." Florence is shocked at such vehemence, since woman should never become angry, raise her voice in public, or run the risk of wounding a man's pride, no matter how exalted her sentiments. Needless to say, Ned sees Isabelle for what she is, "a living, thinking, feeling soul" perhaps, but not the woman for him. He marries Florence, who knows that woman's place is in the home and whose ideas, if she has any, are articulated by her husband. Isabelle had jeopardized the delicate balance between the sexes on which the proper order of marriage and society depends. Florence makes the perfect wife, as promised by the title; the fate of Isabelle is not revealed. It was probably too dreadful for the gentle readers of the *Ladies' Wreath* to contemplate.[15]

Woman's education was arranged to carry on this same dichotomy of spheres. Nineteenth-century text books stressed masculine authority and feminine submission and inferiority.[16] Female academies trained her not for the learned professions but to be the companion of her husband, the Christian-Mother-Educator of her sons. The pragmatic function of female education was stressed by Charles Butler in *An American Lady*. "The chief end to be proposed in cultivating the understanding of women, is to qualify them for the practical purposes of life."[17] Metaphysics was "too remote from the practical affairs of life to be useful," George Woods, president of the Board of Trustees, warned the graduating class of the Brooklyn Female Academy. He recommended instead *belles-lettres* as "very appropriate, generally, to the character of the female intellect."[18]

A similar utilitarian position was expressed by *Peterson's Magazine*, whose editors were "sick of the cant" about educating women and men in the same way. Clearly their educations should differ since they were being trained to perform different functions: "The province of the one is to cheer our fireside, to educate our children, to regulate our household economy; the business of the other is to toil for the livelihood of those dear beings whom he has left at home, and to protect them against the thousand evils of the world." A woman should "possess general information on every subject of daily life; but it is not necessary that she be scientifically educated. The true relations of life are more important to her than mathematics, astronomy, or the dead languages."[19] These "true relations" were of the sort the *Mental Flower Garden* had in mind when it suggested coyly that "of all studies the most necessary and natural to woman, is the study of men."[20]

John Greenleaf Whittier's poem "In School Days" is a case study of "true relations." It tells of two young scholars, a boy and a girl, competing in a spelling contest; he missed a word and she spells it correctly, replacing him at the head of the class. Afterwards she timidly approaches him:

> He saw her lift her eyes: he felt
> The soft hand's light caressing,

And heard the tremble of her voice,
As if a fault confessing.

"I'm sorry that I spelt the word;
  I hate to go above you,
Because,"—the brown eyes lower fell,—
  "Because, you see, I love you."[21]

The young lady did right to confess; she had committed a grievous offense against her female nature. Women properly excelled in affection, not in competition, and any apparent confusion should be immediately resolved.

Women of genius (an encomium applied to virtually every woman who was able to get one of her effusions published) were urged to make it clear in their lives and in their work that they understood this same order. Their domestic duties came before their work and "literature was the garnish of their life, not its food."[22] Although writers of popular verse and novels proclaimed themselves wives and mothers first, and writers only afterwards, a woman whose gifts were really extraordinary was regarded with curiosity and pity. *The Young Lady's Companion* admitted reluctantly that there had been "women whose minds have been equal to any human undertaking," but "happily these giants of their kind are rare."[23]

If a woman, no matter how gifted, debated her rights or bewailed her wrongs in a public place, she deserved everything she got: a short unhappy life, dementia, death, and a total lack of respect from men or virtuous women were among the milder punishments meted out in popular fiction. *The Mother's Magazine* observed pleasantly: "These Amazonians are their own executioners. They have unsexed themselves in public estimation, and there is no fear that they will perpetuate their race. We treat insanity in all its forms, with allowance."[24]

Over and over again, in every organ of the pulpit and the press, the differences between men and women were detailed. Essentially they were the differences between an intellectual and an emotional nature. "Man's strength lies in his bold mind, in his indomitable purpose, in his strong arm," defined the Reverent John Abbott. "While woman's power lies in her gentleness, in her soft and affectionate voice, in her retiring delicacy, in her unobtrusive readiness to minister to suffering wherever found."[25] Timothy Arthur advised young men that while the fair sex was superior in perception and intuition, they should reserve for the males the more rational, if not the better part. "In the graver things of life, a man's judgment is more to be relied upon than a woman's, because here a regular course of reasoning from premises laid down is required, and this a man is much more able to do than a woman."[26] Horace Mann was repetitive but succinct: "His might is in muscles and logic; hers in fascination and pathos."[27]

This complete acceptance of radically different natures based on a dichotomy between rational and non-rational powers, permeated even the liberal pages of *The Present*, a periodical which promoted the doctrines of Fourier. Here the categories which divided the Male from the Female were:

MALE	FEMALE
man	woman
truth	love
knowledge	wisdom
ignorance	folly
history	poetry
labor	amusement
head	heart
laws	commandments
action	re-action
thinking	reflecting
justice	mercy
mind	soul
intellect	understanding
talent	genius[28]

These distinctions, while more subtle than those of the woman's magazines or the moralists, were essentially the same. The womanly virtues of wisdom and understanding have conclusions reached through intuition, while the male virtues of truth and knowledge come from the intellect. Man sins through ignorance, through "not knowing"; woman through folly, willful disregard of knowledge. Man labors and learns facts in history; woman is made for lighter tasks and responds emotionally to poetry. Man is a doer, an actor. Woman reacts, she reflects rather than creates, is the moon to his sun. He makes laws and she obeys commandments. Man's mind leads him to truth while woman's soul informs her of the higher wisdom. Man has skills and talents, but woman's gifts, like her knowledge, come from a deeper source and do not respond to training or practice since they are the product of genius. Man reasons and is just; woman loves and is merciful.

Woman could be regarded as anti-intellectual in another, more profound sense. She was trivial in conversation and superficial in accomplishment, always absorbed in the infinite detail of domesticity. Perhaps no real intellectual could afford the price of a happy but cluttered existence, and the presence of woman might distract man from weightier achievements.[29]

At the same time that woman was exalted as a more spiritual being than man, she was also recognized as in some ways more physical. She was more conscious of her body, more limited by it. Thus she could remind man whose intellect might soar beyond the frail tolerance of his flesh, that he too was mortal. One of Hawthorne's heroines is aware of her feminine ability to make man earthbound, and asks her scholarly lover if she may not be "the tie that shall connect you to the world."[30]

Real American women received these strictures of their nature, capacity, and role, with mixed emotions. An extremely popular work of the period was the autobiographical novel, *Corinne*, by Madame de Staël. The pseudonym "Corinna" was much favored by literary ladies, who were quick to identify with the plight of the heroine, a woman of extraordinary powers, great gifts, and deep feelings. Corinne in the novel is a brilliant *improvisatrice* who fled conventional tea-cosy life in England for the freedom of Italy, where her inspired singing, playing and acting won her renown. She is abandoned by her lover Oswald, who follows his father's wishes and marries Corinne's half sister Lucilia, innocent, ordinary and thoroughly feminine. Lord Neville's dying wish is honored by his son, who accepts his father's conclusion that Corinne could never be happy in England, where his son must remain to carry on the family name. "In those countries, where political institutions give men so many honourable occasions of shewing themselves in active life, women must remain in the shade." Corinne, her heart broken, dies, a martyr to her own uniqueness.[31]

Her fate was perhaps similar to the one reserved for Isabelle, the antagonist in "The Model Wife," for if Lord Neville's statement about woman's role in England was true, how much more difficult was the lot of a gifted woman in republican America. The interpretations of the novel here do not distinguish the fact that Corinne was in fact no intellectual; her performances were the result of inspiration not cerebration. The problem she posed was the problem of the exceptional woman's role in society.

Two American women who sought, as Corinne had, to reconcile their gifts and their womanly natures, were Emma C. Embury and Margaret Fuller. Emma Embury was a writer of popular romances for the ladies' magazines. In her essay "Corinna" she explained how her own life paralleled the de Staël heroine, for she too had had a loveless youth, surrounded by family and friends who were unsympathetic to her sensitive poetic gifts. Like Corinne, Mrs. Embury feared that her literary talents "were perilous ones" because they set her off from other women and might interfere with her first desire, "the gratification of a womanly heart." She knew that no achievements, no matter how great, could bring happiness to a woman "unless there was pure, true affection" as well."[32]

Mrs. Embury made her peace with her talent and society by placing her heart before her mind, as she admitted in a dedication of a manuscript volume of her poems addressed to her future husband: "Would they were worthier; but, alas! my power is but a woman's power and since I cannot bring before you the glorious visions of a poet's soul, let me hope that my humbler gifts may not be rejected when thus offered by the purest friendship of a woman's heart."[33] A contemporary biographer praised the "beauty of her domestic life which equalled the beauty and purity of her writing." Mrs. Embury regarded "the good order of her household, and her duties as affectionate wife, tender mother, and sympathizing friend," as of greater importance than her "muse."[34] She was a True Woman and thus deserved a happy ending.

Margaret Fuller, frequently styled "The American Corinne," did not solve her conflicts of talent and nature so easily. She risked her reputation and her livelihood by an imprudent marriage and precipitate motherhood, and was punished in life, as she would have been in fiction, by a tragic and early death. However, in the eyes of her contemporaries her marriage was her only possibility of redemption; the punishment came for all the years when she campaigned so strongly to enlarge woman's scope and role.

In her youth as a Massachusetts girl who looked in the mirror and decided that she couldn't help being plain but she *would* be clever, Margaret had protested woman's passive acceptance of her lot. With horror she recounted the anecdote of a woman who lived on a lonely mountain for forty years and was asked why she was there. "It was the man's notion," was the laconic response of this humble representative of True Womanhood and Margaret's blood was chilled. She wanted, or at least she said she wanted, for woman to be free to develop as a human being, in whatever sphere she chose—"Let them be sea captains, if they will," was one of her famous dictums—and to use her intellect not to make her a better companion for man but for her own sake. "Now," she had concluded bitterly, "There is no Woman. Only an overgrown child."[35]

The answer to Margaret Fuller, as to Madame de Staël and Emma Embury, was to give them a home and a cradle to rock, and they would forget their questions and accept their role. Madame de Staël's own life in some ways justified these predictions,[36] and so perhaps did Margaret's last years. Long before her marriage she had written in her Journal: "I shall always reign through the intellect, but the life, the life! Oh my God! shall that never be sweet!" She had poured out her heart to Emerson, to Caroline Sturgis, to a lover who had betrayed her, and they all left her craving for love unsatisfied. In her child she found the peace and happiness even her most intense relationships had not provided. In a letter home she wrote: "What shall I say of my child? All might seem hyperbole, even to my dearest mother. In him I find satisfaction, for the first time, to the deep wants of my heart."[37]

In other letters she talked as before about achievement and her book on Italy which she hoped would make her wealthy and famous.[38] Hawthorne noted some Roman gossip that she had never finished this manuscript, had barely, in fact, begun it, so far had she swung from the intellectual to the domestic life. Having noted this, he reflects "On the whole, I do not know that I like her the better for it; because she proved herself a very woman after all, and fell as the weakest of her sisters might."[39] Hawthorne was inclined to forgive her her trespasses, since they were the sins of the flesh, so much less serious to him than the sins of the intellect.

Marriage and motherhood might have enhanced Margaret Fuller's gifts; it might have eclipsed them. The shipwreck in which she and her husband and child drowned ended, as Corinne's death had ended, the question of whether a gifted woman could return to her homeland. Those who, like Hawthorne, had censored her in life, were more gentle after her death precisely because they felt that in the conflict between her intellect and her heart, her heart had won. Sarah Josepha Hale, editor of *Godey's* and staunch advocate of woman's traditional role, wrote approvingly that Margaret had lost her taste for German literature before her death, which might be a sign of redemption.[40] A British reviewer magnanimously concluded that "from the time she became a mother till the final tragedy . . . she was an altered woman and evinced a greatness of soul and heroism of character so grand that we feel disposed to extend to her whole career the admiration and sympathy inspired by the closing scenes."[41] Margaret Fuller may have tried to live her life as an intellectual. Those who came to bury her could only praise her by maintaining that she died a true and unthinking woman.

The American Corinne's life had a certain dramatic rightness, like the Greek tragedies in which unsolvable questions posed by mortals are swept away by the mighty tides of fate. But a woman physician writing in the 1850's protested the innumerable domestic tragedies, without grandeur but equally disastrous, which were the result of woman's non-reasoning role. Most of her patients were mentally, not physically ill, their "minds were atrophied through disuse" and their bodies suffered accordingly. "We wonder at the Hindoo widow burned on the funeral pyre of her husband," wrote Dr. Harriot Hunt, "But we wonder not at the Christian wife who starves her mind to death, and moves about her house a living corpse."[42]

Whether tragedy or pathos, Electra or *Dot the Waif*, the insistence on woman's immutably anti-intellectual nature posed problems for anyone who challenged this thesis. Woman's role in society was based on this conception of her nature and her role was linked in turn with the pervasive anti-intellectualism of the period. Woman as exalted in her affectionate and life-giving functions of wife and mother was indeed heaven's last best gift, an example

Dimity Convictions

of virtue and happiness, which is virtue's reward. If she was unhappy, it was her fault, for in this particular vicious circle happiness depended on properly fulfilling her nature, and remaining in her natural habitat, the home. Home was increasingly idealized as the center of man's joys and the repository of earthly happiness, and home was woman's sphere, where her gifts and values triumphed.

If women's education and occupations changed without a parallel change in the definition of her nature, then, no matter how high a premium society might eventually place on the creative intellect, woman was still faced by confusion and self-doubt. For if, with her new knowledge and opportunities, she strove for that particular brass ring, she would be faced by the same dilemma that confronted the women of a previous generation: by definition she could not be truly womanly if she was truly intellectual.

6

THE FEMINIZATION OF AMERICAN RELIGION
1800 - 1860

The relationships among nineteenth-century reform movements in the United States, their overlapping of personnel, and their disparity and similarity in motivations and results are popular themes in social history.[1] In the women's movement, which concentrated on obtaining suffrage but had more specific and more diffuse goals as well, almost all of the leaders and most of the followers were active in other reforms. Indeed, the abolitionist, temperance, and peace societies depended on their women members to lick envelopes, raise money through fairs, and influence their husbands and fathers to join in the good work. Although sometimes frustrated and even betrayed by these other reform movements, the woman's movement on the whole benefitted from the organizational experience, political knowledge, and momentum generated by other reforms. At the same time American religion, particularly American Protestantism, was changing rapidly and fundamentally. Although not overtly tied to the woman's movement, these religious changes may have had more effect on the basic problems posed by women than anything which happened within the women's organizations or in related reform groups. Because of the nature of the changes and the importance of their results to women's role, American religion might be said to have been "feminized." The term is used here, like the term "radicalization," to connote a series of consciousness-raising and existential, as well as experiential, factors which resulted in a new awareness of changed conditions and new roles to fit these new conditions.

For the historian to attempt an analysis of the relationships between institutions and movements at a given point in time is a fascinating exercise in social history. It may well be an exercise in futility, however, because he lacks sufficient knowledge of the society he studies, or because the theories of change and social dynamics are applicable only to the present, or at least not to the particular segment of the past which he explores. The hazards of the sociological vocabulary, the limited number of sources (or the overwhelming magnitude of sources in some areas), and the difference between sociological and historical logistics and time are significant barriers.[2] Within these limitations we can discuss the process of "feminization," to apply this definition to religion in America in the first half of the nineteenth century, and to explore the results of a "feminized" religion.

In some ways the allocation of institutions or activities to one sex or another is a continuation of the division of labor by sex which has gone on since the cave dwellers. At certain times survival required that the strongest members of society specialize in a given activity. Once the basic needs of survival were met, other activities, not of current critical importance, could be engaged in. These more expendable institutions became the property of the weaker members of society which, in western civilization, generally meant women.[3] In the period following the American Revolution, political and economic activities were critically important and therefore more "masculine," that is, more competitive, more aggressive, more responsive to shows of force and strength. Religion, along with the family and popular taste, was not very important, and so became the property of the ladies. Thus it entered a process of change whereby it became more domesticated, more emotional, more soft and accommodating—in a word, more "feminine."

In this way the traditional religious values could be maintained in a society whose primary concerns made humility, submission and meekness incompatible with success because they were identified with weakness. At the same time American Protestantism changed in ways which made it more useful to American society, particularly to the women who increasingly made up the congregations of American churches. Feminization, then, can be defined and studied through its results—a more genteel, less rigid institution—and through its members—the increased prominence of women in religious organizations and the way in which new or revised religions catered to this membership.

American churches had regarded it as their solemn duty to lead

in building a godly culture, and the "city on the hill" which symbolized American aspirations had clusters of church steeples as its
tallest structures.[4] In the nineteenth century the skyscraper would
replace the steeple as a symbol of the American dream, and the
ministers of God fought against this displacement. Politics cap-
tured the zeal and the time once reserved to religion, and the pul-
pits thundered against those men who mistakenly served power
itself and not the Source of Power. The women's magazines and
books of advice also warned against politics as a destroyer of the
home. Cautionary tales equated the man who squandered his
energy in political arguments with the man who drank or gambled;
both were done at the expense of the home and religion.[5] Women
and ministers were allies against this usurper, from which they
were both excluded. Women were forbidden to go into politics
because it would sully them; the church was excluded for similar
reasons. Increasingly, in a political world, women and the church
stood out as anti-political forces, as they did in an increasingly
materialistic society, dominated by a new species, Economic Man.
For women and the church were excluded from the pursuit of
wealth just as much as they were kept out of the statehouse, and
for the same rhetorical reasons. Both women and the church were
to be above the counting house, she on her pedestal, the church in
its sanctuary. Wealth was to be given them as consumers and as
reflections of its makers.[6]

Democracy, the novel by Henry Adams, gives a fascinating insight into what happens when a woman ventures near the source
of power, politics, and Washington. In venturing so near the sun
she burns her wings and, limping badly, heads for home.[7] Human nature as defined by the church and human nature as defined
by the state seemed totally different in the eighteenth century
when the idea of original sin conflicted with the Jeffersonian hopes
for perfectability through democracy. During the nineteenth century the churches moved toward the eighteenth-century premise
of progress and salvation. Democracy, on the other hand, seems
to have reverted to a more cynical or perhaps realistic view of
human nature, closer to the Calvinist tradition. Women, however, precisely because they were above and beyond politics and
even beyond producing wealth, much less pursuing it, could
maintain the values of an earlier age. If women had not existed,
the age would have had to invent them, in order to maintain the

rhetoric of eighteenth-century democracy. As the religious view of man became less harsh, it meshed nicely with the hopes of Jefferson and Jackson.

The hierarchy, ministers, and theologians of most religions remained male. There were almost no ordained female ministers—Antoinette Brown Blackwell was an exception and not too happy a one—and few evangelical or volunteer female ministers.[8] When Orestes Brownson growled about a "female religion" he was referring largely to the prominent role which women played in congregations and revivals. However, he was also sniping at the tame minister, whom he caricatured with such scorn as a domesticated pet of spinsters and widows, fit only to balance teacups and mouth platitudes. Brownson's solution, to join the Church of Rome, undoubtedly was motivated by a number of personal and ideological reasons. Not the least of these, however, in the light of his contempt for feminine and weak Protestantism, was the patriarchal structure of the Catholic Church.[9]

Besides their prominence during services, women increasingly handled the voluntary societies which carried out the social office of the churches, by teaching Sunday school, distributing tracts, and working for missions. This was only the external sign of the internal change by which the church grew softer and the religious life less rigorous. Children could be baptized much earlier. The idea of infant damnation, which Theodore Parker rightly said would never have been accepted had women been in charge of theology, quietly died around the middle of the century.[10] These changes were of great benefit to women's peace of mind. Now, if a diary recorded the loss of a child, at least the loss was only a temporary one. Women had found the prospect of parting forever from a beloved child, because there had been no baptism or sign of salvation, almost unbearable. The guilt with which these women so often reproached themselves at least need not concern eternal suffering, and the difference mattered to a believer.

The increasing softness and flexibility in the American churches were reflected in their role in social stratification as well as in their theology. The highly touted classless society of the Revolution was becoming increasingly stratified and self-conscious. The churches represented all different stages in the transition from wilderness to social nicety. The revivals had to fight not only hardness of heart but the lack of social prestige they entailed.

Anglo-Catholicism had stood for a softer life both materially and spiritually since at least the time of the Glorious Revolution. It was also to a degree partially identified with higher social and economic status. The Episcopal Church and the Presbyterian Church were increasingly the churches of the well-to-do, and they offered their members a higher social status to correspond with their wealth. Women used their membership in a more prominent church as an important means of establishing a pecking order within the community.[11]

The male principle was rarely challenged by Trinitarians or Unitarians—whether three or one, God was male (and probably white). However, during the first half of the nineteenth century two ideas gained popularity which showed an appreciation for the values of femaleness—the first was the idea of the Father-Mother God and the second was the concept of the female Saviour. The assignation to God of typically female virtues was nothing new. Presumably a God who was defined as perfect would have all known virtues, whether or not he had a beard. The Shakers went farther, however, and insisted that God had a dual nature, part male and part female.[12] Theodore Parker used the same theme, in pointing out the need for female virtues, particularly the lack of materialism, and finding these virtues in a Godhead which embodied all the symbols of mother's mercy along with father's justice.[13] Joseph Smith consoled his daughter with the thought that in heaven she would meet not only her own mother, who had just died, but she would also "become acquainted with your eternal Mother, the wife of your Father in Heaven." Mormon teaching posited a dual Parenthood within the Godhead, a Father and a Mother, equally divine.[14]

This duality of God the Father with a Mother God almost necessitated the idea of a female counterpart of Christ. Hawthorne in *The Scarlet Letter* has Hester muse on the coming of a female saviour. She reflects that because of her sin she is no longer worthy to be chosen.[15] The female saviour is an interesting amalgam of nineteenth-century adventism, the need for a Protestant counterpart to the cult of the Virgin, and the elevation of pure womanhood to an almost supernatural level. If the world had failed its first test and was plunging into an era of godlessness and vice, as many were convinced, then a second coming seemed necessary. Since the failure of the world also represented a failure of male laws and male values, a second chance, in order to effect change, should produce a different and higher set of laws and values.[16] The role was typecast for the True Woman, as the Shakers and the Mystical Feminists (and later the Christian Scientists) were quick to point out.

The changes in interpretation of Christ which made him the greatest of humans and stressed his divinity in the sense that all men are divine were also interpreted as feminine. The new Christ was the exemplar of meekness and humility, the sacrificial victim.[17] Woman too was the archetypal victim, in literary and religious symbolism. If Christ was interpreted as a human dominated by love, sacrificing himself for others, asking nothing but giving everything and forgiving his enemies in the bargain, he was playing the same role as the true woman in a number of typical nineteenth-century melodramatic scenarios. As every reader of popular fiction knew in the early nineteenth century, woman was never more truly feminine than when, on her deathbed, the innocent victim of male lust or greed, she forgave her cruel father, profligate husband, or avaricious landlord. A special identification with suffering and innocence was shared by both women and the crucified Christ. "She was a great sufferer," intoned one minister at a lady's funeral, "and she loved her crosses."[18]

The minister who interpreted this feminized Christ to his congregation spoke in language which they understood. By 1820 sermons were being preached on the "godless society" which spent its time and money on politics and the pursuit of wealth, "and were seen in church only at weddings and funerals."[19] Observers of the American scene noted frequently that American congregations were composed primarily of women and that ministers spoke to their special needs. Mrs. Trollope cast her cold eye over the flounce-filled pews and remarked that "it is only from the clergy that the women of America receive that sort of attention which is so dearly valued by every female heart throughout the world . . . I never saw, or read, of any country where religion had so strong a hold upon the women, or a slighter hold upon the men."[20] One reason for this prominence was, she felt, that only the clergy listened to women, all other ranks of man's society and interests were closed to them.

The hymns of this period also reflect the increasing stress on Christ's love and God's mercy. The singer is called upon to consider Christ his friend and helper. (To some degree, if the period before the Civil War is seen as one of feminization for Protestantism, the period following it might be termed a period of juvenilization, for increasingly the child as the hope and redeemer of his parents and society is stressed.) Woman's active role in the writing of hymns used in the Methodist, Presbyterian, Episcopal and Congregational hymnals at this time is very small. They contributed almost no music but did quite a few translations, particularly from the German. They were represented best in the lyrics to children's hymns.[21] It is perhaps significant that a hymn which became extremely popular at weddings had words written by a woman. "O Perfect Love" exhorts the young couple to emulate the perfect love of Christ in their own marriage:

> O perfect life, be thou their full assurance
> Of tender charity and steadfast faith,
> Of patient hope, and quiet, brave endurance,
> With childlike trust that fears nor pain nor death.

This was a pattern for domestic bliss much favored by women and the church, since it required the practice of those virtues they both cherished so highly—and which were found increasingly in only one partner of marriage. The implication is one which was made more explicit in the women's magazines: the burden of a marriage falls on the wife; no matter how hard her bed, it is her duty to lie on it. Marriage, and life itself, were at best endurance contests and should be entered in a spirit of passive acceptance and trust.

Another great favorite, "Nearer My God, to Thee," written by Sarah Adams in 1841, carried the same message: "E'en though it be a cross, that raiseth me; Still all my song would be, Nearer, My God, to thee, nearer to thee."[22] The hymns of the Cary sisters, Phoebe and Alice, repeated this theme with variations: "No Trouble Too Great But I Bring It to Jesus," and "To Suffer for Jesus Is My Greatest Joy," for example.[23] Another favorite stressed the total dependence of the singer on Jesus: "I Need Thee Every Hour."[24] The lyrics to this lend themselves all too well to the *double entendre* as those of us forced to sing it in Sunday schools remember to our shame, but in fairness to our interpretations it is true that the imagery in many of these hymns seems very physical. In the desire to stress the warmth and humanity of Christ, he becomes a very cozy person; the singer is urged to press against him, to nestle into him, to hold his hand, and so forth. A love letter to Christ was the only kind of love letter a nice woman was allowed to publish, and sublimation was as yet an unused word. If Julia Ward Howe had called her book of love lyrics a book of hymns even Hawthorne (who thought her husband should have whipped her for the book) would have approved.

The ultimate in such expressions of total absorption in Christ and a yielding up of an unworthy body and soul to his embrace is the widely-sung "Just As I Am, Without One Plea."

> Just as I am, without one plea,
> But that thy blood was shed for me,
> And that thou bidd'st me come to thee,
> O Lamb of God, I come, I come.
>
> Just as I am, though tossed about
> With many a conflict, many a doubt;
> Fightings and fears within, without,
> O Lamb of God, I come, I come.
>
> Just as I am, poor, wretched, blind;
> Sight, riches, healing of the mind,
> Yea, all I need, in thee to find,
> O Lamb of God, I come, I come . . .
>
> Just as I am: thy love unknown
> Has broken every barrier down;
> Now to be thine, yea, thine alone,
> O Lamb of God, I come, I come.[25]

Since so many of women's problems were presumably physical and thus, like the weather, beyond help, it behooved them to endure what they could not cure. The "natural" disasters of childbirth, illness, death, loss of security through recurrent financial crises—all made "thy will be done" the very special female prayer, especially since submission was considered the highest of female virtues. In their hymns women expressed this theme of their lives, as a kind of reinforcement through repetition. However the woman who wanted a more active role in religion than enduring, or even than teaching Sunday school, had several possibilities open to her at this time. She could become a missionary, she could practice an old religion in a new setting, or she could join a new religion which gave women a more active role.

The Christianizing of the West, indeed the domesticating of the

West, was probably the most important religious, cultural, and political event of the first half of the nineteenth century.[26] So long as the West was unhampered by the appurtenances of civilization, including women with their need for lace curtains, for coffee cups and Bibles and neighbors within chatting distance—it was an unknown and possibly dangerous phenomenon. All the Protestant religions and Catholicism as well considered it their special duty to bring God and woman westward as soon as possible. Law, order, and consumers were enhanced by the presence of churches and women. Missionary work appealed to women as a way to have an adventure in a good cause, although the Mission Boards which passed on applications were firm in ruling out "adventuring" as a satisfactory motive. Missions to far off China or Burma were usually denied to the single woman, but the determined girl could quickly find a husband in other zealous souls determined on the same career. The majority of American missionaries in the period before the Civil War stayed within the continent, taking the Christianizing of the Indians as their special challenge and duty.[27]

Mary Augusta Gray reflected on the interior dialogue with which she came to her missionary vocation:

> Ever since the day when I gave myself up to Jesus, it had been my daily prayer, "Lord, what wilt thou have me do?" and when the question, "Will you go to Oregon as one of a little band of self-denying missionaries and teach these poor Indians of their Saviour?" was suddenly proposed to me, I felt that it was the call of the Lord and I could not do otherwise.[28]

The missionaries to China usually went with a sense of doom and impending martyrdom, and the heroic exploits of such women as Ann Hasseltine Judson were fodder for this belief. Mrs. Judson had died, as she knew she would, far from home but near to Jesus, and thus her story became one much favored in children's biographical literature.[29] However even the home missions carried the same possibility for martyrdom, as the fate of Narcissa and Marcus Whitman proved.[30] There is no question but that the aspiring missionary was aware of this possibility and that he welcomed it. Part of the reason for this is perhaps the theology of the period which taught that the death of a martyr assured heaven. The desire for death in the service of the Lord seems in the cases of some missionary women to be their strongest motive.

Eliza Spalding, a Connecticut girl who had been converted at an early age, found that distributing tracts and doing visiting among the poor was not enough for her. She asked divine guidance about her future and received the impulse to go to Oregon. When her husband tried to dissuade her she replied: "I like the command just as it stands, 'Go ye into all the world,' with no exception for poor health. The dangers in the way and the weakness of my body are his; duty is mine." Mrs. Spalding survived the trip, leaving the following diary entry:

> Oh, that I had a crust of bread from my mother's swill pail. I cannot sit on that horse in the burning sun any longer. I cannot live much longer. Go on, and save yourself and carry the Book to the Indians. I shall never see them. My work is done. But bless God that He has brought me thus far. Tell my mother that I am not sorry I came.

Her husband wrote to the Mission Board: "Never send another white woman over these mountains, if you have any regard for human life," but of course they did, for the women clamored to come to the Indians and to death, if need be.[31]

Although the West has been seen as a fertile ground for democratic innovations, this was not necessarily true for woman's role. Simply because of the lack of numbers, most western churches gave women the freedom to participate in church services, and the West was the natural breeding place for such woman evangelists as Carry A. Nation and Aimee Semple MacPherson. However there was still pressure to conform to the traditional female role within religion, as Narcissa Whitman wrote shortly before her death:

> In all the prayer meetings of this mission the brethren only pray. I believe all the sisters would be willing to pray if their husbands would let them. We are so few in number, it seems as if they would wish it, but many prefer the more dignified way. My husband has no objection to my praying, but if my sisters do not, he thinks it quite as well for me not to.[32]

In the West, but especially in the East, the spirit of revival was strong during this period. The language, like that of the hymns, was sexual in its imagery and urged the penitent to "stop struggling and allow yourself to be swept up in His love." Obviously this kind of imagery had a familiar ring to women, for it was in similar language that they were encouraged to submit to their husbands. Whether in the divine or human order, woman was constantly urged to be swept away by a torrent of energy, not to rely on her own strength which was useless, to sink into the arms of Jesus, to become absorbed and assimilated by the Divine Will— in other words, to relax and enjoy it. The fantasies of rape were nourished by this language and by the kind of physical sensations which a woman expected to receive and did receive in the course of conversion. "A trembling of the limbs," "a thrill from my toes to my head," "wave after wave of feeling," are examples of female reaction to the experience of "divine penetration."[33]

Mrs. Maggie N. Van Cott, who called herself the first lady licensed to preach in the Methodist Episcopal Church in the United States, told in her autobiography of receiving the "great blessing of fullness" as a result of which she was "perfectly emptied of self and filled with the Spirit of God." In showing her the way, God had announced "I am a jealous God; thou shalt have no other Gods before me," which she interpreted to mean that her Master wanted her complete devotion.[34]

Ellen G. White had a similar vision in which she was shown a steep frail staircase, at the top of which was Jesus. As she fell prostrate, her guide gave her a green cord "coiled up closely," which she could uncoil to reach Him. From that time "my entire being was offered to the service of my Master."[35]

Particularly interesting are those first-person accounts which discuss these experiences and then go on to say how little her husband understands her and how he tries to interfere with this wholehearted commitment to Christ. "Oh, the bliss of that moment, when my soul was enabled to cast all her care upon Jesus and feel that *her* will was lost in the will of God," rhapsodized Myra Smith at 4:14 a.m. one Sunday. Soon after she wrote: ". . . I find sweet comfort in doing the will of God instead of my own . . . I feel that God calls me to labor in a more special manner than he usually does females . . . I am not understood by my husband and children but I don't murmur, or blame them for it. I know they can't tell why I seem at times lost to everything around me."[36] Richard Hofstadter points out that revivalism was one of the manifestations of a pervasive anti-intellectualism in mid-nineteenth-century America.[37] However it can be further annotated by means of the popular custom of dividing qualities into male and female categories. By this nomenclature all the intuitive and emotional qualities are most natural to women, all the cerebral and intellectual policies of linear thought the prerogative of men. When in terms of religion a more intuitive, heartfelt approach was urged it was tantamount to asking for a more feminine religious style.[38]

Although at the intellectual and, therefore, presumably "masculine" end of the scale, Transcendentalism might also be considered representative of certain feminine standards. One hanger-on to Transcendental circles and ardent feminist, Caroline Dall, saw Anne Hutchinson as the first Transcendentalist and, by extension, the first feminist in the American colonies.[39] Her argument was that antinomianism was an open door to the exercise of individual rights, by either sex or by any group. If God, not the ordained clergy, picks His spokesmen, then women are as likely as any to be among the chosen, for as any popular novel or sermon would have it, women are more religious, more noble, more spiritual than men— so all the more likely to be a vehicle for God's message. Besides, if one adheres to the principle of autonomous conversion, then there is no way to second-guess the Almighty; any soul may receive Him, no sex barred. In the Quaker religion the Inner Light was expected to be equally indiscriminate in the choice of vessels to illuminate, and the Society of Friends practiced theoretical religious equality from its beginnings.

The Transcendentalists accepted a similar definition of equality before God. All souls were equally divine, without regard to sex or race. As Nathaniel Frothingham points out, Transcendentalism was a part of the Woman's Rights Movement in the most profound sense in that it posited her as an innate equal, whose potential had been hampered by society. Ralph Waldo Emerson went through a number of phases in the formulation of his own position on women. His theoretical approach, contained in a number of essays, was sometimes at variance with the way in which he actually coped with his Aunt Mary, his two wives, and the irritatingly untheoretical presence of Margaret Fuller. In an essay, "Woman," Emerson tried to analyze the religious style of females. He concluded that ". . . the omnipotence of Eve is in humility." This, he continued, was the direct opposite of male style, which was to stress the necessity and potency of the male to the object loved. Religion perforce requires humility, since God does not depend on human strength. Women also, according to Emerson, possess to a high degree that "power of divination" or sympathy which the German Romantics prized so highly. They have "a religious height which men do not attain" because of their "sequestration from affairs and from the injury to the moral sense which affairs often inflict. . . ." It was therefore not surprising that "in every remarkable religious development in the world, women have taken a leading part."[40]

The idea of a regenerated reconstituted society was important to most members of the Hedge Club, and they looked optimistically towards an America in which man would leave behind his chains and emerge closer to nature and nature's God. The concept of ideal manhood and of ideal womanhood was often discussed at these meetings, and, of course, in Margaret Fuller's Conversations.[41] Womanhood was believed to be, in principle, a higher, nobler state than manhood, since it was less directly related to the body and was more involved with the spirit; women had less to transcend in their progress. "I trust more and more every opportunity will be offered to women to train and use their gifts, until the world finds out what womanhood is," wrote William Henry Channing. "My hope for society turns upon this; the regeneration of the future will come from the exalting influence of woman."[42] Most of these Transcendentalists were unconvinced about woman's role in politics, but they were totally convinced that she represented the highest and best parts of man.

Margaret Fuller contributed another important idea to the feminization of religion in her stress on the importance of the will. As historians such as John William Ward have pointed out, this belief in the power of the American will was typical of Jacksonian America. Like other aspects of the so-called American character, however, it did not necessarily hold true for all groups within the society. (David Riesman, for example, has reconsidered some of his statements about American character because of the remoteness of the female half of the population from his producer economy.)[43]

For Margaret Fuller the will was the instrument to power for women even more than for men, and she set out to convince her world of this fact. Woman traditionally was urged to negate her will, or at least to yield it up to her father, her husband, and her God. Margaret Fuller told her to actively pursue her goals, to "elect" her destiny. Miss Fuller possessed Emerson's "spark of divinity" by which she was able to convince the young girls and wives who flocked to her that they too were divine and could go out and accomplish great (but unnamed) things. This preaching to women of their worth before God and man was sound Transcendental doctrine, but the stress on female worth, on transcendent womanhood, was a personal interpretation of Margaret Fuller. She gloried in her role of Sibyl, and relished all references to her as Delphic and/or Oracular.[44] The cult of the will, as Donald Meyer writes, found its triumph in Christian Science, also the religion of a woman, in which even death bows to positive thought.[45] Margaret Fuller's intent and fervid preoccupation with the making-over of the self presented a considerable threat to the men in her circle. For if sex itself, as well as health, family, education, income, all counted for nothing—what standards remained? It was perhaps the vicious circle of antinomianism after all; a religion open to the vagaries of God's choice or the boundaries of the human will is a religion without class lines and certainly without sex discrimination.

The Transcendentalists sought concrete expression of their philosophy in the community of Brook Farm, and the setting up of ideal communal societies was one way in which nineteenth-century religion expressed its dissatisfaction with past religious styles and its hope for the future. The equal rights of Transcendentalism were much in evidence at Brook Farm. One participant in that noble experiment recalled hearing a lecture on women's rights during his time in residence. The young lady speaker:

> . . . was much put out, after orating awhile, to note that her glowing periods were falling on dull ears. Our womenfolk had all the rights of our men-folk. They had an equal voice in our public affairs, voted for our offices, filled responsible positions, and stood in exactly the same footing as their brethren. If women were not so well off in the outer world, they had only to join our community or to form others like it.[46]

In the constitution of Brook Farm, as in many other communal societies, there are promises to the women members that they would be liberated from the tyranny of men and of the stove, and given greater freedom to develop their own identities. Charles Nordhoff, writing on the influence of women in Utopian communities in 1875, found that women's participation in discussions gave them "contentment of mind, as well as enlarged views and pleasure in self-denial." Women in communal life found stability, which they needed and wanted, and many small comforts provided by the men

for which "the migrating farmer's wife sighs in vain." The simplicity of dress typical of many groups was "a saving of time and
trouble and vexation of spirit." Their greatest contribution to communal society was their "conservative spirit," which operated in the
aggregate as it had in family life. Nordhoff concluded that women
expressed the basic excuse for being of the communist society, for
her "influence is always toward a higher life."[47]

When the commune moved from the planning stages to the land
itself, somehow or other, women ended up in the kitchen or the
laundry. Men might serve on these committees, but the overriding
principle of the division of labor mandated their presence outdoors.
In the communal societies whose records I studied, there is no record of any complaint on the part of the women, nor was there any
recorded instance of women challenging their husbands on a given
vote. There seems also to be no pattern of a woman's bloc.[48] But
the actual role of women is less important than the way in which
the changed pattern of social life was supposed to bring true equality to both sexes and liberate man from his own tyranny at the
same time woman was freed from the conventional bonds of family
life.

The Fourierist philosophy, which, so far as recorded sources tell,
was never completely followed in the United States, provided for a
good deal of sexual freedom within a definition of human nature
which relied on "natural affinities." Parts of the human race were
exempted from monogamy because they had "natural affinities"
towards several members of the opposite sex. The fact that women,
as well as men, might be expected to have these preferences was
regarded as "peculiarly French," and not relevant to the American
Phalanx.[49]

Within the Americanized version of Fourierism there was much
"wholesome intercourse" between the sexes. The opportunity to
work and study and talk together was rare enough for middle-class
American youth, and the Phalanxes gave them much more freedom
than most families allowed. The great charm of the communal life,
one remembered fondly long after the community itself was a thing
of the past, "was in the free and natural intercourse for which it
gave opportunity, and in the working of the elective affinities."[50]
The young women who participated in these experiments were em-
boldened to pursue lives as teachers or reformers after they left
the Phalanx. The Transcendental idea of the infinite worth of the

individual and his ability to work out his destiny was greatly appealing to these young women. Even if women continued to do woman's work and find their greatest individual destiny in monogamous marriage, there was a statement of equality and of alternatives on the record.

The experiment at Oneida, conducted by John Humphrey Noyes as an example of his Perfectionist religion, was a particularly interesting application of new religion to women. One of the avowed purposes of the Oneida Community was to give women "extended rights" within "an extended family." The way in which Noyes defined these rights was sharply criticized by his contemporaries and has not received very sympathetic treatment from historians. In many ways he really was, as he claimed to be, "Woman's best friend." Noyes believed that the search for complete perfection began with control over one's own body. For women this was a complicated phenomenon, involving not only the marital rights but the right to choose whether she wished to have children. Noyes spoke very cogently about the trauma of the nineteenth-century woman, who bore her children with such pain and hope, and saw them die as infants.[51] In a society which defined woman as valuable largely in relation to her ability to bear children, it was logical that women thought of their own worth in those terms. When a child died it was an affirmation of personal guilt and possibly sin. What have I done, the bereaved mother asked her God, that I should be punished? Pages of women's diaries are filled with personal recriminations. For months she flagellated herself with the remedies she might have used, the errors of judgment she could have avoided, the ways in which she might have offended a jealous God. Noyes proposed to define her worth in different terms: she was a loving companion and "yoke-fellow" on the road to perfection. Childbearing was only part of her duty, to be engaged in sparingly and under controlled conditions, and to be separated from sex.[52] In terms of woman's self-image this proposal was one of the most radical of the century.

The form of birth control used by Noyes, which he called "male continence," consisted in "self-control" which prolonged intercourse but stopped the act short of ejaculation. Interestingly enough, this insistence on control was only for the man; there was no limit to the amount of pleasure a woman was allowed to get from the act. Moreover, sexual intercourse was accepted as a good in itself, completely outside the propagation of the species, and as an important means of self-expression for both sexes. Noyes went so far in identifying the sex act with perfectionism as to assert that sexual intercourse was practiced in heaven. This insistence on the joys of sex was rare enough, but, couched in terms of a conjugal relation which promised equal rights of choice and no penalty of childbearing on the woman, it was extraordinary. Perfectionism stressed the "giving, not the claiming," the act of loving, rather than the social and economic benefits of marriage.[53] In these ways, it acceded to the feminine spirit and role. The nineteenth-century belief that "love is a game, nothing more to a man/ But love to a woman is life or death," that "love is woman's whole existence," was applied by Noyes to both sexes. "We should pray, give us this day our daily love, for what is love but the bread of the heart. We need love as much as we need food and clothing, and God knows it. . . ."[54] In the popular jargon of phrenology, Noyes separated "amativeness" from both "union for life" and "procreativeness." In the phrenological manuals, amativeness was considered to be particularly well developed in men; the other two qualities, along with "philoprogenitiveness" to be peculiarly suited to female skulls.[55] Noyes stressed love for both sexes and freedom of choice for both, which gave to women the continuation of her preoccupation with love plus the right to a repetitive use of her loving. Marriage at Oneida was a working out of the feminine rhetoric of love on a sequential basis.

Although Mormonism was treated as a great foe of women's rights, and even its female proponents agreed that it placed the male in a dominant role, it had certain components which made it part of the overall movement towards "feminization." Like Perfectionism it claimed to be acting in the name of a better life for women. "No prophet or reformer of ancient or modern times has surpassed, nay, has equalled, the Prophet Joseph Smith in the breadth and scope of the opportunities which he accorded womanhood," wrote a dutiful and satisfied daughter of both the Prophet and Zion.[56] Mormonism required its followers to accept the words of their spiritual Father without murmur, and to obey the precepts of authority. The important concept of the Mormon priesthood is one which excludes women (as well as blacks by some interpretations). However, Joseph Smith, when the women of his group asked him for a written constitution for their Relief Society, told them he would give them "something better for them than a written con-

stitution . . . I will organize the sisters under the priesthood after
a pattern of the priesthood . . . The Church was never perfectly
organized until the women were thus organized."[57]

Thus the women of the Church of Jesus Christ of the Latter Day
Saints claimed that they were admitted as "co-workers and partners" in the important work of attaining salvation. They were in the
priesthood only when taken by their husbands and only with their
husband could they enter into a special heaven. Their consent was
required for plural marriage, which became their passport—again,
only with their husbands—to the highest stages of celestial bliss.
And yet, patriarchal as it was, women were not ignored by this
new religion. Indeed, they were given explicit and critical directions
for salvation. No man could get to heaven alone, by any combination of faith or good works; he had to come bringing his family with
him. Women could legitimately claim that Mormonism recognized
their importance more than any other religion because it tied them
to their husbands for all time and eternity. Motherhood was stressed
in Utah even more than in the rest of American society, but it was
the importance of producing souls not bodies that counted. Since
every woman, in theory, could be united to the man of her choice,
she could go to heaven with her love, not her forced compromise.
Recognizing the fact that society gave women status only as a
married woman and as a mother, the Mormons gave each woman
the opportunity to have that coveted status in this life and in the
next. What is surprising is not the formulation of Celestial Marriage, but the fervor with which Mormon women defended it as
important to their ideas of themselves as valuable and valid persons.[58]

Like the Church of Jesus Christ of the Latter Day Saints, Roman
Catholicism during this pre-Civil War period had both masculine
and feminine manifestations. The patriarchal system of authority,
which so pleased Orestes Brownson, has already been mentioned.
The diatribes against Rome which were prevalent in the 1830s
and 1840s stressed this authoritarian and antidemocratic aspect
of the church. In other words, Catholics were not allowed to exercise their masculine prerogatives of intellectual autonomy and independent judgment. When a modest number of conversions to
Roman Catholicism occurred during the last days of Brook Farm,
some observers found the cause to be the discouragement and
disappointment which the failure of that experiment created in its
members. Most of the converts were female, and disparaging state-

ments were made about the need to abandon the heritage of the New England Protestant (masculine) church to find solace in a more soothing, structured (feminine) religion.[59] The letters of the converted Fourierists do nothing to deny that they found the Church of Rome more suitable to their needs, but their emphasis is not on feminine dependence but on womanly warmth. Sophia Ripley wrote to a sympathetic friend that she found "the coldness of heart in Protestantism and my own coldness of heart in particular" to be repugnant. After her conversion she saw herself clearly for the first time: "I saw that all through life my ties with others were those of the intellect and imagination, and not human heart ties; that I do not love anyone. I never did, with the heart, and of course never could have been worthy in any relation." Catholicism united her for the first time with humanity, and that chill intellectual pride which New Englanders wore like Lady Eleanor's mantle at last melted away. "I saw above all that my faith in the Church was only a reunion of my intellect with God," and not a union of hearts. To her mentor Bishop Hughes she poured out her fears that "this terrible deathlike coldness" had produced a "heart of stone" which even the love of Christ could not melt. He reassured her that if she had been born in the Church perhaps her nature would have been softened, but she must offer to God not the heart she coveted but the heart she had: "Oh God, take this poor cold heart of mine, and make of it what thou wilt . . . This heart of yours is a cross which you must bear to the end if needs be."[60] Catholicism, then, at least to some of its members, incorporated the love and warmth so characteristic of women and so necessary to them.

Like Mormonism, Roman Catholicism was also regarded as a religion for the many, not the few. This sense of religion as a means of keeping down intellectual arrogance and spiritual pride is one which accords with a subtle but important aspect of female definition during this period. In Hawthorne's stories and novels the woman is the symbol of the earth, the tie with domestic detail and bodily warmth which prevents man from soaring too high or sinking too low.[61] Louis Auchincloss has called women "guardians and caretakers" because of their role in preserving literary and cultural traditions.[62] Inasmuch as religion is concerned they might as well be termed "Translators and Vulgarizers." In the Transcendental novel, *Margaret*, Sylvester Judd says of woman: "She translates nature to man and man to himself."[63] Women, in religion, as in popular taste, take the bold and bitter and make it bland. One critic of American conformity blames the low standards of American culture on the fact that women are the audience and arbiters. "Averse to facing the darker brutal sides of existence, its uncertainty and irrationality, they prefer the comforting assurance that life is just bitter enough to bring out the flavor of its sugared harmonies."[64] Women in the first half of the nineteenth century took Christianity and molded it to their image and likeness.

"The curse of our age is its femininity," complained Orestes Brownson. "Its lack, not of barbarism, but of virility."[65] These changes, which annoyed Brownson as much in literature as in religion, made women as well as men conscious of their virtues. Womanhood and virtue became almost synonymous. Although the values of the nineteenth century have predominated during the twentieth century, it becomes increasingly more clear that they are not the only values and that the so-called feminine virtues may assume more than rhetorical significance. The giving over of religion to women, in its content and in its membership, provided a repository for these female values during the period when the business of building a nation did not immediately require them. In order to do this, it was necessary first to assign certain virtues to women and, then, to institutionalize these virtues. The family, popular culture, and religion were the vehicles by which feminine virtues were translated into values.

Religion carried with it the need for self-awareness, if only for the examination of conscience. Organizational experience could be obtained in many reform groups, but only religion brought with it the ultimate definition of who you were and where you were going. Women in religion were encouraged to be introspective. What they found out would be useful in their drive towards independence. The constant identification of woman with virtue and with religion reenforced her own belief in her power to overcome obstacles, since she had her own superior nature and God's own Church, whichever it might be, behind her. Religion in its emphasis on the brotherhood of man developed in women a conscious sense of sisterhood, a quality absolutely essential for any kind of meaningful woman's movement. The equality of man before God expressed so effectively in the Declaration of Independence had little impact on women's lives. However the equality of religious experience was something they could personally experience, and no man could deny it to them.

7

DEFENDERS OF THE FAITH
Women Novelists of Religious Controversy in the Nineteenth Century

Popular novels often fade quickly, their idiom and their ideas easily forgotten. Yet the best-seller is frequently an index of the values of a particular period. It sells well because it reenforces and reassures, frequently in response to some challenge or change in established patterns of behavior. Often the moment of a particular book is the moment of historical transition from one such accepted pattern to another, and from this vantage point can be seen changes in institutions not easily susceptible to documentation. When an idea or attitude formerly ignored or negatively presented becomes the preferred choice of the protagonist in a best-selling novel, it signals no longer the chill of disapproval but the more pleasant shock of recognition. The reader can relax and enjoy the changes in his own life which probably already existed but lacked the sanction of fiction, that seal of approval which gives nature the license to imitate art. The cultural, class and sectional discrepancies and time lags in the United States of the nineteenth century can be partially charted through the response to such novels. Women, so often the popularizers of ideas and the levellers of abstract theory to the common denominator of human experience, wrote about one-third of the best sellers during this period.

The nineteenth-century novel written by women often served as a vehicle of protest, one of the ways in which women could express opinions without being open to charges of "unsexing" themselves. Temperance, women's rights, prolabor and antilabor, slavery and abolition, were all treated fictionally, but it was rare for an overtly reform novel to reach "best-seller" status. Only Harriet Beecher Stowe's *Uncle Tom's Cabin* combined specific reform with great popularity. The heroines of these books, however, were all women of unusual character and ability.

In the period from the Civil War to the end of the century the best-seller lists had many more novels written by women which were tracts for or against social change. Frances Hodgson Burnett popularized Christian Science and New Thought in her work; Martha Finley's child redeemer Elsie Dinsmore pleaded with her father to keep the Sabbath holy and the sideboard unprofaned by the presence of liquor; Louisa Mae Alcott warned against the destructive urban values and admired the Jeffersonian rural virtues of the "Old-Fashioned Girl"; Helen Hunt Jackson offered Ramona's saga as a protest against the treatment of the American Indian; and Marietta Holley's sharp-tongued Samantha Allan was a humorous proponent for her "sect's" rights and for temperance.[2] During the same period three American women wrote best-selling novels which dealt with the most frightening and perplexing of all changes, the controversies facing American Protestantism. These books offered a resolution of the dilemmas faced by the church in an age of science and materialism. They also suggested the role which women should perform in this resolution, and their heroines combined the piety and strength of an earlier period with new talents and power, acceptable rather than alarming because this expanded consciousness would be used to defend the faith.

In an age when religion was still the most serious and important of concerns, or at least proclaimed to be so, all change within the churches was regarded with suspicion. Public behavior was strongly linked in the minds of Americans with the deterrent power of religious sanctions, and attempts to mitigate or liberalize doctrine were feared as openings for political and social turmoil. Women, increasingly the guardians of public as well as private morality, were assumed to be the staunchest and most numerous members of America's churches. It was natural that women should respond to the challenge of suggested doctrinal, as well as social, change. In the novels of religious controversy the relationship between religion and woman, already accepted myth and practical reality, is made more specific and more fundamental. Reforms which concern women are sanctioned, if they are sanctioned at all, largely because they increase the power of woman to save the church from its enemies. The specific religious controversies and the resolutions assigned to them in these novels are particularly favorable to women.[3]

The novel was only one of several ways in which women's opinions of religious change were disseminated among the American people. Another was the "how-to" book, perennial best-sellers in an optimistic society impressed with the strength of its will. The blueprint for personal holiness varied with the author and the season, but all promised the rewards of a tranquil heart in this world and, of course, joy everlasting in the next. Among the most prominent of these manuals in the nineteenth century were Phoebe Palmer's *The Way of Holiness* (1845) which explained the possibilities of perfectionism to those who sought it; *Stepping Heavenward* a novel by Elizabeth Prentiss (1860) which adapted Fenelon and Thomas à Kempis to the needs of harassed wives and mothers, who wanted desperately to be good but found the low threshold of domestic trivia far removed from high holiness; and *The Christian's Secret* (1883), in which Hannah Smith shared the Quaker ideal of silent prayer and reflection with a generation which had grown busy and troubled about many things.[4] Unlike these directive and explicit works, the religious novel offered a dialogue before the resolution and implicit and indirect choice among values. In the novels the addition of attractive and compelling characters, particularly the tension between the religious values of men and women characters, linked the resolution of religious doubt with the resolution of personal problems. The happy ending consisted in the reconciliation of love of God and the love of some particular man.

Augusta Evans Wilson, Elizabeth Stuart Phelps Ward, and Margaret Deland wrote novels of religious controversy which attained best-seller status. These three women were separated by approximately a decade each in age, although their works overlapped in publication. They represented three separate creeds, three sections of the country, and three different life styles. Yet the works of all of them were conservative of the religious and female traditions. Each posed essentially the same questions and although the answers varied, they remained within the same pattern of choices. The difference lies in the author's satisfaction or lack of satisfaction in the disposition of the questions, whether gladly or ruefully she contemplated the results of the lives she had created.

Augusta Evans Wilson (1835-1909) wrote as a life-long Southerner, Methodist, and opponent of women's suffrage. She had, however, undergone a period of painful skepticism, and she had strong convictions about women's spiritual superiority. At thirty-three, already an established writer, she married an elderly widower with grown children, and devoted herself to the elaborate routine of his household. She had no children of her own, and participated little in organized reform. Her most popular novels were *Beulah* (1859) and *St. Elmo* (1867), but her ideas on religion are also important in her other novels, especially *Inez: A Tale of the Alamo* (1855), *Macaria* (1863), and the much later *A Speckled Bird* (1902).[5]

Inez is an anti-Catholic tract, along the lines of *Maria Monk* but with special pleading for Southern churches and Southern women. Nativism, as David Brian Davis suggests, united the fear of countersubversion with the fear of sexual perversion (or perhaps even of sexuality).[6] The defense of the Alamo provides a noble opportunity to combine patriotism and Protestantism. From the arguments of Mary with the villainous Jesuit Father Mazzarin it becomes clear that one of the beneficial results of female education is the ability to out-argue the seducer, whether of body or soul. The wily Jesuit competes with the Methodist heroine for the soul of her cousin, who is also her half-sister, as revealed in one of the tortuous subplots. Mary pleads with her cousin to exert her "individuality," her Protestant American will. "Florry, you have been blinded, deceived . . . But oh! there is a source of rest and strength, and comfort, which is to be attained not by confession, or the intercession of the dead or living, but by repentance for the past, and an active, trusting faith in the meditation of our blessed Lord Jesus Christ." The unwary English have meekly swallowed "Puseyism" and the Oxford Movement, naively failing to realize the poison is "stealing silently but very swiftly to the very heart of their ecclesiastical institutions, and total subversion will ultimately ensue." American institutions will be similarly subverted unless the country becomes more vigilant. The Alamo and Texas must be saved for Protestantism, as Florry must be settled in a healthy Protestant marriage. Mary as a kind of sacrificial victim dies, exhausted from her salvage efforts, and her own lover is killed in the Alamo.

In her second novel, *Beulah*, the heroine grapples with Darwinism and skeptical thought, the dangers to religion which have supplanted the Jesuit threat. Beulah loves the distinguished Dr. Hartwell, a gentleman and a scholar but with the flaw of unbelief. Rather than accept a loving living God he has been swayed by "geological and biological tomes" until "truly God was dead, re-placed by a subtle Pantheism." Beulah refuses Hartwell's proposal —"I cannot rest on your rock of negation,"—and begins serious study to defend her God against those insidious voices claiming the world was created in more than the Biblical four thousand and four years. In the same spirit, although with different inten-tions and results, Lucy Stone studied Greek and Hebrew at Ober-lin so that she might read the Bible in its original languages and determine the extent of its apparent antifeminism. After thought and study Beulah is confused. "The more I read and study the more obscure seem the questions that I am toiling to answer. Is this increasing intricacy the reward of an earnestly inquiring mind?" The price of being an intellectual, of seeing more than one side of an issue, of finding little which is perfectly clear and much that is ambiguous, is too high. "Oh, better die now than live as I have lived, in perpetual struggling! What is life without peace of mind, without hope . . ." Sleepless, she muses, "Oh, philosophy! thou hast marked my hungry soul . . . starless night . . . cold metaphysical conjectures . . . My God, save me! Give me light! Of myself I can know nothing!" And, purged of ego, in this cere-bral counterpart of the discredited conversion experience, the il-luminating love of Christ enters her soul and she believes, through love, what she cannot understand. "Her proud intellect was hum-bled, she fell on her knees and prayed." Secure and happy she marries Dr. Hartwell, and under her influence his "cynicism melted insensibly away." To show that even his male intellect ought to bow before the mysteries of the universe, she poses the question, "Sir, can you understand how matter creates mind?" He is ponder-ing as the book ends, with the prayerful wish on the final page, "May God aid the wife in her holy work of love!"

Replying to a critic of Beulah's experience, the author wrote, "The truth of the whole matter lies in a nut-shell—our religious states are determined by *Faith, not Reason* . . . Beulah consti-tuted her reason the sole criterion of truth, but found on all sides insolvable mysteries—found that unaided by that Revelation—which her reason had ignored that she was utterly incapable of ever arriving at any belief . . . and discarding the belief that Rea-son alone could discover the truth, she rested her spent soul in the Ark of Faith! whereby she was enabled to receive the sublime teachings of inspiration!"[7] Beulah, in rejecting masculine approaches to the mysteries of God, and accepting her feminine intuition as superior, was reaffirming woman's place and nature, and giving these traditional values new importance. God's mysteries cannot be understood by the masculine mind; they are penetrated only by the female heart. What women had, if they only realized it, was better than what men had. And this in a generation spared the vocabulary of castration complexes and penis envy!

In *Macaria*, published in the Confederacy in 1863 (and republished in New York in 1868) the theme of the woman serving American Protestantism is joined to the theme of Southern superiority. The North represents the worst of the masculine character, its avaricious, materialistic, soulless side. The South has the humanistic, unselfish and honorable values of the women it has put on a pedestal and the religion they cherish. Irene, the "Flower of the South," bids her lover farewell saying, "I want your promise that you will so live and govern yourself that, if your soul is summoned from the battle-field, you can confront Eternity without a single apprehension." She can face his death if she has "the conviction that, in that noble death, you found the gate of heaven." Her prayer is that God will "accept the sacrifice, and crown the South a sovereign, independent nation!" When in fact her lover is mortally wounded, he eagerly awaits Heaven. "Oh, Irene, but for your earnest piety this precious anticipation might never have been mine." After his death Irene plans a life of good works, "with the hope of promoting God's glory, and of contributing, as far as one feeble woman can, to the happiness and weal of her fellow-creatures." The suffering of the South, like all female suffering, receives meaning in the context of religion, and the injustices of this life where male vice is frequently favored over female virtue, just as the South may be crushed by the North, will be righted in the next world. Southern defeat and female tears, followed by a reconstructed life of prayers and good deeds, are all that remain of temporal existence. But they shall both, the South and its women, laugh in the latter day, when religion triumphs over politics and economics. Augusta Wilson believed as strongly in the South as she did in her God and in the strength of womanhood. She served as a nurse throughout the Civil War, but *Macaria* was her most important war work. According to her biographer, it was the most popular novel published in the South during the War and, an even surer pledge of its orthodoxy, it was considered dangerous contraband by General Thomas, who burned any copies he found.

Her fourth and most popular work, *St. Elmo*, has a heroine distinguished by "love of nature, love of books, an earnest piety and deep religious conviction." Her guardian's son, St. Elmo Murray, is a handsome cynic with "a lordly, brilliant intellect." Edna, granddaughter of a blacksmith, is given over to Mr. Hammond to be educated, although he warns her at great length against becoming a bluestocking, one of those awful women "whose fingers are more frequently adorned with ink-spots than thimble" and who are "ugly and learned and cross; whose hair is never smooth and whose ruffles are never fluted." Edna calmly rejoins, "I do not understand why ladies have not as good a right to be learned as gentlemen." The rest of the book defends that right. Women should be educated, even at the risk of ink-stained fingers and wrinkled ruffles, to enable her to defend religion more effectively.

Edna refuses a good man's offer of marriage because, although she respected him and "liked his society," she did not love him passionately. Her tutor remarks that she must marry only when she has "learned to love, almost against her will. Some strong vigorous thinker, whose will and intellect masters hers, who compels her heart's homage, and without whose society she can not persuade herself to live." As in the Gothic novel, the apparently beastly man must be tamed by woman, whose beauty of soul and body brings him to his knees. Once he subdues his nature in order to win her he can happily master her ever after. In the religious novel the woman must bring about the erstwhile beast's submission to Christ before accepting her own role as submissive wife. Edna is deeply in love with St. Elmo but can not countenance his skepticism. He explains that he was trifled with for his fortune by his fiancée. He himself deserted a bride at the altar which still bears the stains of her dying hemorrhage. His own guilt seems too great for Christ's redemption and, besides, he has lost his faith in human nature.

Vowing that "rather than become the wife of a sacreligious scoffer . . . I will, so help me God, live and work alone," she goes to New York to work as a governess and write a novel. The purpose of this book will be "to discover the only true and allowable and womanly sphere of feminine work." In it she argues against "the tendency of the age to equality and communism," and warns "of the dangers to be apprehended from the unfortunate and deluded female malcontents." Women were encouraged "to become sculptors, painters, writers, teachers in schools or families," all acceptable positions. If they could not master these new roles they should "remain mantua-makers, milliners, spinners, dairymaids." But never, "at the peril of all womanhood," should they "meddle with scalpal or red tape." The woman doctor, the woman orator were all part of an alarming "tendency to free and easy manners and colloquial license" which was "rapidly destroying all reverence for womanhood" and "was placing the sexes on a platform of equality which was dangerous to feminine delicacy, that God-built bulwark of national morality."

St. Elmo, convinced by her example (her honesty in not opening a locked box goes a long way to restore his faith in human nature) and her best-selling novel, becomes a minister, having accepted God's offer of forgiveness and future saving grace. They prepare together for a life of good works in God's service but he tells her, she will write no more books for her time belongs to him. His final words are an apostrophe to their future together. "Loving each other, aiding each other, serving Christ, through whose atonement alone I have been saved from eternal ruin." Religion provides the personal, the sexual and the societal salvation. Woman in her sphere will exert her great influence to keep God in His heaven. If woman became a mere man, at her ease in the dissecting room and at the ballot box, the whole fragile edifice by which female purity preserved national morality would topple. A well-educated woman uses her mind to convince her family and, if she chooses to write, her public, to resist the changes which could bring on this destruction. Augusta Evans Wilson saw literature as admirable precisely for its ability to convey moral truths. "Art should elevate, should refine, should sanctify the heart," she wrote, and vowed "to combat skepticism to the day of my death, and if possible, to help others to avoid the thorny path I have trod ere I was convinced of the fallibility of human Reason."[8]

When people read *St. Elmo* they could work through with him the puzzling maze of scientific arguments about the creation of the world and reformers' harangues about the nature of women. When, with him, they reached the other side they found to their joy that they could have knowledge, science, revealed religion, and beautiful young Americans. If, that is, woman would continue to play her ordained role, and guide men to follow her heart, not his head, when it came to the Almighty. She for her reward would get the reformed and masterful St. Elmo, who was far closer to the average maiden's prayer than was his nearest rival, Susan B. Anthony.

A Speckled Bird, her last full-length novel, was Augusta Wilson's most explicit statement of Southern womanhood and piety opposing the unsexed godless North. Eglah is presented as a graduate of a woman's college, but vehemently opposed to suffrage and, incidentally, to trade unions. A broadly comic suffragist, Ethelberta Higginbottom, taunts Eglah with her old-fashioned Southern standards, and her neglect of "women's rights." Eglah replies proudly, "Indeed, I have the most affectionate and jealous regard for every right that inheres in my dower of American womanhood. I claim and enjoy the right to be as cultured, as learned, as useful, and—if you please—as ornamental in society and at home as my individual limitations will permit. I have no wrongs, no grievances, no crying need to usurp lines of work that will break down the barriers God set between men and women. I am not in rebellion against legal statutes, nor the canons of well-established decency and refinement in feminine usage, and, finally, I am so inordinately proud of being a well-born Southern woman, with a full complement of honorable great-grandfathers and blue-blooded, stainless great-grandmothers, that I have neither pretext nor inclination to revolt against mankind." Eglah is rich, beautiful and, finally, successfully wooed by an equally affluent and attractive man. Again, success is the best proof in these novels that virtue's own rewards come in this life as well as in the next. Woman suffrage seemed, at the end of the novelist's long career, to be the most dangerous enemy religion had yet faced, before which Jesuit tricks and Darwinian theories appeared quickly unseated challengers. The Priest and the Scientist had failed, but the New Woman of the twentieth century was a truly formidable enemy, knowing, as she did, so many of the passwords,

Elizabeth Stuart Phelps Ward (1844-1911) was brought up in Andover where her father was a professor in the Seminary. Her mother, Elizabeth Stuart Phelps (whose name the young author adopted) was a popular writer of fiction during her brief life. She died when her daughter was eight, the victim of "her last book and her last baby." The demands that real life make on the gifted woman were a matter of thoughtful discussion to Mrs. Ward, as were the demands of the Andover version of Calvinism on the nineteenth-century Christian. Her own marriage in her forties to a much younger man produced no children and, apparently, little happiness. Her causes were numerous and pursued with enthusiasm—dress reform, temperance, and, most passionately advocated of all, antivivisection legislation. Her personal creed softened to a general religion she called "Christlove." Her religious novels, *The Gates Ajar* (1868), *Beyond the Gates* (1883) and *The Gates Between* (1887) and *A Singular Life* (1895), were popular enough to be considered best sellers. Among the more than fifty volumes she wrote of novels, short stories, and nonfiction, were two works on religion, *The Story of Jesus Christ* (1897) and *The Struggle for Immortality* (1889). Her books for children, especially the very popular Gypsy Breynton series, presented a little girl who struggled hard to be good and who possessed plenty of spirit and courage, so that her brother Tom noted approvingly that she neither fainted nor cried. The special relationship between religion and women was treated in *The Story of Avis* (1877), *Doctor Zay* (1882), and the anonymous *Confessions of a Wife* (1902).[9]

Her most popular and controversial work, *The Gates Ajar*, was the story of a devoted sister mourning a brother killed in the Civil War. The object of the book, as Mrs. Ward wrote in her autobiography, was to comfort "some few of the women whose misery crowded the land." She did not think much of the suffering of men but of "the helpless, outnumbering, unconsulted women; they whom war trampled down, without a choice or protest; the patient, limited, domestic women who thought little, but loved much, and, loving, had lost all."[10] Among the many ways in which the Civil War affected women was to provide them with a future in which no man offered economic, or emotional support. For some women the war was a test of all the authority they had accepted unquestioningly, father, country, God. When Elizabeth Stuart Phelps wrote that her "little book . . . stole forth trembling . . . into that great world of woe," she was not exaggerating the need it filled. The war, combined with the confusion and doubts of Protestantism confronting change created both skepticism about male potency and a desire for some meaning from the holocaust.

Elizabeth Phelps Ward presented in fictional form the beliefs she evolved for herself, "I believe in the Life Everlasting: which is sure to be; and that it is the first duty of Christian faith to present that life in a form more attractive to the majority of men than the life that now is." The second item of belief in her personal credo was closely tied to the first: "I believe in women; and in their right to their own best possibilities in every department of life."[11] Most of her religious thought and writing stresses not only the pleasures but the sexual democracy of heaven. This is seen not as a substitute for the imperfect society on earth but as a paradigm of those Heavenly Cities which forward-thinking and progressive nineteenth-century Americans should be constructing.

In *The Gates Ajar* Mary is pictured as so crushed by her brother's death that she has no interest in this world and little hope for the next. God is forbidding and austere, and her well-meaning orthodox minister only makes her grief more complete by his rambling about the spiritual bliss and bloodless joys of heaven. Her Aunt Winifred, accompanied by her daughter Faith, arrives to visit and comfort her. Aunt Winifred has just buried a beloved husband, whose brilliant mission work was cut off by a lingering death. But Aunt Winifred, far from being bowed under fate's blows, is all peace and joy. In the long conversations which form most of the book she explains her philosophy to her niece, careful to note that she "conjectures nothing that the Bible contradicts." For Winifred the dead are "only out of sight . . . not lost, not asleep, nor annihilated." And being so near, they go right on loving as they did in life, thinking of, caring for, hoping for, praying for the ones they left behind, "not less out of a body than in it." The absent dead can still be relied upon to counsel and to love. Her faith in the continued presence of those she loved is based on her idea of the humanity of Jesus, with whom she has a loving intimate friendship. In these talks the human Christ, who loves and comforts women, is the real God who will not fail them. Mary sees that though "he was once an abstract Grandeur which I struggled more in fear than love to please," now He has "become a living Presence, dear and real."

The child Faith is carefully being trained to identify heaven and death and Jesus only with the things she likes best, like gingersnaps and pink building blocks. Generations of Presbyterian children echo in Winifred's condemnation of "the hours of death that children live through, unguessed and unrelieved." The duty of Christian mothers is to replace these dark terrors with the night light of happier bedtime thoughts, so that the child "shall learn to see in God the centre of all possibilities of joy." After convincing Mary of these future pleasures, whose intimations are always about her, Aunt Winifred dies of breast cancer. Mary and Faith remain cheerfully "waiting for the morning when the gates shall open."

The presentation of the human Christ, so prevalent in nineteenth-century writing from Renan to William James, is, of course, a statement of the self-satisfaction which its citizens felt in themselves, an acceptance of Emerson's invitation to share Christ's divinity as He had deigned to share their humanity. For Elizabeth Phelps Ward, Christ was not only human but a human male purged of that sex's insensitivity to female values and virtues. The new Christ is the ally of women against the insensitivity of other men. Like Tolstoy, she stressed Christ's democracy, his great love of the poor, "the deference of strength to weakness." But whereas Tolstoy admired Christ's compassion for the have-nots of the world, Mrs. Ward was impressed by his kindness to women. For her, Christianity in its new forms must provide answers to the "Three key-notes in the great discords of life: the cruelty of nature, the mystery of sex, and the misery of the poor."[12]

Not everyone shared these views, and one member of the established church felt strongly enough about the damage done by a popular novel to write *Antidote to 'The Gates Ajar'* in order to draw attention to the "dangerous errors which abound in *The Gates Ajar*" and to "incite others to come forward and present or counteract the diffusion of its unscriptural views." While the author admitted a natural curiosity to know what kind of place his "eternal home" might be, he was firm in his belief that "For wise and inscrutable reasons the Almighty has not satisfied these cravings; for were we to have even one glimpse of the inconceivable glories of the other world the sight would so dazzle us as to unfit us afterward for our every-day existence." Dangerous overtones of spiritualism and even Romanism lurked in Mary and Winifred's musings. Once the beloved dead were spoken to, these women might ask for advice "and perhaps pray to them." If the saved were hovering around, the unsaved might be lurking too, "What a horrible idea!" Firmly the author concluded that "After all, our duty is not to speculate, but to act."[13]

Undaunted, Mrs. Ward continued to speculate in *Beyond the Gates*, in which heaven is described in the same loving detail that the numerous travelogues of the nineteenth century used for the

less exotic sights of this planet. The story is narrated in the first
person by another Mary, this one a forty-year-old spinster, a believer in the Christian religion "but not a devotee." Mary confessed that she "had not the ecstatic temperament, and was not
known among my friends for any higher order of piety than that
which is implied in trying to do one's duty for Christ's sake,
and saying little about it or Him." Lying ill, the narrator sees her
dead father beckoning her to follow him.

Her first insight into the mores of the Celestial Kingdom is that
God "expects nothing of us but to be natural." Whereas in her
former life she submitted to God "not because I wanted to, but
because I had to," she now finds it easy and natural to give up
her will to divine wishes. After all, being dead was quite pleasant,
since she was "dead to danger, dead to fear" and "alive to a sense
of assured good chance that nothing in the universe could shake."
It was, literally, the best of both worlds; all the joys of spirit and
body she had known were still present, their anticipation unmarred
by forebodings, their achievement unblemished by disappointment. Immortality, she exults, is "the gift of Jesus Christ to the
human soul." Christ, whom she meets, is the perfect Friend, and,
following a long chat in the meadow she announces "Now, for
the first time in all my life, I find myself truly understood."

Heaven, on closer inspection, is a highly organized busy community, rather like Andover, where one continues "definite
duties as well as assured pleasures." Social life consists in "a
series of subtle or acute surprises." Beethoven entertained with a
new oratorio and Raphael supervised a magnificent art exhibit.
(It was rumored that Leonardo was present to see it, but Mary
missed him.) Everywhere the reality of the "close Theocracy" is
the hope of the New England conscience, "Live! Be! Do! Because He
lives, you live also. Grow! Achieve! Hope! . . . Having fought—
rest. Having trusted—know. Having endured—enjoy. Being safe—
venture. Being pure—fear not to be sensitive . . . Dare to be
happy!" The new theme song, sung at every gathering, is the new
chorus of nineteenth century Protestantism, "God is love, *is* Love
—is LOVE!"

In one aspect, however, Heaven surpassed even Andover. Mary
is surprised to observe that few of the happy couples on the heavenly streets had been partners on earth. In heaven, she is informed, one meets one's true soul-mate, according to "the Laws of

Affiliation." Only about a third of earthly marriages are so rati-
fied. She finds herself unaccountably lonely and a man for whom
she had always cared appears. To the strains of "The Wedding
March" he takes her in his arms. Mary asks about "her," the
wife he had on earth, and is told that she is irretrievably earth-
bound and has remarried. His true destiny and "heaven-mate" is
Mary. At this moment she awakes, finds herself again in her sickroom, surrounded by her anxious family. The first words she hears
are her brother's asking why she looks so disappointed.

In this version of Heaven all the sexual inequalities are removed.
The unloved spinster, so cruelly treated in literature and life,
found her mate. The unsung heroism of women's daily lives at last
received a reward. Mary noted that the biggest homecoming
celebration during her heavenly visit occurred in the aftermath of a
train crash, whose only victims were the heroic engineer who
sacrificed his life to save his passengers and a timid woman who
died of fright. This poor soul, unnoticed on earth, had been "notable among celestial observers for many years." She was the
"household saint," who, "silent, never thinks of herself, scarcely
knows she has a self—toils, drudges, endures, prays."

A third volume, *The Gates Ajar*, dealt with the limbo between
this world and the next. Dr. Esmerald Thorne is catapulted "between the gates" in a carriage accident on his way to a patient.
He leaves behind him many grateful men and women who were
healed by his skill, and a wife and son whom he had treated far
less nobly. Having pursued and won his "fair Helen" and vowed
always to adore her, Thorne "imperceptibly blunted his awareness" in his relationship with her as his wife. In fact, on the night
of his accident, his last words to her had been harsh and impa-
tient ones, coupled with his refusal to examine the boy, whose illness he dismissed as "mere female foolishness." As he wanders
between the worlds Thorne is made to realize the overwhelming
importance of these domestic relations and to regret his "be-
trayal" of his love. He meets his son in this nether-world, although
he fails to recognize him until helped by a friendly neighbor. Here
again, his wife had been right and he wrong for the boy had died
of the illness his father had dismissed as trivial. The doctor puts
in a journeyship of helping others adjust to their new life and, as
his last assignment, brings Helen through the gates, happily discovering that she has completely forgiven him.

This preoccupation with the next life was a vindication of a new kind of Christianity in this life, since the kingdom of earth should be patterned on the kingdom of heaven, as man's life was patterned on Christ's life. A more natural and joyous existence, where God is loved not feared, where domestic virtues are ranked above wealth and power, is the goal of the nineteenth-century Christian woman. Novels of that world are criticisms of this one, a reminder that God intended a different order of things and man the clumsy oaf has blundered off the path. It is fitting that woman, man's traditional judge and example, should point out these discrepancies through the traditional medium of the popular novel. Mrs. Ward has her women both accept the new social Gospel and point out how firmly rooted it is in true Christianity. "Our modern dream of humanity is nothing else than Christianity in a mask domino," she wrote.[14] In order, however, for Christianity to continue, women must be allowed to expand their roles in society, so that they may influence men and defend the faith. In the group of novels in which Mrs. Ward looked at the struggle of the modern woman to enlarge her sphere she found much less hopeful evidence of permanent change.

In the biography of Austin Phelps, Elizabeth Ward had said of her mother, "A wife, a mother, a housekeeper, a hostess, in delicate health, on an academic salary, undertakes a deadly load when she starts upon a literary career. She lifted it to her frail shoulders, and she fell beneath it."[15] Her mother's writing, she noted, without complete approval, was done from simple necessity of self-expression. "She wrote because she couldn't help it." And yet, by giving in to the compulsion of genius, she left behind small children "who couldn't understand why their mother had gone to Heaven, when she was needed so much in Andover." This was the unhappy result, common in the "rich and piteous lives" of those gifted women "torn by the civil war, of the dual nature which can be given to women only."[16] In *The Story of Avis* and *Doctor Zay* two such gifted women are discussed.

Avis, an artist of extraordinary ability, has always been far more independent than the other girls in the New England college town where her father teaches. "Why shouldn't a woman have a latchkey?" signals her first revolt from the strictures of sex. She is happy in her work until Philip Ostrander, a young professor, lays siege to her heart. She protests that her true love is reserved for her art and that she could never devote herself solely to his wishes. Philip argues, "Suppose a man and a woman had been made and led and drawn to one another, just to show that the tolerance of individuality, even the enthusiasm of superiority, could be a perfectly mutual thing." Avis protests that marriage causes "a civil war" in a woman between her responsibilities to her family and to herself. But when Philip returns, a pitiful wounded veteran, she responds to his pleas. The marriage goes just as badly as she expected. Two children are born. She puts off painting to attend to them and to the house. Philip complains about the coffee. After one of their quarrels he apologizes. "Avis, I was a brute." "No," she said bitterly, "you were only a man." After he is dismissed from his job for shirking his responsibilities, and has hurt her by flirting with other women and neglecting the children, she accompanies him to Florida, where he dies, reconciled through her devotion both to her and to God. After the funeral she reflects that "It seemed to her the great triumph of her life that she could love her husband just as God had made him." She determines to live for her daughter (the son having died during one of Philip's prolonged absences) and will hope, for her, a better life. Avis will teach art but will never paint again. Her fingers and her imagination have "stiffened and hardened."

Doctor Zay raises the same questions—whether a gifted woman can or should marry. Perhaps mercifully it ends before the marriage takes place. A beautiful and extremely skillful homeopathic physician, Doctor Zay, who happens to be a woman, treats rich, idle young Waldo Yorke after an accident. He falls in love with her, completely convinced of her superiority and the value of her work, which shows him "what all the little feminine protest in the world could never have made patent to his imagination: a woman absorbed in her business, to whom a man must be the accident, not the substance, of thought." When he asks her to marry him she refuses, sorry for his misfortune in loving "a new kind of woman. The trouble is that a happy marriage with such a woman demands a new type of man." No matter how good his intentions, Waldo had not progressed beyond his genes and "would not know how to cultivate happiness with a woman who had diverged from her hereditary type." He insists that their marriage would be a historic first, and she succumbs. "Mr. Yorke," asks the Doctor tremulously,

"Are you sure? . . . That it is *me* you want,—a strong-minded doctor?" He corrects her—"A sweet-hearted woman," and they are committed to the experiment.

Both *The Story of Avis* and *Doctor Zay* were written before Mrs. Ward's marriage. The anonymous *Confessions of a Wife* came from bitter personal experience. Marna Trent, not a woman of genius, but a strong and capable person, is finally and reluctantly brought to marriage with Mr. Herwin. "Oh, teach me how to make you happy! I have everything to learn I know. But believe me that I care for nothing else." The marriage degenerates into routine and her health suffers. "Men are so busy and so insolently strong. There is something cruel in their physical freedom . . . No woman deity would ever have constructed this world." She is unwell, weary with nursing a sick baby; her husband tells her she should make herself more attractive intellectually. Marna pleads that "All a woman wants is to be considered, and to be valued. All she wants is love—all she wants is the Life Eternal. I suppose this is an immoderate demand—something like the demand of a moth for personal immortality." She remembers her free and independent life when she called herself "Wilderness Girl." Having deserted her, Herwin returns, a heroin addict, whom she cures and redeems through her prayers and nursing. Again, men who neglect their wives are punished—in this world, as well as in the mists surrounding the next.

Elizabeth Ward was realistic in her sense of the pace of some social changes. She believed that so long as marriage, motherhood and men remained virtually unchanged, all the changes in women's education and ambitions were likely to signify only a few clanging cymbals. On the other hand, she was able to hope for a new religion which might bring about the desired changes in men to enable women to take their proper place in the world. In *A Singular Life* her hero is a young minister, Emanuel Bayard, who preaches temperance and Christ's love in a town so much like Gloucester that Mrs. Ward offended at least one citizen.[17] Bayard found his education irrelevant to parish life. "Predestination, foreordination, sanctification, election, and botheration,—and never a lesson on the Christian socialism of our day, not a lecture to tell us how to save a poor, lost woman, how to reform a drunkard, what to do with gamblers and paupers, and thieves, and worse, how to apply what we believe to common life and common sense." Bayard is killed by a stone thrown by the saloon keeper's son, but his widow will carry on his church, "Christlove."

The power of a woman to cure men and to keep them righteous extends to all reforms. In one story of dog-napping the heroine announced firmly, "No true woman could love a vivisector." There is hope for a religion of love and for intelligent reforms like homeopathy, dress modification, prohibition and anti-vivisection. But help for the gifted woman who wants marriage, children, sympathy and her work remains more illusive and visionary. Until the nature of men partakes more of the nature of Christ, and love, not power, is the moving force on earth, the "civil war" between body and soul and men and women will continue.

Margaret Deland (1857-1945) was brought up in southern Pennsylvania, the Old Chester of her novels, although her adult life was spent in New England. She married Lorin Deland, reformer and pioneer in "creative business' in 1880. The marriage was extremely happy, although "the children we waited for never came." She converted Lorin, born a rather grim Unitarian, to her own Episcopal faith which she in turn outgrew. In later years, especially during her widowhood, she turned for comfort to New Thought and spiritualism. She shared her husband's interest in social and civic reform, especially his scheme to help wayward girls by having them raise their own illegitimate children while giving them honest work. She favored a "limited suffrage," for both men and women, and was dubious about the techniques of the suffragists, although sympathetic to some of their demands. *John Ward, Preacher* (1888) was her first best-seller among the thirty-seven volumes she produced. Two later volumes, *The Awakening of Helena Ritchie* (1906) and *The Iron Woman* (1911) achieved this popularity. Her ideas on religion, and on woman's role in religion, are also expressed in *Sydney* (1890), *Philip and His Wife* (1894), and the Old Chester Tales (published from 1888 to 1928) about the parishioners of Dr. Lavendar.[18]

John Ward, Preacher appeared within a few weeks of another best-seller, *Robert Elsmer*, by Mrs. Humphry Ward. The American version of religious change was often compared to the English one, but in some ways the differences are more interesting than the similarities. Mrs. Ward's hero, Elsmer, is a young minister who, after much soul searching, realizes that he can no longer be-

lieve in miracles. His wife, Catharine, is the best type of old-fashioned Christian, possessing a simple faith. Elsmer's conviction
may, he realize, cost him not only his parish but his marriage. He
receives sympathy from his former professor at Oxford who knows
that "to him who has once been a Christian of the old sort, the
parting with the Christian mythology is the rending asunder of
bones and marrow. It means parting with half the confidence,
half the joy of life." Nonetheless Robert makes his painful confession to his horrified wife. "I can believe no longer in an Incarnation and Resurrection . . . Christ is risen in our hearts, in the
Christian life of charity. Miracle is a natural product of human
feeling and imagination; and God was in Jesus—pre-eminently, as
He is in all great souls, but not otherwise—not otherwise in kind
than He is in me or you."

Catharine's love is equal even to her husband's unbelief. "I
know so little of books, I cannot give them the place you do,"
she says, but nonetheless, "I will be your faithful wife unto our lives'
end." Patiently he instructs her in his new ideas until she cries,
"I will learn my lesson; I will learn to hear the two voices, the
voice that speaks to you and the voice that speaks to me." Together they do settlement work and Catharine's ideas change so
that she "had, in fact, undergone that dissociation of the moral
judgment from a special series of religious formulae which is the
crucial, the epoch-making fact of our day." Elsmere and his friends
create a new religion, The New Brotherhood, but he soon gets
tuberculosis of the larynx and dies. Although he fails to give his
wife the words of reassurance about immortality which she wants,
he dies happily, convinced that "He cannot lead us to the end and
disappoint the craving He himself set in us." The sales of Mrs.
Ward's book were helped greatly by a review by William Gladstone
denouncing it. When Mrs. Deland's publishers begged for the same
favor, the former Prime Minister refused, since he felt that *John
Ward, Preacher* was doctrinally sound.[19]

In the American novel it is the young preacher who remains
true to the old religion and his wife who firmly espouses the
new. There is more ambiguity in the Deland book; the reader
feels sympathetic with both characters and, to some degree, with
both points of view. When she wrote it, Mrs. Deland had passed
under the influence of the sonorous humanism of Phillips Brooks,
but of the Episcopal Church she said, "I had outgrown it as a

child outgrows Santa Claus." When her family learned the topic
of the novel she was writing, her stepfather protested that "Maggie knows no more about hell than a kitten knows about a steam
engine," and promised her two hundred dollars if she would burn
the manuscript. She decided to ask her uncle, Dr. William Camp-
bell, former president of Rutgers and an official of the Dutch Reformed Church, for his opinion. Uncle William approved thoroughly. "I only wish there were more John Wards in the Church."
Pleased with the support, Mrs. Deland felt her uncle had somewhat missed the point. "The deduction I had hoped might be
made from the book was that all such good but misguided men
had better be weeded out of the churches." Obviously the message of the book depended on the reader. A Maine fisherman,
for example, refused to sell land to the Delands, explaining to
Lorin, "Your woman has wrote a bad book—yes, sir! 'Gainst
religion!"[20]

The book, expressing Mrs. Deland's "rebellion against the fetters
of religious dogma," presented the confrontation of religious values
between two people who loved each other. John Ward believed that
"Death is better than sin," and is appalled when he realizes that
Helen, his adored young wife, rejects hell, predestination and any
other tenet which does not accord with her hopeful view of human
nature and divine mercy. He vows to try, "little by little, to show
her what I believe, and turn her thoughts to Truth." Helen brushes
off his tentative sermons, telling him not to trouble himself about
what is purely a personal matter. "I mean, it does not make any
difference to me what you believe. I wouldn't care if you were a
Mohammedan, John, if it helped you to be good and happy. I think
that different people have different religious necessities." This lofty
anthropological perspective is anathema to John, who protests,
"But dearest . . . to deliberately turn away from the search for
truth is spiritual suicide." He begs her, "Just let me tell you how
the scheme of Salvation makes the mystery of salvation clear and
right."

But Helen in her own gentle way is just as stubborn as her husband. "No, I cannot talk of it. I should be wicked if I could believe
it; it would make me wicked." John continues to preach on hell and
righteousness while his wife stays home with her sewing. It is his
duty, because "even if it were not for her own soul's sake, I must
not let my people starve for the bread of life, to spare her." The

town drunk is killed in a fire after rescuing a child and Helen assures the widow that Tom's good deed has saved him. John Ward regretfully but firmly contradicts her; the man died unsaved, his sins unforgiven; he is in hell. The gulf between the two widens, and the leading elder of John's parish, the self-righteous Brother Dean threatens to "session" Helen and denounce her lack of faith to the congregation. John is forced to send her away to spare her the humiliation. Her guardian, Dr. Howe, an Episcopal rector who sometimes prefers comfort to conviction, pleads with John to relent and temper his justice with mercy. But John remains adamant, sending for Helen only when he is dying. After his death she returns to her uncle's home. "And so Helen Ward's duty came to her, the blessedness and helpfulness of being needed . . . She would be necessary to her uncle, and to be necessary would save her life from hardness."

The novel is a *De Profundis* for the old religion, not a *Te Deum*, rejoicing in its death. There is no high enthusiasm for a "New Brotherhood," only sorrow at the inability to unite the good qualities of the old and the new order. John Ward is an impressive figure. Margaret Deland faced the possibility, which many Americans feared, that much of the progress and steel of America was due to its Calvinist rigor. Helen survives in her more rational, more modern creed of *laissez faire* and social consciousness, but there is the lingering regret for the John Wards of the past and the feeling we may not look upon their likes again.

Calvinism was firmly buried by 1888, however, and the novel provided only the last shovel of earth on its grave. *Harper's Magazine*, although it admitted the work to be impressive and "when it comes to dealing at close quarters with the impassioned and the grotesque, it is a greater book than *Robert Elsmer*," considered it an anachronism. "This is not saying that there are not probably such survivals into our time, but the scheme loses verisimilitude through Mrs. Deland's failure to accent Ward as an instance of atavism."[21] *Harper's*, rather like Uncle William, missed the point. It was precisely because the majority of Americans had already accepted the reality that they enjoyed the rhetoric so thoroughly and so guiltlessly. American Protestants in 1888 admired the rigors of Calvinism in the same nostalgic way in which they admired the hardships and sturdy characters of the almost defunct frontier, and from the same safe distance. From the comfortable armchair of the easier religion and life, they remembered and eulogized the past.

Mrs. Deland's next novel, *Sydney*, expanded her views on religion and gave even more theological acumen to the heroine. Sydney Lee has been raised by her father Mortimer to reject all revealed religion and to deny God's existence. Since he suffered the unbearable pain of his wife's death, he is determined to spare Sydney false hope in God's mercy and immortality. He also wishes to spare her love, since death ends life and love. Sydney is "to seek for truth, to do without illusions; to look the facts of life full in the face. She was to judge, emotionally, first whether it was probable that there was a beneficient and all-powerful Being in a world which held at the same time Love and Death; and next, with inexorable logic, she was to find a universe of law, empty of God." Mortimer Lee pointed out how the myths and absurdities of the Bible left no hope of personal immortality, and destroyed the Christ of Christianity. His philosophy "demonstrated that morality and expediency were synonymous . . . counseled negation instead of happiness. More than all, it pointed out the mad folly of love in a world where death follows love like its own shadow." A young doctor, Alan, arrives with his patient, Robert Steele, slowly being brought back to health after a struggle with morphine addiction. Alan falls in love with Sydney, declaring "that life is beautiful and good where there is love,—I mean, the love of a man and woman; it is not always fierce and terrible; it does not of necessity involve the unreason of passion; and it does glorify existence." To prove the consistency of his own ideas, Alan cheerfully admits that he is doomed to die an early death from heart disease.

Different characters in the novel contribute different varieties of their religious experience, from which Sydney draws conclusions. Miss Sally, the sweet and simple aunt who raised her, believes only that "if they remember the dear Lord they can trust the rest. If they just take God into their lives, darling, they needn't fear death." An admirable young woman, Katharine Townsend, represents a more intellectual view of traditional Christianity. After vicissitudes necessary to the plot of a nineteenth-century novel Katharine at last finds love and prosperity. Sydney, searching, as always, for the truth, asks this thoroughly modern and independent young woman if she is happy. Katharine says that she is and to Sydney's next question, "But what of death?" she responds, "first there is life, and then heaven." When Sydney pushes her further about immortality Katharine bursts out, "because life would be too terrible if it were not true! It must be true!" This comment elicits the rather acid interpolation by the novelist that "Although not aware of her mental processes, Katharine had curtailed her perceptions to fit her need, knowing, without having taken the trouble to reason about it, that she could not stretch her creed to contain her perceptions. As a result, she was quite happy, and found the endeavor to live up to her religion far more comfortable than would have been the effort to understand it." The reformed morphine addict, Robert Steele, makes a series of blunders due to his particular dilemma, "I cannot seem to see the point . . . at which what is theoretically right begins to be practically wrong." No longer able to trust his judgment he admits, "I understand the comfort of making somebody else your conscience. That is the peace of the Catholic Church." After a period of struggle, during which "he despised his own intelligence which had deprived him of such peace," he capitulates and joins a Roman Catholic brotherhood.

Sydney rejects all these solutions and, during her vigil at her aunt's death-bed, reaches her own synthesis of the old and new. She finds herself needing to acknowledge the existence of a "vague Someone Who Knows," and this conviction seems to her quite wonderful. Denominations irritate her. "I should think that a God would be enough. But they hang all those little thoughts around the one great thought until they almost hide it. I suppose that one could cover a mountain with lace." A series of revelations unfold during her lonely night. She saw "Human existence, like an endless spiral, touching light and darkness, life and death, stretches into eternity." She can accept both sides of the spiral, with her new conviction that "all things work together for good." Her refuge is "the eternal God," who receives her at the end of a long journey. "Oh, weariness of longing which is the expression of the universe, which is eternal! And the deepest longing is for a meaning . . . To see a meaning would be to find a refuge; yes, it would be like arms in which one rested and trusted." Such a meaning would reconcile her even to Alan's "going out into blankness," for he would really be "going back into this mystery, or Cause, to be part of it forever." There would be pain but unlike her father who rejected a God who permitted suffering, Sydney sees that "the pain would be part of the mystery, part of the Eternal Purpose, and so, bearable." Life was worth living "if it were lived struggling for Oneness with the Eternal Purpose of which sorrow was as much a part as joy, death, as life."

When her father enters the room to announce that her aunt is dead, Sydney refutes him. "No, not dead,—there is no death. Life and death are one; the Eternal Purpose holds us all, always. Father, —I have found God." When he protests she responds with the overwhelming evidence of her own need. "Does not the hunger of the body declare that there is bread?" When he appeals to philosophical arguments, she silences him with, "I do not reason, Father; I know." She marries Alan shortly before his happy death, and is able to announce triumphantly that, yes, "He is dead, but he has lived. He is mine, always. Oh, it is worthwhile,—it is worthwhile; the past is ours, and all is—God!"

Like the earlier novels of Augusta Evans Wilson, the resolution replaces male skepticism and reason with Female faith and intuition. Direct contact between the soul and God does not require such male-dominated institutions as the churches. In another novel, however, Mrs. Deland analyzed divorce, a specific social and religious problem, not susceptible to mysticism. In 1869 Augusta Wilson had also treated divorce, in a book entitled *Vashti: or, "Until Death Us Do Part."* Mrs. Deland's *Philip and His Wife* was written a quarter of a century later. Divorce laws were slightly altered, but religious and social pressure had relaxed very little, at least among the middle classes.[23] And yet divorce had great symbolic and practical significance to all those who linked religion and changes in women's role.

In *Vashti* the hero, Dr. Ulpian Grey, master of Grassmere, loves a mysterious woman, whose secret is revealed to be the presence of a living but discredited husband. Vashti found out on her wedding day that Maurice, who loved another, had married her only for her money, and she left him immediately. "Under some circumstances I deemed separation a woman's duty." However when Maurice is reported dying she goes to him. "Like a brave, true, though injured woman," she will do her duty, "no matter how revolting." Maurice and Vashti both die and Dr. Grey is left to bear his loss "with a sublime and increasing faith in the over-riding wisdom and mercy of God." The heroine's name and actions were based on the Biblical character. A different treatment of the same theme is found in Ursula Gestefeld's *The Woman Who Dares* (1892) and in *The Woman's Bible* (1899).

In *Philip and His Wife* it is the husband who is the victim, and who ponders the possibility of ending the marriage. Philip, a decent and rational person, asks when a man's conscience should take precedence over conventions. He knows that his beautiful and sensual wife Cecil is thoroughly bored with him and he has lost all respect for her. "Marriage without love is as spiritually illegal as love without marriage is civilly illegal." In a subplot, the poor hardworked Eliza Todd contemplates separation from her sodden brute of a husband. She dies, bearing her seventh child, without answering the question.

The argument against individual choice as an overriding motive is refuted by Roger Carey, a young lawyer about to marry a wholesome young girl. Carey insists that divorce is "like suicide, not inherently or specifically wrong, but socially vicious; both lower just a little the moral tone of society." Civilization progresses "in direct proportion to our ideas on the sacredness of marriage." Even the innocent have no right to tamper with an institution so manifestly bigger than both of them, the future of the race. "They've got to suffer, that's all. It's a pity, but they've got to suffer." Although Philip and Cecil may go ahead with their plans, the penalty will be exile abroad for her and loneliness at home for him. The sacred duty to marriage vows which kept Vashti from divorce in 1869 has been replaced with a sacred duty to the mystical force of progress in 1894. Insofar as the individuals are concerned, divorce is equally wrong and the social results will be equally punitive.

More muted versions of practical problems confronting old beliefs are found in Mrs. Deland's stories about Old Chester. The cosmic and tragic visions of John Ward, Sydney, and Philip are written much smaller. The inhabitants of the small Pennsylvania town consider themselves "Dr. Lavendar's People" and look to the venerable Episcopal minister for advice and sanctions. In a conflict between the old standards and common sense, or between justice and mercy, the latter prevails. The first story sets the tone for the series. "Old Chester was always satisfied with itself. Not that that implies conceit; Old Chester merely felt that satisfaction with the conditions as well as the station into which it had pleased God to call it which is said to be a state of grace." Individuals among the congregation constantly challenge old standards in their search for meaning and joy in life, and, most of the time, Dr. Lavendar is on the side of happiness. Sometimes the old man has to exert con-

siderable pressure to overcome the opposition of the more traditional of his parishioners.

Old Chester clung to the old ways and the old religion. One tale
begins, "In theory, Old Chester was religiously democratic; it
plumed itself upon its Christian humility, and every Sunday it
publicly acknowledged that Old Chesterians were like the rest of
humanity to the extent of being miserable sinners. But all the same.
. . ." Unlike the people who judge harshly, Dr. Lavendar forgives
a woman with a past, sends the real mother of an illegitimate child
away and awards the girl to the foster mother, tells an itinerant
preacher that he doesn't need seminary training to speak God's
word, and assists at the elopement of an elderly couple escaping
their over-protective children. He refuses to bind everyone to the
same code. In one story a young girl commits suicide because of
the harsh treatment she received from her Quaker guardians. Her
uncle admits, "We tried to make her good in our way, but she had a
right to her own nature." In "The Stuffed-Animal House," perhaps
Mrs. Deland's best story, Dr. Lavendar helps the independent taxi-
dermist Miss Harriet prepare for a heroic death. But as her pain
increases her retarded sister Annie gives her chloroform, the "sleep
bottle" with which Miss Harriet put trapped animals out of their
agony. Dr. Lavendar does not question the superior wisdom of
Annie, confronted with the mystery of God's demands.

The minister is both appreciative of woman's religious nature
and angry at its excesses. In one story an Old Chester girl was
forced by her pregnancy into marrying a weak vulgar man. When
she dies, the widower whimpers, "She was always pleasant. You
mayn't call just being pleasant, religion. . . ." Dr. Lavendar
answers, "I do." When Rose in "How *Could* She?" refuses her
fiancé's request to release him from his promises so he can marry
another woman, Dr. Lavendar defends her against town gossip.
Rose did it to save the man she loved from the clutches of an
unworthy woman. Once the danger is over she proudly dismisses
him. "I will never marry anyone, but you least of all." Dr. Lavendar
counsels the rejected suitor that though he may yet marry Rose,
"you'll never *get* her. She is the stuff the martyrs are made of."
Of another woman rearing her son in fanatical devotion to ideals,
he says, "She was the kind of Spartan mother who would hand a
fox to her child." Vowing that most of the trouble in the world "is
caused by women's consciences" he insists he'll "not have it in

my parish," and tries to liberate women from the blind reliance on convention that interferes with their lives and their right to happiness. Instead of attacking the political or economic system which holds women back, he opposes those clinging mothers, tyrannical fathers, selfish siblings, and thoughtless husbands who chain women to drudgery and subservience.

No course in American thought, no text on American religion mentions Augusta Wilson, Elizabeth Ward, or Margaret Deland. Yet they were read by many more Americans than were Emerson, Rauschenbusch, and William James. Perhaps their sex and popularity, as well as the choice of fiction to convey their ideas, prevent their being taken seriously, even in a footnote. They were by no means creative thinkers, but it could be argued that they filled the important role of lay theologians, popularizing and making palatable religious controversy which had already taken place, and showing a middle way whereby Christianity could flourish even in the midst of social change. Their interpretation of the new Christianity gave women an important role in its maintenance and preservation. A human Jesus was a friend who valued female lives, and the virtues on the Mount were the domestic female virtues, ignored by men only at the peril of their eternal lives. Christian benevolence was an extension of a role already played by women within the churches. Antisectarianism played down the authority of minister and elder and stressed a personal communication between the individual soul and God which existed independently of sex. If science led men into error, nature showed women the truth. It is interesting that Doctor Zay was a homeopathic physician, whose remedies came from nature not drugs. Once only kings and crusaders could be called Defenders of the Faith. Now American women could claim the title.

8

MURDER MOST GENTEEL
The Mystery Novels of Anna Katharine Green

The development of the literature of detection written by women, and, particularly, the creation of the role of the female detective, signified some important changes in the stereotype of nineteenth-century womanhood. The female detective and the woman who wrote of crime and its solution dealt in problems susceptible to reason, in action, in reality which might include blood and death—in other words, in many areas from which the traditional definitions of women's abilities and nature might exclude them. On the other hand, as the genre grew and flourished, it combined many traditional qualities of women's nature with these new skills. Intuition, the acute knowledge of human behavior and sensitivity to people and place, the use of the homely detail to make an analogy—all these domestic skills become a part of the female detective and a feature in detective stories written by women, as devotees of Miss Marple and Miss Silver and Troy Allyn and Amanda Campion and Harriet Vane know and relish.

From 1878 to 1923 Anna Katharine Green consistently produced best sellers in a genre which she virtually created. She was avidly read by several generations on both sides of the Atlantic, but such is the transitory nature of taste that she is noted only briefly in a few specialized literary histories. Anna Green was the first American to write murder mysteries in an American setting, featuring the detective work of an American policeman.[1] She was also the first to create a woman detective[2] and to invent a number of what have become the clichés of the criminal mind.

The last decades of the nineteenth century were a time of considerable nervousness and fear for the security of person and property. The newspapers and periodicals bristled with tales of sinister conspiracies, anarchist plots, and international gangs.

130

Closer to home, metropolitan police forces dealt with increasing numbers of strikes, riots, robberies, and assaults, and the press viewed it all with alarm. The detective story, which had lain fallow since the time of Edgar Allan Poe, arose to meet the challenge. Louise Bogan defined the central element of these stories as "a nameless sense of apprehension characteristic of men living in an insecure civilization."³ Julian Symons, in his history of the detective story and crime novel, remarked that "It is impossible to understand the romantic aura which spread around detective departments and bureaus, without realizing the thankfulness felt by the middle class at their existence."⁴ All that a bourgeois society held dear, as Erik Routley points out in *The Puritan Pleasures of the Detective Story*, "were their property, and rights, and loss of these was their greatest fear."⁵

The formula of the detective story, as it was worked out over the next fifty years, promised that the application of rational thought to problems could restrain irrational acts, and that violence could be controlled by superior intellects working on the side of law and order. Death could be mocked; it was the beginning of a successful process, not the end of existence. The hazards of assassination, war, and madness could be discussed, grappled with, and solved instead of being freefloating anxieties, too terrible to be named. William O. Aydelotte in "The Detective Story as a Historical Source," finds that these novels describe the world "as simple and understandable, meaningful and secure." The criminal is the scapegoat. Once he is discovered, the rest of society goes free. The intellectual, ill at ease in a chaotic and absurd life, seized the detective story as his "hope for his survival in an alien world."⁶

Anna Katharine Green wrote her first criminal detection novel in 1878 and her last in 1923. When she began her work only Edgar Allan Poe had written in this vein in America. Wilkie Collins was writing novels about crime, but without a central detective hero.⁷ Sir Arthur Conan Doyle was almost her contemporary, followed by a number of lesser but popular writers—Baroness Orczy, M. Mc Donnell Bodkin, Mrs. Meade, Mrs. Braddon, Fergus Hume, Mrs. Henry Wood, and finally the early works of Mary Roberts Rinehart, Jeanette Lee, Mrs. Belloc Lowndes, Gilbert Keith Chesterton, Agatha Christie and Dorothy Sayers.⁸ By the time she died in 1935 the detective story was at the height of its popularity and most well-known writers tried their hand at constructing one, even if they hid behind a pseudonym.

Critical evaluation of her work, almost nonexistent by her contemporaries who read but did not ask the reason why, is also lacking today. One of the first to attempt to analyze her popularity was Grant Overton who said, in 1918, that while she was a most marvelous storyteller, "the simple truth is that she can't write."[9] Howard Haycraft more chivalrously hailed her as "the first woman to practice the form in any land or language" and to do it "at a time and place when feminine literary output was slight at best and confined chiefly to sentimental verse and similar lady-like ephemera."[10] That this could be written after a century of the Brontës, George Eliot, and Mrs. Gaskell, not to mention Mrs. Humphrey Ward, Margaret Deland, Harriet Beecher Stowe and other ladies of impeccable and unblinking seriousness of purpose, shows, one assumes, ignorance not malice.

Anna Green's importance, writes Willard Huntington Wright, lay in the fact that her work "went far toward familiarizing the English-speaking public with this, as yet, little-known genre." Wright considers that she possessed "an excellent style," as well as "a convincing logic" and "sense of reality."[11] Dorothy Sayers, on the other hand, while considering the novels "genuine detective stories, often of considerable ingenuity" finds them "marred by an uncritical sentimentality of style and treatment which makes them difficult reading for the modern student."[12] Sayers admits their influential role on later American writers, and other commentators remark particularly on her creation of a detective who is a man of the people, Ebeneezer Gryce, the forerunner of a whole school of matter-of-fact, hardworking policemen.[13] A French critic notices that she not only shows the working of the police, but the influence of crime on the soul and the illumination of the mind as a result of shared guilt.[14] John Dickson Carr in his classic "The Locked-Room Lecture," pays tribute to a colleague who not only developed a locked-room mystery, but also was the first to have a murderous secretary kill his employer and to use an icicle as a bullet.[15]

A renewed interest in the history of American women and the questions raised about the relationship of gender to reputation make some further analysis of these novels an exercise in the history of popular culture and, particularly, of one woman's role in creating an extremely popular and profitable genre. The continuing importance of women writers in the field of detective fiction, and the concomitant, perhaps causal, relegation of the literature to the back bench of scholarly reputation, is a further area for research and analysis.

In her first and most famous novel, *The Leavenworth Case: A Lawyer's Story* (1878), Ebeneezer Gryce is introduced as a master of all disguises except for the one role he cannot play, "that of a gentleman." The portly little detective, meek when wearing his own face, bold when disguised as another, forces a confession out of the murdered man's secretary. His first clue was his belief that no woman could have committed the crime, because no woman would have cleaned the gun afterwards. In this novel two types of women appear, who are used frequently in Green's work. One is Mary Leavenworth, "a woman of high regal beauty, very strong and proud." She, and all the women like her in the stories which follow, is destined for trouble. Her cousin, Eleanore, is the choice of the young lawyer and hero of the tale. Eleanore possesses "a smaller, paler trembling beauty." Mary will never find happiness, at least not in these novels, because her ambitions are a man's ambitions: she wants money, fame, and power. Instead love for her causes the murder and the story ends with her realization of the havoc she has wrought by her demands on a weak man. It was for love of her that Trueman Harwell shot his employer, and the guilt is equally hers.

Another theme that runs throughout Green's novels is the weakness of woman's intellect and will before the overpowering dominance of her emotions. In *A Strange Disappearance* (1880), in which Mr. Gryce tries to find a missing wife, the heroine defends her actions by saying: "I am a woman and therefore weak to the voice of love pleading in my ear." Mr. Gryce generally assumes that women act only according to the dictates of their hearts, with the possible exception of the spinster, Miss Amelia Buttersworth, whom he recruits to help him.

Although Mr. Gryce usually speaks good sense and prose, some of the novels have poetic flights of gothic horror. In the labyrinthine plot of *The Mill Mystery* every turn reveals another unpleasant event, with some strong descriptions for 1886. The fiancé of pretty Ada Reynolds drowns in a mill vat and Ada, dying, wills her room-mate Constance Sterling her lifetime savings of $500 to clear his name before she too expires. Constance discovers that the unfortunate man had seduced Rhoda, another of that type of girl too proud and self-willed for her own good. "I was swept round and round into the whirlpool of passion till not earth nor heaven could save me," Rhoda confesses, admitting her own guilt. Baerus, regretting his cowardice, had gone to the vat thinking he would starve to death slowly over a ten day period, but the vat was filled and he died instantly. A final twist has Rhoda poison herself rather than face dishonor when she is tricked into going to a house of ill repute. The inexorable punishment for illicit sex remains the same as in Hannah Foster's *The Coquette* (1798) and all subsequent stories of seduction and death, but the tracking down of the criminal through clues and the vivid descriptions of violent death are new embellishments.

The novels of earlier women writers like Mrs. E.D.E.N. Southworth had plenty of violent incident, but the element of detection and in particular the creation of a detective character who functions in several different stories is an innovation of Mrs. Green's. Her completely American settings, her characters, and the motives which impel them to murder, are also unique.

Another example of her favorite theme—two women, one too proud and one of democratic ordinariness—is carried out in *A Matter of Millions*, published in 1890. In this book the young artist Hamilton Degraw catches sight of a face in a crowd and cannot rest for love of it until he finds the young girl again. In his search he neglects to notice that Hilary Aspinwall, a wealthy and philanthropically inclined young woman, has fallen in love with him. Her more sober qualities are diminished by the flame of Jenny Rogers' exotic beauty. Hilary, with "generous sympathy and womanly sacrifice" helps him find her rival, to whom he proposes marriage. All seems resolved until he asks to see a copy of a letter his fiancé has: "A wife is so sacred to her husband! He wants to feel that she holds no secrets from him—that all is clear between her soul and his." Jenny is forced to reveal that she tricked him as part of a complex plot to enable her to inherit money and is so shamed that she kills herself. This form of honor among women who have been untrue to their ideals or who have been betrayed by men is characteristic of Green's plots. Hamilton Degraw has learned the snare of fatal beauty and excess of passion; Hilary "is now the comforter of the artist's grief, . . . who will live to be the angel of his home."

The woman herself becomes the victim of her passionate nature in *Cynthia Wareham's Money* (1892). Hermione, "fiercely
beautiful and fiercely proud" and her gentle sister Emma are
prisoners in an old house in Connecticut. Hermione, morbidly
sensitive about a scar on her face (caused by Emma as a child)
had, in a flaming temper, vowed that she would never leave her
house because her deformity had been mocked by the man whom
she thought loved her. The girls' father, a mad scientist, holds
Hermione to her vow, from which she is released only when the
house burns.

Another woman of frightening force of character is the title
character of *Miss Hurd: An Enigma*, written in 1894, "the story
of a strange, impenetrable, fascinating woman." In the novel
"Miss Hurd" (whose real name is Vashti, the Biblical heroine so
dear to the feminists of the nineteenth century for her defiance of
her husband) flees her husband through assuming a series of professions and disguises, including a stint with the Protestant Ministering Sisters. The story is interesting for the paucity of alternatives available to the woman who wished to disappear, as well as
for the way in which the power of her personality is revealed
to be such that anonymity is impossible for her.

Part of the plight of these strong and passionate women is that
there are no men to match them, the dilemma written about in
real life by Margaret Fuller and Charlotte Perkins Gilman. In
Agatha Webb (1899), the heroine declares, "I cannot, I dare not,
marry where I am not held in a passionate, self-forgetful subjection. I am too proud, too sensitive, too little mistress of myself,
when angry or aroused . . . Strength only can command my admiration or subdue my pride. I must fear where I love, and have
for husband him who has first shown himself my master." However, convinced that the man she loves is her family's enemy,
she marries the gentle, passive Philomen. Five of their children
die in infancy and, believing their marriage cursed because she
was untrue to her nature, she gives the sixth, a son, out for adoption; on his return as her heir hangs the complex plot. When
she discovered that her father and Philomen had tricked her she
cursed herself and her children. In order to help her son, whom
she has found stealing from her, she makes him her heir and kills
herself.

A happier ending awaits the awakened soul of Gilbertine in *The
Amethyst Box* (1905). The narrator loves sweet calm Dorothy but

is himself desperately loved by brilliant beautiful Gilbertine. Gilbertine lets her nasty old aunt take poison, justifying her actions by saying that she never had a mother and was allowed to read too many romances. Once it is established that dear Dorothy is the heiress and Gilbertine is penniless, she is able to reform and marry the truehearted Mr. Sinclair, who has loved her not for her brilliance but for the soul he knew she possessed, which could be liberated only if she were freed from the tyranny of riches.

In all these stories the theme of the intense and passionate woman of mystery, a theme celebrated by Hawthorne and later by a series of famous women detectives, is present, but linked with violence and death. Woman as victim of her own nature, as well as of a cruel society and brutal men, is necessary for the working out of these plots.

Another theme which runs through Green's work is fear of the doctor and of scientists playing God and making choices of life and death for women which ought to be reserved for the Almighty. A demented doctor is the anti-hero of *Dr. Izard* (1895), who had killed a man because he refused to let Izard perform an autopsy on his wife's body. Dr. Mollesworth in *Behind Closed Doors* (1888) refuses to marry the woman he loves unless she retains her position in society, and proves in the long run to be capable of loving only his mother and his friend. The only doctor who emerges as a really positive figure is in a short story, "A Mysterious Case," published in *The Old Stone House* (1891) in which a jealous woman tries to poison a noble young woman doctor's patient.

Another set of conventions explored in these novels is the political plot, a favorite of readers of Wilkie Collins and Arthur Conan Doyle. In *The Chief Legatee*, written in 1906, a secret organization drains the life and energy of Georgian Ranson, who is forced to create a dual identity of her own twin Anitra in order to escape the tentacles of political vengeance. The Cause is left vague, but its advocates believe it "will triumph" over the petty reforms which are doomed to failure. In a short story, "The Bronze Hand," published in *A Difficult Problem* (1900), a more specific conspiracy involving the North and South is hinted at. The bronze hand is a complicated mechanism which is kept in the office of Dr. Merriam, to be activitated when a ring is placed on its finger, the signal for a political assassination. Irene, who is a part of the group of avengers, admits to her lover, "I have meddled with matters few women could even conceive of." He interrupts her, "You need not go on, I quite understand. But you will be my wife?" In fact, Irene is herself a victim of the political murders.

Two attempts at the historical novel of deduction are *Marked Personal* (1893) and *The Forsaken Inn* (1890). In the former, the atmosphere of a California mining camp is invoked as the setting for the death of a young boy at the hands of two men. In a stroke of masterly revenge, his father claims their lives but tells them he will wait until they have children of their own, so they too can know the pain of loss. The bereaved father tries to collect his due in 1863 but is prevented by the riots of that year, and only later do the two deaths take place.

The Inn, in the title of the earlier novel, is a colonial hostelry, the scene of a romance of the American Revolution. The woman of the couple denounced the United States, "so new, so crude, so democratic! I should like to live where I could ride over the necks of common people." Clearly her end is going to be an unhappy one. She has, it appears, connived at the murder of Honoria Urquhart, killed by her husband who becomes the Tory's lover. After sixteen years the unreconstructed Loyalist returns with her daughter. The guilty woman dies in the secret room where the bones of Mrs. Urquhart repose. The daughter prepares to marry a French Marquis, who is not only willing but eager to give up his title and live in the new republic.

In many of these novels the Americans live up to their reputation for mechanical ingenuity. John Dickson Carr was impressed with the use of an icicle for a bullet, the murder weapon in *Initials Only* (1905). In the story Edith Challoner is killed by her lover, a radical and scientist—he was working on a mechanism to send an air car straight up from its mooring place—who is pictured as having great sympathy for "our toiling, half-starved, downtrodden brothers and sisters in the lower streets of this city." His sympathy extends to killing one of these toilers with a practice icicle, a washerwoman "with nothing to look forward to."

The Filagree Ball, written in 1903, is bizarre even in the context of the other novels. It tells of a fiendish device, in which members of a family got rid of unwelcome guests in their parlor by releasing a spring which turned the crank on a lethal weapon, then returned it safely to its hiding place until another family member got in trouble. The secret of the device could be deciphered in writing on the outlines of an old picture, when looked at with a magnifying glass. In this case the girl who did the deed, a bride of two weeks, committed suicide afterwards. She had killed the man she thought was her first husband (it was, in fact, his brother) who had returned to confront her with bigamy.

Perhaps the first American use of the release of a catch by the production of a musical tone is found in *Three Thousand Dollars* (1910) in which the perfect secretary Grace Lee sings the aria from *The Magic Flute*, ending on the high note that opens the safe door. In "The Little Steel Coils," reprinted in *Masterpieces of Mystery* in 1913, a mysterious death is explained by the finding of a mechanical puzzle, a particular weakness of the murdered man, in the form of a little steel coil. This one, however, had "the deadly secret poison, woorali," on its tip. Another story in the same volume, "Room No. 3," is an early version of the missing scene of the crime, to be used so effectively later by Edmund Crispin in *The Moving Toy Shop*. In this story the murderers change the paper in the room; thus baffling the murdered woman's daughter.

In "The Staircase at Heart's Delight," a much-anthologized favorite written in the 1890s, the death trap for unwary travellers is very effectively presented. And in "Midnight in Beauchamp Row" there is the use of concealed identity and accidental discovery in a manner reminiscent of O.Henry when a young bank clerk poses as a Negro robber, having left his wife with the payroll, and is, in his turn, killed by a second and real robber. A final convention of the period and every other period is in *One of My Sons* (1901) where the presumed typed note of the dying man, "ONE OF MY SONS" is revealed to be "NONE OF MY SONS", the initial letter omitted through his weakness as he slumped over the keys in death. A further convention is the fact that the murder was not committed by a son because the butler did it.

The most important innovation of Mrs. Green was the creation of a series of detective characters. Ebeneezer Gryce, the inoffensive little man whose eye was not proud, is the best known among them. One memoir of the detective story remembers a case featuring Gryce as the only mystery sanctioned by the author's mother, since "Mr. Gryce was such a nice man."[16] His first role, *The Leavenworth Case*, was supposed to be the favorite reading of Prime Minister Stanley Baldwin.[17] Besides Gryce, Anna Green created Detective Sweetwater, who lived with his "Mamsie", played the violin, was interested in electric gadgets and had premonitory dreams about his cases. But the most original of all her detectives were the two women in the field, Amelia Buttersworth and Violet Strange.

In 1897 the heroine of *That Affair Next Door* begins her tale with the prophetic words, "I am not an inquisitive woman, but . . ." thus beginning the career of a lady detective. Miss Amelia Buttersworth, "of colonial ancestry and no inconsiderable importance in the social world" is recruited by Mr. Gryce to help him solve the murder of her next-door neighbor. "Women's eyes for women's matters," says Mr. Gryce, who also appreciates the fact that the well-connected Miss Buttersworth can enter doors forever closed to him no matter what his disguise. Miss Buttersworth is the fictional sister of that staple of nineteenth century fiction, the humorous spinster, well-known in Frances Whicher's *Widow Bedott*, as Samantha Allen in Marietta Holley's series and even in Henry James' Henrietta Stackpole—a lovable but laughable lady, inquisitive, sharp-eyed and sharp-tongued. Miss Buttersworth becomes the fictional model for the host of spinster sleuths of the twentieth century, Rachel Inness, Hildegarde Withers, Emily Seeton, Miss Marple, Miss Tyler, Miss Silver, and so on into an infinity of characters, armed with umbrellas, knitting needles and equally sharp elbows and wits.

In the sequel published in 1898, *Lost Man's Lane*, Amelia returns, against her better judgment but persuaded that "an opportunity came for a direct example of my detective powers in a line so seemingly laid out for me by Providence that I felt I would be slighting the Powers above if I refused to enter upon it." Tracking down a series of unexplained disappearances, Miss Buttersworth comes upon a strange household, inhabited by many of the characters in *Arsenic and Old Lace*. Once held a prisoner she is annoyed that she must "await events like any other weak and defenceless woman."

Gryce has chosen her for "my knowledge of persons . . . my knowledge of their fears, their hopes, and their individual concerns." She proves worthy of his trust, tracks down the murderer and collects two proposals of marriage on the way. Miss Buttersworth is ever ready to defend herself as a True Woman, no matter how many murders she is involved with, but she rejoices that she

has few of her sex's weaknesses "and none of its instinctive reliance upon others which leads it so often to neglect its own
resources." There is nothing of the languishing lady of the Gothic
tale about Miss Buttersworth; when necessary she uses her corset
laces to effect an escape. ("Pardon me. I am as modest as most
of my sex, but I am not squeamish. Corset laces are strings, and
as such only I present them to your notice.") She confesses to two
weaknesses only, a dislike of barking dogs and a deepseated distrust of mechanical devices, including the telephone. At one point,
in order to check a set of footprints she puts tacks in a suspect's
boots so he will have to change them and wear the pair she suspects made the imprints.

Miss Buttersworth makes her final appearance in 1900 in *The
Circular Study*. "That most respectable of ladies," who proclaims
herself "intensely feminine, sir, in all my instincts," gets mixed
up in another murder, which she solves through keen observation
and mingling with the suspects who cannot distrust such a "refined and sympathetic listener" and therefore tell all their guilty
secrets. At the conclusion of the case, although she vows never
more to put her finger "in the police pie," she admits to "a
quiet complacency which argued that she was not altogether dissatisfied with herself or the result of her interference with
matters usually considered at variance with a refined woman's
natural instincts."

Amelia Buttersworth illustrates those qualities which make the
fictional heroine of the novels featuring a woman detective important as a countervailing force to the stereotype of impotent
and passive females. Although it is "An Unsuitable Job for a
Woman" (the title of an excellent novel by P.D. James published
in 1971 and featuring a professional woman detective) Miss
Buttersworth makes a success of it, without destroying her social
position or feminine instincts.

The second of Green's female detectives, Violet Strange, whose
problems formed the chapters of *The Golden Slipper* (1915), belonged to a different category of sleuth. Violet, like Dora Myrl,
Lady Molly Robinson-Kirk, and Florence Cusack, in the stories by
M. Mc Donnell Bodkin (1900), Baroness Orczy (1910) and Mrs.
L. T. Meade (1899 and 1900), is a "slip of a girl" with a special
mission on which to use her detective skills. Violet had become
a detective in order to finance the singing lessons of her older

sister Theresa, who had been banished from their home when she married a man against her father's wishes. Once Theresa makes a successful debut, Violet can retire from the profession.

In the "Problems" Violet is used as an auxiliary of an unnamed private detective, who believes in setting "sex against sex, and, if possible, youth against youth" in matching detective to criminal. Violet, the daughter of the wealthy but self-willed banker Peter Strange, finally takes her brother into her confidence and lets him accompany her when she goes to a place of dubious reputation. She solves her problems by putting herself in the victim's mind and recreating the scene of the crime. "Miss Strange hated murders and it was with difficulty she could be brought to discuss them," but nonetheless she solved several important crimes. Although slight, "almost childish" in face and form, Violet has enormous sensitivity and great common sense. It is part of her ability to seem "but a girl of fashion" when in reality her hands, "those little hands so white and fluttering, so seemingly helpless under the weight of their many rings, and yet so extremely capable" were stretched out to help anyone who asked her.

Nonetheless, some crimes are too disgusting, and she denounced her employer: "When, for reasons I have never thought called upon to explain, I consented to help you a little now and then in some matter where a woman's tact and knowledge of the social world might tell without offence to herself or others, I never thought it would be necessary for me to state that . . . I should not be asked to touch the sordid or the bloody . . . What do you see in me, or miss in me, that you should drag me into an atmosphere of low-down crime?" And her employer answers: "Nothing, Miss Strange. You are by nature, as well as by breeding, very far removed from everything of the kind. But you will allow me to suggest that no crime is low-down which makes imperative demand upon the intellect and intuitive sense of the investigator." In this passage are recapitulated the arguments against women entering most phases of real life at the beginning of the twentieth century, as well as the arguments against reading murder mysteries.

In her fourth problem Violet meets the melancholy young Roger Upjohn, depressed because of his fears that his beloved father killed his wife. After that case "her interest had been reached and her heartstrings stricken as never before in her young life. She would never be the same Violet again." Violet discovers that the crime was committed by his father's too faithful servant.

The last three of her cases become increasingly more frightening. Violet, already "in a state of secret despondence" over Roger is present at the unpleasant accident whereby the blind Doctor Zulriski kills his wife, in attempting to prove he had not committed a murder two years earlier. In her final escapade she goes into a secret room in search of a missing "page thirteen" of a scientific formula and comes across the skeletons of her host's parents, who had dueled to the death over his custody many years before when he was a child. Violet frees the old man from his memories through her compassion and understanding: "There is no suffering like a child's, terrified by a secret which it dare not for some reason disclose."

In the final chapter she explains her career to Roger, who has diffidently approached her with an offer of marriage. "You wonder why, with all the advantages I possess, I should meddle with matters so repugnant to a woman's natural instincts," she begins, but he accepts her in advance of an explanation. She then tells him her secret struggles to support her sister, admitting the strain and sacrifice it caused her but confessing to a sneaking enjoyment through it all. Violet may now retire to a profession, more suitable for a woman—wife and step-mother. "Such a union as ours must be hallowed, because we have so many persons to make happy besides ourselves."

The transitional novel of Mrs. Green's, using the romantic conventions of the Gothic tale and the increasing involvement with problem-solving which became the modern detective novel, often ends on some such pious note. But in the intervening pages there is a good strong plot, complex motivation, and frequently, particularly interesting female characters. She is the first of the women who made this genre their own and one of the most prolific. Like other women who wrote detective fiction she was responding to popular interest in gory details and writing for the same generation that so relished the news of Lizzie Borden.

Most women writers have written popular fiction because they needed to support themselves, and in her early years this was true of Mrs. Green.[18] If, as most commentators believe, detective fiction was a response to Victorian anxieties, then women in writing it were fulfilling their traditional function as guardians and conservators of traditional values. But the novels of Anna Katharine Green, however conservative in their stress upon American detectives solving crimes and making American cities safe and happy, are also immensely innovative. While the role of woman as guardian and popularizer was accepted, the idea of her being an innovator in any creative field was more often challenged.

In her treatment of women Mrs. Green also both adhered to conventions and created new images. In her theme of the fiercely proud and passionate woman, whose intensity cannot be matched by man or society, she demands an adjustment to domesticity and submissive conformity for survival. Sigmund Freud made the same demands on his female patients to bring them to grips with "reality." But in Anna Green's novels, however relentlessly she punishes such women, she at least creates them in all their magnetism and strength. Read in the context of some of the feminist novels of protest of the late nineteenth century—*The Woman Who Dared* and *Is This Your Son, My Lord*, for example—the inability of these women to find a mate who can match them is their tragedy, and the reason they must mute their splendor to endure. American society exacted a levelling of its citizens, female as well as male, as the price of equality, and both the exalted high and the debased low nature must melt into an undistributed democratic middle. But the society was not so bland, as perhaps Poe had feared, that crime could not flourish in it, and frequently there was crime proportionate to the material wealth, high ideals of women and marriage, and political intrigue.

Mrs. Green was also highly conventional in favoring careers for young women, but insisting that their natural destiny and only chance for real happiness was at home. The opening pages of *The Mill Mystery* contain an apostrophe to single blessedness which begins, "Oh, the deep sadness of a solitary woman's life!" In *The Woman in the Alcove* (1906) the narrator, young, wealthy and beautiful Rita Van Arsdale trains as a nurse, much to the surprise of her family and friends. However, in the course of finding the murderer and thief who threatens the man she loves, Miss Van Arsdale realizes that her training has all "been for home joys and a woman's existence." Violet Strange must put down the fascinating but frightening pursuit of crime when she marries her melancholy widower. But Amelia Buttersworth, spared from domesticity (but not from True Womanhood) by her years and temperament is allowed free expression of her instincts and intellect. There is nothing "deeply sad" about Amelia, and her spinster's life is filled with humor and incident. If women miss their natural destiny and end up as detectives, then they are allowed to relax and enjoy it.

In her pious endings and romantic entanglements Anna Katharine Green followed the traditions of the nineteenth century popular novel. In her trapped and haunted women, her treatment of American character and criminals, her use of place and personality to establish mood and motive, her Yankee cleverness in dispatching her victims, and her use of women detectives, she was very much a part of that popular twentieth century literary form, the murder mystery.

9

MYSTICAL FEMINIST
Margaret Fuller, a Woman of the Nineteenth Century

The woman who lived in the nineteenth century was besieged by periodicals, novels, and religious tracts defining and explaining her nature and her role. One of the most perceptive and most important of these books of advice was called *Woman in the Nineteenth Century*, Margaret Fuller's urgent assessment of her own sex in her own time. The life of the author and the arguments of the book intersect, and show how even in this most cerebral and transcendent of American women the themes and values of the age persisted. Margaret Fuller's book attempted to bring women of the nineteenth century into a wider, stronger world. Her life showed these same women the hazards and pitfalls which such changes might create as well as their triumphs and satisfactions.

Americans respond eagerly to the how-to book, with its promise that each individual, no matter how poor or clumsy, can do what he puts his will to, whether make a million dollars in the stock market or build his own harpsichord. According to the do-it-yourself manual, no obstacle of education, background, or nature can stand up to the determined American character. These promises of the good American life date from the colonial period. The promise of a new country meant the promise of a new man to inhabit it, and whether it was John Smith, Hector Crevecoeur or Benjamin Franklin describing the unlimited opportunities which awaited the early to bed and early to rise, the resources are pictured as limitless and the potential of the free will in a free nation inexhaustible. In the expansiveness which marked most of the country's history until the twentieth century, limitation of the human spirit seemed unnecessary and undemocratic—as unnecessary and undemocratic as limiting the accumulation of wealth or the use of land and resources. Conservation was a negative concept, at a time when positive thinking and what William James called the "will to be-

145

lieve" hoped to conquer mountains, history, and human nature. To exploit the land and the human resources to their utmost was an aim for each American. The cultivation of the mind, like the cultivation of the soil, was part of the duty and privilege of life in the new Republic. In New England, that difficult and rocky place, the idea that each individual must wrest from his time-span as many fruits as possible, that constant pruning and winnowing of the intellect and character were necessary in order to have a bountiful harvest, was particularly strong.

The New England woman, daughter of the Puritans, wife of the capitalists, was an important force in this reclamation project. Much of the history of this period is the history of New England, transplanted in place but maintaining its characteristics. Therefore it is fitting that the first important book on American women came from the pen of a New England woman, whose own life was an example of constant, unremitting effort to become what she and her country considered a high goal, a new American woman. Margaret Fuller's *Woman in the Nineteenth Century* was published in 1845 and sold out its first edition within a week. Its importance was in its timing as much as or more than in its arguments or examples. Like many important books it reenforced, rather than created, opinions in the process of change and reforms in the process of achievement. The woman who read it saw herself, and, according to her own insights, courage, and luck, arranged her life accordingly. Its value to the women to whom it was addressed was not so much the specific means it advised but the fact that it postulated as a desirable and possible end, a human being, equal to the glories and demands of the nation, who was a woman. The author, Margaret Fuller, possessed the particular power, in her person and her prose, to create this sense of the possible, the attainable goal. By her conversations and her writings she touched the women she knew, or who knew her through her work, and told them there was more in themselves than they had ever known, and they should dream dreams even as men did. She told them to know more, do more, expect more than their mothers had, and to take pleasure in their accomplishments. As an antidote to so much of the mentor literature of the period, preaching submission and resignation, she gave women egos and told them to enjoy them. Women in the nineteenth century, and women now, identified both with the book and perhaps even more, with the author's own life.

The early years of Sarah Margaret Fuller, the first of the nine children of Timothy and Margaret Fuller, are known largely through the autobiographical works she wrote. Her birth in 1810 was the first of her father's long series of disappointments—he wanted a boy. It is amazing how many nineteenth-century feminists announce knowing they were a second-choice sex. That an overwhelming preponderance of these women were first-borns, and that they had a close, although frequently ambivalent relationship with their father, is part of this same knowledge. In her youth Margaret Fuller did what many of the young people she knew in Cambridge did—criticized severely the way in which she had been brought up and reached into her childhood to dredge up stories of early traumas and later problems which arose from them. Her autobiographical work, whether disguised as fiction or presented factually, is filled with blame and recrimination for the way in which her parents, particularly her father, handled her childhood. In the letters and memoirs of many of this group of young people are found similar stories, for introspection and preoccupation with one's own development of self, was a necessary means to self-knowledge. As so often happened, Margaret's stories are more intense and dramatic than anyone's. What we cannot, of course, know, is whether they are accurate.

Timothy Fuller's education of Sarah Margaret was according to the eighteenth-century man's knowledge of classical learning. She started Latin at six and read only the classics. Her recitations were given to her father late in the evening, after he finished his work, and the strain of the performance added to the excitement of the material itself, made the little girl afraid to sleep for fear she would dream of Virgil's forests dripping blood, or horses trampling her. She had offended her father by her very existence, and each day she feared to offend him again by falling short of his standards. Timothy Fuller was often frustrated in his political, economic, and social aspirations. He was determined to have one unqualified success, a learned daughter. Margaret would reflect, as his prospects did not, his real abilities.

Timothy Fuller had been admitted to the Massachusetts bar, was a representative to Congress in 1817 and in 1824 became speaker of the Massachusetts House. His mistake was in choosing John Quincy Adams over the rising western star of Andrew Jackson, and his political and personal eclipse followed quickly upon Jackson's election. Margaret called her father "a man of business, even in literature" with a kind of snobbism towards mercantilism which New England intellectuals favored. Insofar as his business training was reflected in his passion for accuracy and his insistence that Margaret produce summaries and critiques of everything she read which were not only precise but analytical, it was not a bad substitute for a normal school. In many ways all that was strongest in Margaret Fuller's later writing lived up to the standards he set. In imposing them on a young female, and in not making allowance for the enormous imagination and sensitivity which Margaret (somewhat proudly) acknowledged she had, Timothy Fuller created a monster, a "physical wreck" when he intended only a learned man. There is a certain irony, lost to Margaret, that her father made no concession to feminine delicacy at all. No matter how troubling her migraine, her nervous stomach, her "periodic pain," he insisted on his essays and his abstracts. He gave her taste in an age when the predominant writing, certainly that considered suitable for children and women, was bland and insipid.

During Margaret's youth the theories of child rearing were changing from the more rigid approaches of the eighteenth century to the more flexible standards of the nineteenth. Much of what Margaret Fuller blamed her father for doing in her education was no more nor no less than was done in most eighteenth-century families, of middle-class educated New England or English backgrounds. Margaret's friends had different emphases—they believed in the overwhelming power of persuasion and love, the importance of the mother's role as teacher and exemplar, the natural and gradual development of the human organism. Precocity, so cherished in previous generations as an indicator of godliness or intelligence, was to be shunned as a deadly disease, the herald of madness or early death. These were the new standards of the American middle-class, like most child-rearing theories a reaction against the mistakes made by their own parents, and, again like most such theories, a series of new mistakes to be righted, in their turn, by the next generation of mistreated youth. Margaret received the same kind of education most American and English men of achievement received before the 1830s, and she was indignant at it. Love and not force, nature and not intellect, were the guidewords of her generation and the home should be presided over by the strong yet gentle mother. Timothy Fuller did everything wrong; Margaret even rejected the name he chose. She refused to be called Sarah—that was an "old maid name" and she said she would not use it until she sat in her rocking chair with her knitting, Miss Sarah Fuller, that worthy old soul.

Nonetheless under his guidance she learned to know of Roman virtu, the paramount importance of will, perseverance and family duty. In the Greek myths, which she said she knew better than Biblical parables, she saw beauty and worthy passion. She read ancient history and debated modern politics, and she was saved from much that was second-rate and banal. The stereotypes of pious children dying young and girls reforming their lovers, those staples of popular literature, were not of her upbringing. Whether or not she surreptitiously read sentimental novels, as another generation of intellectuals' children might sneak comic books or television viewing, is another question. Even so, she knew that they were not the stuff on which her mind fed, and in her later advice to her sex, she followed a very similar reading program, supplemented by the visual and dramatic arts.

While still under the tutelage of her father she met the first woman with whom she could really identify, a lovely English visitor to Cambridgeport. Margaret was thirteen, ripe for a schoolgirl crush, as she continued to be throughout her life, and the visitor's accent, voice, clothes and manner so fascinated Margaret that she followed her everywhere. She also tried to copy those things which she most admired, as was again to be her style. For the first time she saw female beauty, of form and dress and speech, as well as a cultivated mind. The possibility of lesbianism, latent or overt, has often been discussed in connection with Margaret Fuller. She continued this interest in women throughout her life and formed extremely intense, possessive relationships with several of them. Wherever she went, to the Great Lakes or to Italy or just to buy gloves in Boston she noticed the way in which women acted, what they said and wore and how they were treated. When she criticized pictures she often talked about the portrayal of women and her book reviews invariably single out the writer's attitudes and portraits of females.

Her interest in women was a vital part of her, perhaps her core, for Margaret was interested in what every woman could be or was and might become. This feminism was a reflection of her consuming interest in herself, in the making and the becoming of a person which was a life-work. The process of growth was, as she said, "all" to her. All women were part of the woman she was, and she was part of them. This was the mystical element of her feminism, increased by the Romantic philosophy she espoused in its German and New England forms, but fundamentally part of her own nature and background. But at the same time—and this is why lesbianism is irrelevant, as well as impossible to document— in both Margaret's writing and in her life is the theme that this process of growth, this making of self into the most that could be, was to a dual purpose: it was complete in itself, an achieved person, but it was also part of some further completion by union with an equally divine and complete male nature, which would complement and sustain her own nature. The allusions and hyperbole in her writings about herself as the chosen bride of Apollo, the outbursts to her One Love, her God, her sense that Christ might prove her only worthy Bridegroom, even her choice of a talisman flower, the heliotrope, bride of the sun, showed this groping towards some union between the male and the female, elements of which were both in her nature. And there is always that typical female fear that it would all be for nothing, a barren culture, that "no one has ever loved me, will ever love me," and she would be "Miss Sarah Fuller" after all, the last leaf on her own ancestral tree.

Shortly after this first intense love she was sent to the Misses Prescott School in Groton, Massachusetts. There she suffered the pains of being different in a group of conformists. The affection and admiration which she wanted, needed, and so often received from young women was conspicuously lacking in this academy, which offered a curriculum including natural philosophy, astronomy, fine needlepoint, and harmony, but paid little attention to the Latin and Greek classics. Margaret tried to force herself on the girls she met and on her teachers, but was met with coldness or laughter. Her achievements counted for little in that surrounding, and so she tried to make herself into a popular girl. According to her story, she resorted to clowning, to bizarre dress, and then to malicious gossip in her effort to be accepted. She might tell herself that she was resigned to being "ugly but wise" but she had a tremendous need for acceptance and admiration, based, she felt, on the deprivation of "natural affections" in her "unnatural childhood." In Margaret's story, Mariana, who has tried to court favor by sowing discord among the girls and telling vicious tales about some of them, is made to face the girls she tried to defame. In the confrontation she falls senseless to the stone hearth, seized with brain fever. In the period of delirium and recovery, a sympathetic teacher, using reason and love, brings Mariana to face her problems more realistically. Told by the teacher of a similar experience in her own life, Mariana is inspired to reform and to win a place for herself among her schoolmates by the approved means of character and benevolence.

This story, with variations, is a stock ingredient of many of the novels which Margaret presumably never read. Whether such a confrontation actually occurred, or whether, as often happens in fiction, Margaret saw this as the denouement she wished had happened, and the teacher as the wise, loving parent she had never had and wished to become, we cannot know. It is somewhat unusual that, with all the notoriety of Margaret Fuller's life and death, and the abundance of memoirs which saturated this period in American history, no one of her real-life schoolmates ever stepped up to separate fact and fantasy in the story. This was well before the tell-all atmosphere which surrounds such personality cults as that of Sylvia Plath, but to know Margaret at all, in the nineteenth century, usually brought with it the communication of an opinion on her. Probably certain elements of the story took place and others did not, but the residue of the experience in Margaret's life was a feeling that she had tested the limits of sanity, and endurance, and feared what lay beyond. Her portrayal of neurotic adolescent behavior rings true, and could be corroborated by the works of Mather and Freud. Throughout her life she was able to excuse outrageous behavior in women, whether from her friends, the prostitutes she visited at Sing Sing, or herself, on the grounds that this bizarre action stemmed from "perverted pride," a pardonable and necessary sense of self-worth which had gone unrecognized or was contradicted by society.

Perhaps because she felt she understood how normal behavior and reason itself could be pushed by fierce pride, Margaret urged any woman she met, however fallen, to pick herself up and try again. In a life crammed with duties, always pressed for time, and drained of energy, she took endless hours to listen to tales of woe from Brook Farm girls, casual friends, girls she met in shops, women in the prison hospital in New York, and to give them real advice, not hollow comfort. She told them they could do more and be more, that she knew what it was to fail, but that she knew what it was to succeed, largely by the effort of will, sustained by God's love. In her efforts for these women, some close friends but many of slight acquaintance, is a "there but for the Grace of God" quality. She had tested the limits of her own strength and sanity, and she no longer judged, only helped. She felt that her own physical and emotional balance was precarious, achieved and maintained at great cost. This was the price exacted from someone of talent and ambition in this culture, when that person was a female. She knew that for many the price was too great; for herself she was usually sure that it was worth it, but sometimes she wondered.

There was little time for doubt in the rigorous schedule she set herself in the years following her schooling. She was determined to "grow," which for her generation and group meant to grow in character and in intellect: self-study, scheduled literally from dawn to dark, interspersed with lessons to master new languages, conversations with friends engaged in similar pursuits to compare achievements and exchange ideas, and domestic chores, to discharge the duties imposed on all young women, no matter how gifted, as a necessary part of character training. Accomplishments in singing and playing were dutifully and doggedly pursued in this regime, and the day was completed with the ritual diary entry, detailing the struggles and occasional modest triumphs of doing one's best on all fronts. This life of drudgery and plodding towards some obscure goal of personal perfection was directed to the dual ends of personal achievement and possible liberation. Like one of Horatio Alger's heroes, Margaret and other young girls expected to be rewarded for their goodness by being taken away from all the dreary routine and given their rightful place in the sun.

For Phil the Fiddler or Paul the Peddler liberation would come in the *deus ex machina* of a wealthy businessman, willing to share his fortunes with them. For Margaret, her fantasies of freedom required some young prince ("I think that I was born to be a princess") or, the alternative, even more fantastic choice, liberation through her own work. She did not know, as yet, what she would do, but she supposed some kind of writing, probably poetry, since that was the highest form of literature, and the will to self-culture would not concede defeat in its pursuit of the highest goals just because of a few troubling details like the complete lack of any lyrical or metrical gifts.

In 1826 the Fuller family moved to Dana Hill, a pleasant district near the Harvard campus, where many young men were available for intense discussion and long rides through the woods. Timothy still hoped to salvage something from his political career, and he entertained a great deal in the new, more elegant home. There seems to have been an effort at this time, in which she cooperated, to turn Margaret into that peculiarly American phenomenon, the bluestocking belle. Both North and South had examples of the young girl, well born and well educated, who dazzled with her knowledge of Latin tag-ends, as well as with her dimples. The belle, in order to be really celebrated in the United States in the period before the Civil War, was expected to be witty (although, of course, not cruel) and wise (although never competitive), as well as pretty and stylish (natural, not artificial, and, if possible, in American-made finery.) One summer night, Margaret, in bright pink silk, was present at her father's ball. One of the guests, Mrs. Eliza Farrar, wife of an ailing Harvard mathematics professor, was impressed at the potential of the young girl —here was wit and intelligence to spare—but decided that the body which housed this "splendid young soul" needed redoing. Mrs. Farrar, whose etiquette book would be one of the most sensible published during this period before the Civil War, believed that it was the duty of American girls to show off the superiority of their nation. Therefore she took them in hand, and taught them how to dress and behave in order to make their native intelligence, modesty, and good sense shine all the brighter in an attractive setting. Mrs. Farrar sometimes let her passion for improvement get the better of her, as when she wrote a children's version of *Robinson Crusoe* in which the hero's language and deportment were reformed to make him more suitable for her young readers.

With Margaret she had more success. A diet, curbing nervous mannerisms, finding a style and color of dress which suited her, made an enormous change in Timothy's daughter. She would never be beautiful, as she had always known, but she was bright and she had been made presentable. In a period when it was hard for an ugly woman to enter into the kingdom of matrimony, or even to get into the right drawing rooms, this kind of self-improvement was important. From the time of Mrs. Farrar on, Margaret began to acquire the polish and the style which she needed, in order to "grow" socially, as well as intellectually. To be able to converse with the most cultivated people in the world, to understand them and to contribute to them, was a lofty aim for a near-sighted pudgy daughter of a second-rank politician. Mrs. Farrar believed in social and economic mobility as passionately as she believed in the superiority of the American political system, and for many of the same reasons. Margaret was to her an example of intelligence and will applied to natural resources, a "made-in-America" product of which the country could be proud. Her hope was to show off the young girl in Europe, to give her that finishing which the Old World alone could provide. Among her many pieces of sage advice was the warning that improper hygiene and the substitution of ignorance for modesty could give rise to many "female complaints" which were unnecessary.

All her life Margaret suffered from migraine, stomach upsets, "spinal weakness" and excruciating backaches, and a lassitude so profound, accompanied by depression, that any activity was painful. Whether some or all of these symptoms were psychosomatic we cannot know, any more than we can understand why the treatment of "dynamism" or "electrical magnetism" or "sympathetic mesmerism" apparently helped Margaret and her contemporaries. We do know that the "migraine syndrome" and possibly the "migraine personality" seemed to be the occupational disease of the intellectual woman of the nineteenth century and even of our own time. The compulsiveness, perfectionism, and anxiety of the over-achiever, the classic profile of the migraine sufferer, were parts, but only parts, of Margaret's personality. Theories that depression, with its accompanying symptoms, is a manifestation of hostility and repressed anger, fit with what we know of Margaret's background and her resentment of her father. She herself was aware of the connection between her emotional problems and her physical health, and, of course, she was conscious that her illnesses robbed her of valuable working time. Her unconscious desire not to work, so that at some level she "chose" illness, as she "chose" accomplishment, may be, as William James suggested, the negative side of the overriding will. Like Margaret, however, the historian is left with the record of debilitating illness, without understanding fully either the causes or the treatment.

With all of Mrs. Farrar's good advice, these periods of ill health remained and increased, as did certain peculiarities of Margaret's much commented on by her biographers and observers. One was the habit of narrowing her near-sighted eyes to a point and then dilating them so that the iris seemed to emit flashes of light. Margaret found this very effective, particularly when she wished to concentrate all her attention on an individual, either to emphasize her point or to paralyze an opponent. The other habit which attracted an inordinate amount of comment was her way of seeming to extend her neck, so that she could bring her head suddenly forward, then, in one sinuous motion, rear up. William Channing, who rarely gossiped, noted this habit and wondered whether her vertebrae had a special pliancy to enable her to perform this disconcerting (but apparently riveting) feat. People who didn't like her said she looked like a cobra, fixing a victim with a pale cold eye. More sympathetic observers thought it part of her way of reaching out and involving others, of making them feel, by her body and gestures as well as by her voice, that she was speaking only to them and that only they could find the precise, the correct word she sought.

Physical descriptions of Margaret Fuller abound; most of them are unflattering, although even the most harsh concede her style and her presence. It is worth noting that the physical peculiarities of the rest of the Cambridge thinkers are not nearly so well known; the length of Hawthorne's nose, the breadth of Alcott's ears are not the subject of memoir or letter. Was it because females were first and most often perceived in their physical aspects, that all women were to be seen first and listened to only later, if at all? In any case, almost no comment on Margaret Fuller is without its physical description, in which those narrowed eyes, that weaving neck, are prominent, and the pale brown hair, the well-developed breasts, and careful grooming, are only afterthoughts. Oliver Wendell Holmes found that special neck interesting enough to mention in his diary, and to use afterwards in his snake-heroine Elsie Vedder.

One of the mixed blessings Mrs. Farrar brought into Margaret's life was the introduction of the young Anna Barker of New Orleans to the circle of young people in Cambridge. Emerson, dazzled, called her "that piece of divinity," immediately hastening to add that a girl of her background and social graces was beyond his comprehension. Anna had been sent north to be taken in hand by Mrs. Farrar, and here at last was first-class material. Apparently she was extraordinarily lovely and as Margaret rather tritely remarked, "as good as she was beautiful." In the circle into which she was introduced, a literary cliché was regarded as much more damaging that any social faux pas, and it is some sort of tribute to her that almost everyone who knew her said the same thing in almost the same words.

Anna, after a suitable period as a belle, married one of the young men in whom Margaret displayed the most interest, the artistic and cultivated Sam Ward. Their marriage, their home, their life together became a model of the "beautiful people" whom America was beginning to create. The ambivalence with which Margaret regarded the couple stemmed from the fact that she loved Anna with as much or more passion than she loved Sam, and that she was possessed by both envy and horror at this particular style and choice for woman's destiny. Anna had plenty of wit and intelligence of her own, and in the letters of hers which survive we have hints that being perfectly beautiful was not perfectly fulfilling, and that rather than apostrophes to her "eyelids that are like lillies" she might have enjoyed someone taking her ideas more seriously. Margaret paid little attention to that aspect of Anna's character, and concentrated on her as symbol of sweet womanliness which she admired and yet feared.

The intense friendships, of which Anna Barker and Sam Ward were part, formed an important part of Margaret's life during this early period. The ideal of the "platonic" friend was much in her mind, particularly after she read Goethe, but like many young girls each new "platonic" friend was a potential lover, which added immensely to the excitement. After a time it became clear that this particular friendship would remain just that, and so another young man joined the growing list of Margaret's "brotherly companions." The long talks in which she and her friends reveled, and the long letters with which they supplemented these talks when they were even a few miles distant from each other, were filled with the quest for self-knowledge and self-realization. "I am too ardent a spirit . . . I am too easily wounded . . . I am much too strange for the multitude . . ." were comments by which she tried to know herself. Then her friend would respond, frequently largely in terms of his own character, his own problems, but with a few words answering her. Margaret and James Freeman Clarke had a particularly long friendship of mutual discussion and comparison, and her letters to and from Caroline Sturgis during most of her life are also filled with self-analysis and contrasts with the other's perceptions or attitudes.

Sometimes, reading these letters, it seems as if they are more journal entry than communication, that the writers write *at* each other, not *to* each other, and that their concern is with the formulation of their own personality, who they are, who they are in the process of becoming, rather than with the personality of the person they address. This wonder at their own new identity, this preoccupation with self, is a practically universal phenomenon of the adolescent and postadolescent relationship. However, the passion for conversation, for finding out details of life and character from incessant talk, was a part of the mature life of many of this group. The later meetings of the Hedge Club, the Transcendental literary evenings, Margaret's own experiments as director of Conversations, were expansions on this occupation of their youth. The immediacy and spontaneity of conversation made it an appealing vehicle to the Romantic temperament, in many ways superior to the stilted and artificial nature of the written word. Moreover, the stimulus of personalities—particularly, so many said and continued to say, of Margaret's—on others, brought forth ideas and phrases which a lonely sojourn at a desk might not produce. As this group of minds continued to talk and continued to grow and continued to write, it becomes more difficult to assign ideas and interests to one member of the group rather than another. Not until perhaps the Bloomsbury group is there a similar stress on conversation, on trying out ideas and exploring personalities by talking, and perhaps not until that particular group is there a similar preoccupation with the process of friendship, and a proliferation of detail about individual lives, idiosyncrasies, and ideas.

This period of hopeful exploration of friendships in a congenial surrounding came to an abrupt end when Timothy moved his family in with his brother Abraham and then moved the six children and his wife to a farm near Groton, fifty long miles from Boston and civilization. In 1833 it was clear that the Adams' party would not rise again, and Timothy retired to write his memoirs and accept the Jeffersonian dictum that a man was most his own master when he was on his own land. Her mother was in poor health, and Timothy had retired from the teaching business, so Margaret was pressed into service to tutor the younger children and keep the household in order. The life of the oldest daughter often was along these lines, and it was accepted procedure for her to sacrifice herself so that her younger brothers and sisters might achieve. To be a surrogate parent was the usual fate of the oldest girl in a time when childbearing stretched over twenty-year spans and often left the mother ill. Margaret was a very model of a model oldest daughter at this time, doing all that and more than was asked of her for the children and for her parents, at the same time continuing her program of self-improvement, learning German and reading the German romantics in the original, getting up her courage to say something in print about their ideas.

This submission and resignation, so impressive to all who saw her, and so surprising to those who had known her before, may have come about as a result of the religious experience she had two years previously on Thanksgiving Day. "I saw there was no self; that selfishness was all folly, and the result of circumstance; that it was only because I thought self real that I suffered, that I had only to live in the idea of the All, and all was mine. This truth came to me, and I received it unhesitatingly, so that I was for that hour taken up into God." The social value of a conversion experience like this, which even the Unitarians recognized and approved, lay in the effects of usefulness and service it produced. A woman concerned with her own achievements, pushed by pride and riddled with ambition, was unlikely to serve any of the roles her culture reserved for her. On the other hand, a woman dead to self, willing to admit to insignificance, was willing to submit to drudgery. Conversion was part of socialization, or could be made to serve this function. Women were encouraged to negate their own personalities and desires in the service of a higher goal—which, practically speaking, usually meant in the service of their fathers or husbands. The conversion experience was not reserved for women (although it increasingly was to become associated with them) but this particular aspect of it was used to reenforce their traditional place. A proper perspective could be established by seeing the lowly self in relation to God. This could be translated into seeing the lowly self in relation to those familial gods, dutiful daughter, obedient wife, sacrificing mother, in relation to the divine authority of father, husband, son.

Margaret's religious experience, no doubt a genuine one which brought with it a sense of relief and pleasure, made her life in her family easier, even if only for a time. The joy of conformity may be short-lived and self-destructive, but in a patriarchal household, without distractions or opportunities, it may also have been the price of survival. Margaret, in effect, led two lives during the

Groton period: the external one, where she set her lips together and taught the children history (and her brothers, at least, remarked that they fully understood how much she hated the job), and the internal one, nourished by Goethe and Schiller, in which she still dreamed of escape and happiness.

The Furies seemed to pursue the little family trying to escape the changes in the country of which they did not approve—the youngest child died, the boys left home to pursue some sort of reluctant career, the other children were sick and then Margaret herself became ill.

She had just returned from a pleasant visit with the Farrars, and was planning to tell her father of their invitation to join them on an extended trip abroad. She assumed that Timothy would pay for this trip, which was necessary to her intellectually and socially, for she had done what he wanted and asked for very little. Then a minor literary storm arose. Margaret had tried to write a story, based on her own experience with a triangular love affair of her friends. It was a rather banal little piece (and probably had been a rather trite experience in real life, since the participants were good New England Unitarians all), but "Lost and Won" infuriated the people who saw themselves written about, and Margaret, who cherished the esteem of her friends above everything, was plunged into guilty despair. Her passion for friendship, and for knowing intimate details of her friends' lives ("Tell me all about yourself . . . I wish to know you most truly in your secret depths.") meant that she was a repository of many secrets. Sometimes she violated these confidences, always in a good cause, because she was so fascinated by the processes by which her friends lived their lives that she wanted to share her knowledge, which frequently meant sharing her secrets.

Usually people respected her confidences, but sometimes they did not, and, in a small group where everyone knew each other's business, the effect could be devastating. As Margaret was to point out in her later writings, woman's preoccupation with the personal frequently leads her to trivial conversation, which degenerates into gossip, all for want of a genuine goal, a "high object" to her life. Much of what Margaret wrote she had learned through her own experience, of which the contretemps surrounding "Lost and Won" was an example. Margaret's illness, whatever its somatic base, followed immediately this crisis, and was nonetheless serious for being at least partly emotional in origin. In the midst of her fever and pain she heard her father say: "My dear, I have been thinking of you in the night, and I cannot remember that you have any *faults*. You have defects, of course, as all mortals have, but I do not know that you have a single fault." At least these are the words she remembered Timothy saying, and certainly they are the words she wanted to hear.

For someone who had tried to please all her life they were the ultimate expression of success, all the sweeter because, again according to her own testimony, they were her first acknowledgment from her stern taskmaster that all her work with Latin verbs and copying letters and tutoring children had pleased him at all. For someone preoccupied with creating a self as perfect as possible in accomplishment and character they have the ring of godly certitude, fittingly expressed by the source of family authority, her father. It is, in human form, the postconversion experience of sanctification, that attainment of perfection beyond which sin is no longer possible. It was a fitting climax to her earlier conversion experience, and, in terms of religious hopes of Protestantism, a token that she was saved.

She recovered quickly and entered an idyllic period of serving as her father's secretary and companion, the role they both had sought for her. The hours of reading Jefferson aloud and pondering Burke's knowledge of human nature were brief, for Timothy Fuller died quickly of Asiatic cholera in October, 1835. "The fates pursue me relentlessly," she was to write, and it sometimes seemed as if it were true. In the fall of 1835 Margaret faced that crisis so common to the New England girl of the nineteenth century, the problem of making a living. There was almost no money, the boys still needed some support, Ellen was too young to work, and Mrs. Fuller knew as little about how to survive as did Margaret. She was better educated than most, more intelligent than almost any, but her choices nonetheless were narrow. Fiction writing, which rescued many impecunious literary ladies, was either beyond her or beneath her, possibly both. She could have a little shop, but that was equally both more and less than she felt herself to be. Writing on German Romantics was what she wanted to do, and she had made a few tentative steps in that direction, but magazines which published articles like that, even when edited by her friends, did not pay.

There were really only two alternatives—she could teach or be a governess. In the year before she faced this reality, she stayed on at Groton, trying to finish some writing, to reconcile herself to the continuation of a life of supporting herself and others. Later she would write feelingly about the necessity of training girls to find in themselves the resources they needed to survive in a competitive world, and point out that the voluntary subjugation of woman was based largely on the assumption that man could and would provide for her. When man failed in his responsibility the world was left with a "vine with no support." The dream of going to Europe, an absolute necessity to her plans for her own achievement—"How am I to get the information I need, unless I go to Europe?"—faded into those other fantasies of freedom and happiness, of princes and genius.

During this transitional year she made an important friend, Ralph Waldo Emerson, whom she visited in Concord that summer of 1836, as he and Lydian returned from their honeymoon. Of all Margaret's pursuits in the search of "a divine friend" her tracking of Emerson was the most relentless. Harriet Martineau, the English writer of social criticism, whom Margaret had met earlier, had arranged the meeting between the two Idealists. Finally it happened and neither of them was ever quite the same. What each hoped for from the other we cannot know, but apparently, as in most relationships, they were both alternately sustained and disappointed. Certainly Margaret was looking for a mentor, someone who would teach her and would know more than she, not only about literature and philosophy, but about life. She was also looking for a lover, and perhaps hoped they could be from the same source. Emerson always admired good minds, but personalities sometimes frightened him. He took women seriously enough to write at some length about their moral and intellectual nature. Margaret was, perhaps, more woman than he counted on, at a time when his marriage and his career required most of his energy.

The coldness of which Margaret (and others) complained in Emerson's nature came partly from a sense of priority, and Margaret, dogged by the bad timing which characterized much of her life, entered his view too late for his first enthusiasms, too early for his more mellow middle-age. He could not give her what she wanted—it was one of the faults she noted in women, and one she herself possessed, that they expected men to be gods, and were disappointed when they saw their feet of flesh—but he did give her reluctant praise, which she found welcome. He also introduced her to his friends, one of whom, Amos Bronson Alcott, offered her a real job and a chance to move one step out into the world. Emerson reassured her that her "equipoise" was adequate for survival, something which, in that frightened year after her father's death, she often doubted. He consistently admired her strength of character, as well as her ideas. But he made it clear that his idea of a really good intellectual woman was his relative Sarah Ripley, who so agilely rocked a cradle, shelled peas, read a treatise on optics, and helped her husband tutor young scholars for Harvard. "The woman was not lost in the student," he noted approvingly. In contrast, the starvation of Margaret's affections was embarrassingly obvious and since he could do nothing, or chose to do nothing about satisfying them, she made him nervous, for all her gifts. It must have been with a sigh of relief that he passed her on to the ebullient Alcott.

Bronson Alcott, mercurial, improvident, and innovative, had one unfailing gift, he recognized a good teacher when he saw one. The highly charged, insecure, hyper-intellectual Miss Fuller would not have seemed to everyone the right choice to teach small boys and girls how to reason, but Alcott saw in her the qualities he most valued in people, and therefore in teachers, integrity, honesty, and the naive, overwhelming desire to know. Margaret never liked teaching much, but that does not mean she wasn't good at it. Alcott was satisfied, and his Temple School was an interesting outlet for her talents. She admired the respect with which he listened to the children's questions and the way he honestly made them feel they were sharing in knowledge, not acquiring a ready-made commodity from an impeccable source. He praised her patience and her imagination, her memory and her common sense. In his diary he speculated about the air of mystery, of something "secretive," "labyrinthine," "Egyptian" in her personality, which Emerson had noted and found puzzling and disturbing. Hawthorne's character, Zenobia, which most people thought used Margaret shamefully as a model, had the same quality of the unknown and unknowable about her. Part of it was the mystery of the virgin with its concomitant lure to all men to enlighten and destroy. Part of it was a deeper mystery of womanhood, the woman of the fates and the furies, dangerous to man because of knowledge and power beyond his comprehension.

Margaret, because she seemed like other women and yet different from them, fascinated and repelled more than one man. Hawthorne was more explicit than the others, perhaps more threatened. Alcott, less hostile, more humble, called her a "diviner," for she "read instinctively the mysteries of life and thought" and would translate them into "shining symbols to those competent to apprehend them." This quality of showing the student the possibilities of his own thoughts, imperfectly formed, haltingly spoken, was one Margaret exercised with her friends as well as with her students. Alcott, like Emerson and Channing and Greeley, could not resist a rather smug summary that Miss Fuller's problems came from having "the heart of a woman and the intellect of a man." This insight was neither profound nor accurate, but its prevalence tells us something about the views of women of even the most liberal men of Margaret's generation. Margaret herself was aware of the inadequacy of assigning certain traits or abilities by sex, and wrote about the dual nature of human beings very perceptively, but she was not above exclaiming that "it is a hard thing to have a woman's heart and a man's ambition." This rhetoric was very deep-rooted in nineteenth-century culture, and all the reformers and free-thinkers, suffragists and abolitionists and vegetarians alike, at least occasionally accepted it.

Teaching, even for Mr. Alcott, was boring and repetitious, and a long way removed from writing a life of Goethe. She wrote to Emerson, after Alcott's school had been closed down because of the protest following his *Record of Conversations on the Gospels*, that she had served time in a "purgatory of distracting, petty tasks." She looked to a visit with him to "purify and strengthen me to enter the Paradise of thought once more." A brief taste was all she was granted, for an offer to teach at the Greene Street School in Providence, at one thousand dollars a year, could not be refused, even though she rebelled at more "babbling" with the young and Providence, culturally, "might as well be Borneo."

During the two years she spent in Providence she did more than teach; she used her remoteness from the center of American thought to study and to think, translated Johann Eckermann's *Conversations with Goethe*, and, because of Goethe's interest in the visual arts as a means of expanding knowledge and experience, for the first time became aware of music and art. One of her biographers calls this chapter in her life, "The Lady Superior in Providence," which is a paraphrase of Margaret's own words and an apt summary of her attitude. There was always something of the convent about her, and this period of teaching and reflection intensified it. The private mysticism, which increasingly became her religion, projected herself as a kind of devotee at the shrines of learning. The Abbess Gunderode, Goethe's vehicle for mystical thought, purity, and nobility, was her ideal, and she was often annoyed at the way in which Bettina, "too brownie-like for my taste," with her quick insights, her spontaneous nature, appealed more to Emerson and Elizabeth Peabody than did the more spiritual Abbess. When Emerson addressed her as the "holiest nun" he knew, she considered it, as it was meant, a compliment. Her ideas on virginity would change, but she and the men she knew valued it highly.

To be a New England spinster was to be a kind of nun, and while people might pity the lack of a family and the warmth of knowing a husband's or child's love, there was real veneration for the service and selflessness of the spinster aunt, unmarried daughter, or bereaved fiancée. In this generation when the junior high school student bewails the "burden" of her virginity, this preoccupation may seem morbid and unnatural, but in withholding from man this test of her humanity and mortality, woman was exercising a degree of autonomy. The belief that to be a priestess, to have occult powers and to communicate with the divine, meant that it was necessary to be a virgin, was shared by much of the population. Fifty years later Helena Blavatsky produced a medical certificate proving she was virgo intacta (despite the incriminating evidence of a son) in order to validate her role as founder of a new religion. In order to give her role as savant, as critic, and as seer equal validity, Margaret's untouched quality was necessary. At the same time, because of the mystique of femininity, she could claim the intuition and the insight to see more than masculine intellect could discover. Goethe's words, "Think much, feel more," were her guidelines in this increasing stress on insight, as well as on intellect. Goethe was the "liberator, of the soul from the tyranny of intellectual knowledge," and by the time she left Providence Margaret felt it her inspired, her feminine prerogative, to assure Emerson that there were more things in life than were dreamt of in his philosophy.

Her students always brought her back to reality after her flights of Germanic fantasy. "The gulf is vast, wider than I could have conceived possible, between me and my students," she wrote glumly, but true to form, she worked with the material she had and, in the end, the harvest was good. She and her students, especially the older girls who were her chief responsibility, would share mutual goals of "general activity of mind, accuracy in processes, constant looking for principles and search after the true and the beautiful." These girls would become women, not "grown-up children." She believed, and her success in class confirmed her belief, that "young persons can be best guided by addressing their highest natures." She was pleased that she had resisted that constant temptation of the teacher, the desire to court popularity. "Every word of praise had been earned; all my influence over them was rooted in reality; I had never softened nor palliated their faults; I had appealed, not to their weakness, but to their strength. . . ."

She had succeeded, but it meant nothing, because the canvas was too small. Besides, the paperwork and the repetition were deadening. "Every year I live, I dislike routine more and more," she confided to Emerson. Opportunities for growth in the classroom were, no matter how she professed "mutuality," limited to the students. She felt she had shriveled in the process of their expansion. Providence was impossible, there was no one to talk to. "I see no divine person," she wrote to Emerson in their own argot, which has been so often ridiculed because misunderstood, "I myself am more divine than any I see." In her letters she tried to justify a decision she wanted to make, yet lacked the economic and personal security to do quickly. "I have gabbled and simpered and given my mind to the public view these two years back, till there seems to be no good left in me," she complained, and she had to leave while there was still time, before the routine and the recitation and the rhythm of the classroom would be her only choice. She bade a tearful farewell to her students; still weeping, she moved back home. She had formulated a definition of man's nature: "The earth is his school, if not his birthplace; God his object;

life and thought his means of interpreting nature and aspiring to God." She wanted to live and think and interpret, and she wanted to see her friends again.

From 1839 to 1844 she did all those things, she worked at her translations and edited the *Dial*, participated in the experiment at Brook Farm, established her Conversation Series and went to informal meetings of like-minded people. Back in the mainstream of American life, she became interested again in the quality of the political, as well as the cultural, achievements. The intellectual had by no means achieved his classic stance of alienation or isolation from politics, and the role of critic and seer involved political, as well as cultural standards. Particularly she thought about, worried about, and frequently wrote about, the situation of women in America. All of her experiences, the domestic life at home, the subjection of her father, the grim routine of the classroom and the joys of seeing growth in others, plus the wider experiences of these years were fermenting in her mind to bring her to the point where she could make her statement of herself and of all American women.

While trying both to support herself and her responsibility to the self she was destined to become—two tasks which were almost mutually exclusive—Margaret wrote Emerson for advice and received a few paragraphs later immortalized in his essay on "Self Reliance." "Power and Aim, the two halves of felicity seldomest meet," he defined frustration in general and hers in particular. "To feel and be heroic is surely doing something. . . . So let us deal justly, walk humbly, . ." and all the other ringing phrases. Channing claimed that Margaret chose her friends among "persons of scrupulous reserve, of modest coolness, and severe elevation of view" in an unconscious desire to balance the warmth of her own nature. If so, she got what she felt she deserved in this response. The others in the Hedge Club were equally vague when it came to giving her anything specific to do with her life or with her ambition. She was their equal when they met for conversation, but when they went back to their studies, to their parsonages, or, in rare unhappy cases, to their offices, she was only a woman again. Their company meant everything to Margaret, and the very fact of their existence, that there were a few people like herself who cared desperately about religion, reform, art, genius, gave her the most important opportunity of those years, the chance to express herself.

The world outside of Cambridge and Concord was beginning
to notice this group, and named them Transcendentalists, which
meant something vaguely impractical and slightly comic. It was
considered a valid criticism simply to point out that here was a
group of people who did nothing concrete in their lives, in itself to
be condemned in the tide of anti-intellectualism of that period. It
was just as bad for a woman to ignore her everyday duties as for
a man to be involved in such transitory activities as writing, perhaps worse, for it compromised the harmony of the home; if the
lady of the house was busy thinking, when would the socks get
darned? Every literary lady was at pains to point out that she
never lifted a pen until the last dish was done. The suffragists and
lady reformers insisted they never "shirked" a single domestic
duty, and in the same vein Margaret wrote with some asperity
when asked for a definition: "As to transcendentalism and the
nonsense which is talked by so many about it—I do not know what
is meant. For myself I should say that if it is meant that I have an
active mind, frequently busy with large topics I hope it is so—If it is
meant that I am honored by the friendship of such men as Mr.
Emerson, Mr. Ripley, or Mr. Alcott, I hope it is so—But if it is meant
that I cherish any opinions which interfere with domestic duties,
cheerful courage and judgment in the practical affairs of life, I
challenge any or all in the little world which knows me to prove
any such deficiency from any acts of mine since I came to woman's estate."

At this period in her life, Margaret clearly had no intention of
resigning her status as a True Woman, and was, for all her gifts,
very much in the context of her own time, a woman with both her
heart and her mind lacking focus and direction. Ripley would
change his politics, Alcott his reforms, and Orestes Brownson his
religion; Margaret came to change her ideas on womanhood.

When her translation of Goethe was published in 1839 she was
elated; now she was a full-fledged member of the club. From here
on she had a base of achievement, and some credentials for her
criticism. Like her friends she felt that the role of the intellectual
was essentially that of a critic, and she joined them in attacking
the direction of the country and the citizenry. Let the common man
call the Transcendentalists fools, dreamers, parasites. They answered back with Theodore Parker's sermons on the deficiencies
of the Boston merchants, with Emerson's essays on the creeping
blight of materialism, and with Margaret's slashing reviews of

philistine literature and dead souls. They called for a kind of political Reformation, going back to the principle and standards of
the early Republic as Luther had called for a return to the rigors
of the early Church. "Since the Revolution," Margaret wrote,
"there has been little, in the circumstances of this country, to call
out the higher sentiments. The effect of continued prosperity is
the same on nations as on individuals, it leaves the nobler faculties undeveloped. . . ." They wanted change, in politics, in society, and in art, and they talked and wrote and argued inces-
santly in order to achieve it. As a minority they gave up hoping
that freedom of religion and conscience would work on the masses
to produce "liberality of mind" or "vital religion." They would
work "from within outwards" to "quicken the soul" of all who
heard them, and to turn man into the divine being he was meant to
be, the inheritor of this new Jerusalem, rather than the "mere
comfort-loving inhabitant of earth" he had become. Their weapons
were the weapons of intellectuals—words.

Margaret's choice of a vehicle for her reform was one particularly
suited to her talents, the Conversation. Like most women who
wrote or thought, she had often been compared to and compared
herself with Madame De Staël and her heroine Corinna. Corinna
had been an inspired talker, improvising, speculating, drawing conclusions and examining nuances and subtleties lost to the ordinary
observer or to the person so constricted as to need a script. Females were suited to the conversational art, according to Emerson, it showed them at their finest and highest moment. And, like
so many female arts, it defied translation into the material, it lost
something in becoming concrete written prose. There was an element of the seance, the trance, about these performances but it
was fairly rare. Most of the time spent was used in Margaret's
analysis and in the questions and responses it provoked. The Conversation was not only a means to display Margaret's genius, but
a means to advance the cause of womanhood.

From autumn, 1839, until she left for New York five years later,
Margaret offered the women of Boston the opportunity to think
with her about the role of women in the past, the present, and the
future. The "well-educated and thinking woman" of Boston was, as
Margaret knew all too well, given very little real substance in her
intellectual diet, even in the city with the greatest pretensions to
culture in the nation. Margaret intended her Conversations "To

systematize thought, and give a precision and clearness in which our sex are so deficient, chiefly, I think because they have so few inducements to test and clarify what they receive." The women Margaret met seemed to ask the same questions she asked herself daily, "What were we born to do?" "And how shall we do it?" To support herself, she charged a fee for these conversations.

A group of ladies representing the best in mercantile and intellectual Boston came in response to her call. The following year she had a series for both sexes, but the more successful talks were only for the ladies. Helping women help themselves was her true vocation, for which her mysticism and her feminism had long been preparing her. She was determined to have class discussion, as well as the stimulation of lecture and reading. Although she preferred spontaneous oral participation, when shyness or fear of being thought silly inhibited the first sessions she told the women to write down their thoughts, and she read aloud the best comments at the next session, counting on her praise to provoke discussion. Each contribution, shyly and hesitatingly put forth, was received with respect, and would often provoke a flight of fancy on Margaret's part that left the questioner impressed with her own acuteness, unsuspected until now. Margaret never scolded or criticized; helping women, as she knew from her own youth and from her teaching experience, was frequently working with the wounded, where egos had been battered and confidence maimed by male arrogance and a culture which preached submission.

The records we have of these talks are unsatisfactory. Part of the fault may lie with one of the transcribers, Caroline Dall, who felt herself rejected among Margaret's admirers and who constantly bemoaned Margaret's preference for other unworthier souls. This undoubtedly made her a less than accurate secretary. Nonetheless even her imperfect records show that Margaret did, what Emerson had noted she often had the power to do, "detect an Immortal under every disguise in every lurking place." To show women that they had thinking minds, as well as feeling hearts and angelic spirits, was Margaret's special vocation. Her techniques of challenge, response, encouragement, and fantasy resulted in what we would consider the raising of consciousness.

The topics themselves were seemingly far removed from the issues of the day such as abolition, temperance, peace or women's rights. Margaret titled her lecture series, "The Greeks" and talked of the way Greek art reflected their philosophy. But teaching through parable and analogy is nothing new, and the universal application of Greek thought made it possible to say a great deal about contemporary issues without ever mentioning them by name. The women in her classes were vital, interesting people, many of them married to the best minds in America. Margaret would have considered it vulgar to be relevant in her choice of material; with the women in her group, it was unnecessary. The contemporary application of universal principle was left to the individual hearer, when she left the group and went about her domestic routines. A study of the Greeks emphasized Margaret's interpretation of Greek morality, the absolute right of moral choice which conferred with it absolute moral freedom, not to be abridged by differences in sex, race, or creed. An awakened moral sense, combined with a will bound by conscience and a mind trained to evaluate evidence constituted the truly just person, and that power lay in women as well as in men.

For the six years in which she gave her talks she preached on the same theme, although the subjects varied. Always she stressed the value of the individual, the free will, the enlightened intellect, and the awakened sense of moral responsibility. No allegiance to a church could preclude the right of choice, no hiding behind the authority of the man of the house could abrogate the necessity of a right conscience to make its own choices. As revolutionary doctrine it was quite effective, the more so because she did not use the faddish vocabulary of the "isms" of the period, and avoided both revolutionary and transcendental jargon. If the church or the man or even the country was wrong, it must be made right, by principles translated into action. The Greeks no doubt had a word for it; Margaret called it awakening.

After her performances Margaret suffered the let-down of the actress or the medium. Moreover she still had not answered her own questions of vocation and destiny. "With the intellect I always have, always will overcome; but that is not half the work. The life, the life! O my God, shall the life never be sweet?" Hours of attention to the problems of women made her apply her original standards even more intensely to herself. "I cannot be supposed to have felt so much the wants of others, without feeling my own still more deeply," she had written to defend herself against the charges of arrogance. Her students thought her remarkable; she knew how far she fell short of her goals for herself, which were the highest she could formulate. The Conversations exhausted and depressed her in much the same way as had her teaching; she had momentary triumphs only to see how hollow they were; and she knew that the answers which satisfied her students, were only the questions she was beginning to ask of herself.

One interesting question was asked by William White, brother of the first Mrs. James Russell Lowell, Maria White. Why, the young man wanted to know, was Genius Masculine and Wisdom Feminine. Margaret answered that "The very outlines of the feminine form were yielding, and we could not associate them with a prominent self-conscious state of the faculties. Wisdom was like women always ready to fight if necessary, yet never going to it; taking reality as a basis, and classifying and arranging uppermost all that Genius creates—seeing the relations and proper values of all things." Margaret now admitted that she was not to be a genius after all. She had been moving toward that conclusion for several years; it was the theme of a deprecatory poem about herself she wrote on her twenty-sixth birthday and dedicated to William Ellery Channing:

> Since I no longer on myself depend,
> But seek in God the only perfect friend,
> I have been deeply tried, nor wanting found
> In honor, faith, or zeal, by those around.
> But all that early friends might deem
> Genius vanished like the morning's idle dream.
> Long I refused to let the Ideal go.
> But would persist to clasp it here below.
> At last I yield. 'Tis o'er. I feel it now;
> I must live with the little and the low;
> Father! give grace such toils to dignify;
> And let me do them as if done for thee!
> Thus, though unknown and unadmired by men
> I shall with Thee commune, and to Thy plan divine
> Breathe out a deep Amen.

Now she saw herself as the reflective and analytic instrument for making the genius of the world available and comprehensible to others. She believed that she could, in her writing, as in her teaching and conversations, find the best in American and European literature, explain to people why it was good and why it would help them to read it. There is a certain rueful quality about the kind of maturity that admits it will not write the great American novel but it might possibly write a good book review. From this time on, it was her critical, rather than her creative abilities, which she enlarged and developed.

When she took over the editorship of *The Dial*, a quarterly journal of Transcendental thought, in 1840, she offered as her only achievements of thirty years her ability "to form my character to a certain consistency, cultivate my tastes, and learn to tell the truth with a little better grace than I did at first." In other words, she had become a critic. Having decided that her own intellectual bent was in this direction it is typical that she decided that almost all women were wise, rather than geniuses. Her new job required less wisdom than fortitude. She had to cope with deadlines, with writers who wanted to be paid when there was no money, and with the faithful waiting for "the Gospel of Transcendentalism" to be sent to them. She hoped for "a perfectly free organ to be offered for the expression of individual thought and character." This meant it was her duty to offend some of the people all of the time, and she did.

Besides her work as editor she contributed reviews and essays to the periodical. Two were particularly important. The first, "A Short Essay on Critics" gave her high standards for the vocation she had chosen. It was predictable that having decided she was meant to be a critic, Margaret would insist that the profession itself be made worthy of her. Margaret had high hopes for American literature, although as yet they were largely unrealized. She particularly looked to the writers of this new country to treat women realistically and intelligently. Margaret wanted all literature produced in and about her country to be grand, on a scale commensurate with the moral and material superiority of which it was capable, although it fell so short of its potential.

In her years in New York her critical pen grew very sharp; some said as sharp as her tongue. When Channing, that gentle soul, once remonstrated with her for undue severity, she answered that a priestess must reserve her praise for Apollo. If man were given the role of genius, she would accord him his title only if he deserved it fully. She would be in the service only of that which was genuinely divine. Besides, in the flush of national enthusiasm, there was ridiculous praise for everything written by Americans, and that was worse than the wholesale ridicule heaped by many European critics on any "provincial" literature. To say what was true, and expose pretense and sham, was her aim, and it made her a formidable adversary.

The thin-skinned among American poets and writers found her unfair, and worse, unfeminine in her unsparing judgments. American literature was a tender sapling; any spurt of growth should be encouraged; time enough to prune and thin out the plants when they were better established. In these early days, encourage anything that poked its head above ground. But Margaret's standards were too high for chauvinism, whether in the cause of her country or of her sex. She was uncompromising in insisting that only the best was worthy, of a country or of a woman, and she was firm in her conviction that the best was always possible to those who had the will to seek it. In allocating to herself and to her sex the role of mentor, Margaret accepted again a cultural stereotype of woman, as the reformer. Her notion of woman sternly redirecting man was on a higher level than the wife reforming her drunken husband or the little girl remonstrating with an irreligious father, but the role itself was the same. The price man would have to pay for his genius was that it be directed and controlled by female wisdom.

In her criticism she always discussed a book's approach to women. Charles Brockden Brown received her warm approval for what she considered tracts on feminism, since he placed a "thinking royal mind" in a woman's body. Brown's heroines were proof of what she believed to be true, "that *feminine* is not a synonym for *weak*." Alfieri was specially singled out as sound in his handling of female character. Instead of seeing women as a hindrance to male genius and creativity (a point of view which must have rankled Margaret enormously, since it was directly counter to her own division of creative labor, and was expressed by Nathaniel Hawthorne so often, in spite of her best efforts to convert him.) Alfieri thought females "a high stimulus, a pure solace, and an alluring example to every beautiful work."

This allocation of roles, based on what was appropriate to the sexes, figured increasingly in Margaret's writing, and was tentatively explored in a second important piece she wrote for the *Dial* on the relations between men and women, "The Great Lawsuit." Later she would expand this to the much less colorfully and ac-

curately titled *Woman in the Nineteenth Century*. She published
many poems and articles by women, not specifically feminist although perhaps to the discerning eye a poem like Ellen Sturgis'
"Duty and Beauty" was a trenchant commentary on female reality.
Sophia Ripley's article on "Woman," a bitter and militant piece
which deserves to be better known, appeared in the *Dial*. But the
most important statement on feminism came, as was proper, from
her own pen.

This article, as well as any other, shows the difference between
Margaret, as critic, author and Transcendentalist, and Emerson,
who, in what he called a "rotation of martyrdom" took over the
burden of deadlines and unpaid bills in July, 1842. If Emerson
was a Transcendental optimist, Margaret could be characterized
as a Transcendental pessimist. Perhaps the difference in sex is
sufficient explanation for the difference in outlook. Margaret occasionally allowed herself to hope for a better world, but she never
had real faith in it, for all her striving. For her there was the malevolent Daemon who, notwithstanding the beneficent All, was
out to get her and would probably succeed. "I have no belief in
beautiful lives; we were born to be mutilated; Life is basically
unjust," at least if you are born into it as a woman, a point she
made vigorously in "The Great Lawsuit." She half-clung to a
druidic belief that "the Divine Fire" would replace the blood that
life drained, but that offered little consolation for this life. Sex is
the root of pessimism, at least in a sexist world. "Woman is the
flower, man the bee. She sighs out melodious fragrance, and in-
vites the winged laborer. He drains her cup, and carries off the
honey. She dies on the stalk; he returns to the hive, well fed, and
praised as an active member of the community." Since the exercise
of purely female values and virtues led to victimization and ex-
ploitation, it is not surprising that Margaret increasingly explored
the possibility of what Caroline Heilbron has called "the andro-
gynous vision" as an antidote to male/female dichotomy.

The character reader and phrenologist, John Neal, had once
told her, "You are a woman of contrasts, Miss Fuller." Parentive-
ness challenged Ideality and Amativeness struggled with Adhesiveness. "There is man in you as well as woman. There is scholar
in you as well as teacher. There is child as well as mother. There is
love in you, too." This made sense to her in the light of her own
experience, for she had once written, "It is true that a woman

may be in love with a woman, and a man with a man." In her diary she noted an epigram to the effect that woman has a cell less in the brain and a chord more in the heart. While she disagreed with the sentiment, she found correct the notion "that distinction of sex lies not in opposition but in distribution and proportion of attributes. Whether this dualism will always continue I know not but at present we cannot conceive of active happiness without it." And yet, for her, trapped in this conventional view of happiness attained only by fulfilling the criteria of female virtues, there was the problem of her own nature, "man as well as woman." No wonder she asked in her journal, "Will there never be a being to combine a man's mind and a woman's heart?" for only in such a being could her own duality find fulfillment. Deliberately she chose the carbuncle, the "masculine" stone of knowledge and power, as her charm, and wore it always.

In a later love affair she mistakenly used the feminine form of the endearment "mein liebste" and explained the slip by saying, "Was not that mistake an instinct, seeking the woman in you, when myself was in the melting mood?" Men and women were but "the two halves of one thought," and, as she explained in *Woman in the Nineteenth Century*, the development of one required the development of the other. It was unjust and untrue to give all the heroic virtues to men; women had courage and perseverance. Goethe had approved of the noble woman "who could be a father to her children," and Margaret claimed for American woman in particular this right to share a heroic destiny. Sex, after all, was only an accident of birth. In a democracy there is no aristocracy, or rank, whether of wealth, lineage or sex; it is unworthy and ignoble. Still the trap had been prepared and although she admitted her own dual nature, she was not sure the world as presently constituted could fuse these elements. Perhaps in some future glory of the Republic, when discrimination and sexual polarity had been banished, then "from the union of this tragic king and queen, shall be born a radiant sovereign self." In the meantime, she left her responsibilities as an editor and used her energies for her Conversations and for her own writing.

The pessimism with which she viewed her own chances for success somewhat influenced her opinions of George Ripley's experimental commune, Brook Farm. Even Emerson found the scheme impractical, "a French Revolution in a patty pan:" the incongruity of perfect life on a ramshackle New England farm offended his sense of propriety. Ripley wanted to achieve "a more pure, more lovely, more divine state of society than was ever realized on earth," and he wanted his friends to help him do it. Margaret never joined the group, although she was a frequent visitor, and sent her brother Lloyd there to try to curb his intractable behavior. Her major ideological objection to Brook Farm was that it was dedicated to the many and she to the individual; it concentrated on improving society and her whole life was an attempt at self-culture, and at reaching society only through the improved one. More practically, the sparse living that went along with the high thinking did not appeal to her, and it was well known that when Miss Fuller visited she would have the only china cup in the house to drink the several cups of coffee that the majority of the community had rejected as an "unnatural" stimulant.

She gave lectures on women, and found to her surprise that in the "sans culottes" atmosphere which pervaded the commune, her listeners did not give her the upright posture and nodding respectful head she had come to expect of her audience. Instead they sprawled on the floor in various stages of revolutionary undress, yawned when the rhetoric flowed too freely, and wandered in and out as their affinities moved them. Disconcerted and yet intrigued, she modified her approach in order to meet the challenge of these blythe young spirits, but, as she had expected, the group was not for her; her success came with the individual women who sought her out, and confided their emotional and marital problems to her privately. Young girls, like Georgianna Bruce, found her thrilling and an example of what woman could become. She encouraged them to do what they wanted to do, whether get married or go West to teach school, and she spurred the timid to follow their will by stirring anecdotes, confidences of her own or her friends' experiences, and occasionally by the gift of money.

During her Brook Farm visits she tried to know Nathaniel Hawthorne better, but he resisted her advances. She found Hawthorne very much to her taste because he "combined delicate tenderness to understand the heart of a woman, with quiet depth and manliness enough to satisfy her" as she wrote to his fiancée, Sophia Peabody. Perhaps in this case that "penetration" into the depths of another's consciousness, which Channing thought caused Margaret to be "so dreaded, in general society, by superficial observers" went too close to the bone for Hawthorne's comfort. In any case, during her lifetime they had at best an uneasy truce. Sophia was very impressed by Margaret, although she felt that "marriage and a few babies" would have changed many of her views, as well as made her a nicer person. Hawthorne's letters and diary show that he was alternately drawn to and repelled by Margaret's "magnetic" personality. His portrait of Zenobia, which his contemporaries insisted was taken from Margaret's life, was probably a composite of several women seen through his own prism. The friends of a novelist usually resign themselves to being portrayed in some guise in fiction, and take their chances on fair treatment. If Zenobia was a tragic flawed creature, she was the product of a flawed society, and the reader's sympathy is with her for having dared much. In all his "dark" women, Hawthorne admires them for trying to be more than the general, just before he condemns them inexorably for having gone too far.

The novelist's punishment was the same meted out by the Daemons, and Margaret herself would not have quarrelled with its reality, however she protested its justice. Hawthorne's diatribes after her death and the nasty little tirade on her husband tell more about Nathaniel Hawthorne than about Margaret Fuller. Perhaps he had hoped that Margaret could dare the fates successfully, and he was disappointed when she "fell, a very woman." His "blond" heroines, who wore the pearl of innocence rather than the carbuncle of knowledge, keep to their sphere and are rewarded by peaceful lives. Fear that to dare, to risk is the only game which makes life worth living and yet a game the prudent man is afraid to play, may have been responsible for Hawthorne's anger. His frustration was with the gods, who would treat men badly in proportion to their courage, and treat women, so much closer to the center of divine mystery, the worst of all. It was better to play it safe, and not to risk *hubris*, or so Hawthorne said in his work. Margaret disagreed in theory, and the last years of her life were a flagrant contradiction in fact. Hawthorne hoped she might prove the exception to the decrees of fate in a disordered world, and hated her for proving him right after all, since the proof showed how far society needed to go and how unlikely it was to make the changes in his lifetime.

Brook Farm was for Margaret, as it was for Hawthorne, an experiment in which they had high hopes but little faith. Margaret's hopes were partly based on the possibility that the devouring furies were not determined to destroy everyone, that she alone had been picked for their victim. The more she saw of other women, with the possible exception of those few lucky enough to marry men of strength and gentleness, the more she believed that all women were destined for unhappiness, unless change was affected. The most admirable thing about the Farm was its striving for perfection, the goal to which she had dedicated her life. Although she doubted that anything important could be done in a group, she saw that a climate of enthusiasm and support could generate individual will to succeed. Transcendentalism was by no means the only aspect of Protestant thought preaching perfectionism during these decades; it permeated most of the traditional churches and its spirit was in all the institutions of the nation. It was a particularly liberating doctrine for women who could use it as a rationale to throw off the bonds of original sin and predestined, sex-oriented roles. If will power could produce change in this life, and women possessed wills and had religious experiences to confirm them, then women could expect some change in their status and expectations.

Margaret understood this movement towards change, and rejoiced in it. For herself, though, particularly in this period, she felt herself torn between her destiny—that dim sense of unrealized greatness of which she had been conscious nearly all her life—and her daemons, those forces determined to maim and destroy her, perhaps in direct proportion to her success. Her own religion emerged as a blend of Unitarianism, a transcendent faith in flawed but potentially divine human nature to seek its home in God, and her mysticism, a "listening for the secret harmonies of nature." She anticipated the incomplete God of William James, who needed man in order to function, and she inserted her will as a necessary part of her religion. "For myself, I believe in Christ because I can do without him; . . . but I do not wish to do without him. He is constantly aiding and answering me . . . When he comes to me I will receive him; when I feel inclined to go by myself, I will." The sexual component of her mysticism is clearly shown in this quotation, as she creates through her will a bridegroom who ravishes or leaves unsatisfied as she chooses. It is her credo of mystical feminism, the statement of independence and mutuality which, if denied in earthly lovers, she insisted on from her God.

Her period of retreat and reappraisal ended with the welcome invitation of James Freeman Clarke and his sister Sarah to accompany them on a trip West. From May to September 1843 they visited the prairies of Illinois and Wisconsin. To her surprise Chicago was blighted by "the fatal spirit of imitation, of reference to European standards . . ." which checked any original growth, and Milwaukee was dismissed as "almost as tame as New England." Most upsetting of all was "the unfitness of women for their new lot." When the party reached Mackinac Island, the Indian women proved more interesting and impressive. With a degree of anthropological relativity rare in her time Margaret compared the dreary rubber-stamp white culture with the more individual and vital Indian society. "The civilized man is a larger mind but a more imperfect nature than the savage." The results of her observations were in her first original book, *Summer On the Lakes*, published in 1844.

The plight of women in the West occupied her mind. They lacked both domestic or artistic skills and physical strength, and were without even artificial means provided in the city to cover the poverty of their natures. The poorer women, slatterns though they were, could be pitied; the so-called "ladies" were only to be scorned. "Accustomed to the pavement of Broadway, they dare not tread the wild-wood paths for fear of rattlesnakes." Moreover they insisted on sending their daughters back East to be "polished" which was precisely "the measure most likely to make them useless and unhappy" when they returned. It was clear that women throughout the land needed help, and not everyone could come to Boston for her Conversations. As soon as the manuscript of her Western travels was finished, Margaret began expanding her *Dial* article on women's nature and role. She saw this work as patriotic as well as feminist in tone, for, like most of her friends, she was increasingly concerned at the moral turpitude of a nation drifting into imperialism and shutting its eyes to slavery. If the West, the last hope of natural virtue, was producing specimens so inferior, then the time for action was at hand. Her book on the West had one important effect, it caught the eye of Horace Greeley, whose own advice on going West was to be quoted so often, and influenced his offer to her of the post of literary critic on his New York *Daily-Tribune*. During the last months of 1844 she worked on her manifesto on women, and prepared to leave New England and go to New York. When the book was finished she wrote Channing that she felt "a delightful glow, as if I had put a good deal of my true life in it; as if, suppose I went away now, the measure of my foot print would be left on the earth."

Woman in the Nineteenth Century stands with Mary Wollstonecraft's *Vindication of the Rights of Women* as one of the most important statements of feminist method and theory in history. The two books, so often compared, were based on different arguments, although their conclusions were similar. Wollstonecraft's arguments, published in 1792, were the arguments of natural law and the divine right of women to claim their due as children of God and nature. Fuller's reasoning, published in 1845, was that woman possessed the same intellect as man, the same will, and therefore might have similar hopes of self-culture and achievement. The idiom of Margaret's book was totally American, and its success came at least as much from its timing as from its content. The Women's Rights Convention of 1848 found her book as convenient a manual as the Constitutional Convention had found John Locke's treatise on liberty. It wasn't necessary to read it, but it was comforting to know it existed as rationale and reinforcement for doing what you were going to do anyway.

Comparisons between Wollstonecraft's and Fuller's prose are less intriguing than comparisons between the two lives, both cut so short and both so influenced by their backgrounds and their time. The role of an overwhelming external force—the French Revolution and the Italian Republic—and the counterbalance of a brief but happy marriage, make these two feminists virtually unique in their nations' history. The many other similarities (they shared a taste for unworthy men, both found sympathy from a long-suffering publisher, supported their families, and even had the same kind of headaches) which led in both cases to the publication of their books on women, and to their subsequent effort to adapt their lives to their prose as well as their significant and deliberate failure to practice what they preached when their own hearts were concerned, are a commentary not only on the parallels of two important feminists, but on the lack of change over a fifty-year period in two democratic and liberal nations. Mary Wollstonecraft died in childbirth; Margaret Fuller in a shipwreck. Sometimes one is tempted to believe that the Fates did have a special interest in feminists after all.

In her book Margaret ignored the need to vote or to rule. For the present it was necessary "as a nature to grow, as an intellect to discern, as a soul to live freely and unimpeded, to enfold such powers as were given to her when we left our common home." The substance of woman must be recognized first; the accidents —professions, suffrage, changes in family roles—would follow. She considers the fears of those who would deny women the right to self-expression and shows the restraint with which she turned even stupid questions to good account. She concedes that some intellectual women may have neglected their domestic duties in the pursuit of their literary or artistic lives, but this is the unfortunate exception, not the rule, and she gives examples and anecdotes of famous women who were "some of the most devoted mothers the world has ever known, and whose homes were the abode of every domestic virtue." She reassures the man who feared women would take what belonged to him that "Were they free, . . . fully to develop the strength and beauty of Woman; they would never wish to be men, or man-like."

Since marriage was the destiny of most women, Margaret described the four possible kinds of marriage. The first and most common is the "household partnership" where the woman looks for someone "smart but kind" while the man searches for a "capable, sweet-tempered" wife. They have an efficient working relationship, each runs his own affairs competently, and they meet at meals to discuss their separate worlds with affection and respect. "The wife praises her husband as a 'good provider;' the husband, in return, compliments her as a 'capital housekeeper.' " A second type was that based on "mutual idolatry" which was romantic and lovely, but rarely lasted beyond the first year. A third type was of "intellectual companionship," but just as mutual idolatry stressed only the physical side of marriage, so platonic friendship stressed only the mental, and something important was left out of each. The fourth type, "religious marriage" consisted in the "pilgrimage toward a common shrine." It included all the best elements of the first marriage types, but had the higher ingredient of a shared plunge into the divine abyss. Whether through marriage or without it, woman, like man, must fulfill the law of her being and nature. At that moment, once she knows herself, the marriage relationship and all other relationships will be "harmonized" and she can move, self-propelled by her own will, relying on her own abilities now understood and appreciated, to her God-given destiny.

It is not a bitter book, or at least it tries not to be. "Man is not willingly ungenerous," she says gently. "He wants faith and love, because he is not yet himself an elevated being." Three men can in fact be found who were worthy to be called "prophets of the coming age"—Swedenborg, Fourier, and, of course, Goethe. These men appreciate the fact that all of mankind must be improved, male as well as female, and that each must help the other half, according to his special talents and powers. Man has failed rather badly in the way he has used women in the civilization built on his superiority, and prostitution and the marriage of convenience are two concrete examples of his frailty. Because man is only human, woman must not make him her god. She should not cultivate her gifts simply to make herself a better wife or mother, which was a pious aphorism in urging female education: "The intellect, no more than the sense of hearing, is to be cultivated merely that Woman may be a valuable companion to Man." Intellect, like any gift of God, should be developed because "its mere existence signifies that it must be brought out toward perfection." The first voyage for every woman must be the voyage of exploration. She must accept the reality of her own intellect and will, and no longer accept the low estimate put on them by mistaken men in an imperfect world. Once she sees her potential she should move to develop it, and nothing should stop her, not even love, from achieving her highest goals.

In some ways Woman, not Man, was the Enemy, and she must free herself from the chains she has helped to forge by agreeing with the dichotomy of values and roles, and accepting moral superiority in exchange for intellectual and volitional equality. Pleasant though it may be to be "led and taught by men," women must exert self-discipline and do it, all of it, herself. She should not fall by the wayside, in thrall to the love of one man, but continue her journey, alone if necessary, until she is "good enough and strong enough to love one and all beings" from the "fullness not the poverty" of her achieved self. "I would have her free from compromise, from complaisance, from helplessness." As she emerged to a new consciousness of womanhood she would see, as Margaret herself increasingly saw, the constant merging of the sexes. "Fluid hardens to solid, solid rushes to fluid. There is no wholly masculine man, no purely feminine woman"; at least there need not be. But as things were presently constituted "the lot of Woman is sad. She is constituted to expect and need a happiness that cannot exist on earth. She must stifle such aspirations within her secret heart, and fit herself, as well as she can, for a life of resignation and consolation. . . . The man is not born for the woman, only the woman for the man."

Woman could not change herself, without changing society, and Margaret told women to speak out against slavery, to tell men that unless they behaved morally they were not fit fathers, lovers, sons. The work that was needed to be done would be done by women, for women. Men need only remove the "arbitrary barriers" which, in their pride and ignorance, they had erected, and which now stood in the way of their own perfection, more than in the way of woman's achievement. Perfection of the race can come only when both sexes are free, and when the inequities done to the Red Man and the Black Man, as well as to women, are righted. The United States must fulfill its special destiny as "the chosen land for moral law." And as part of that fulfillment "woman's turn must come, it is the destiny of the land, the inexorable epic law." The inevitability of American greatness and female equality emerges as a major theme of Margaret's book, the drive to greatness that admits no barrier, geographic, political, or sexual. The destiny of Americans is equality before God, and "there is no sex in souls."

There is an autobiographical passage where Margaret acknowledges her debt to her father for his gift of "a dignified sense of self-dependence," (and, one might add, for leaving her in the position of having to depend on herself in order to survive). If one woman could do it herself, then all women who chose independence should be granted the right and the means to achieve their aims, without artificial rules or roles standing in their way. Rather than standing by taunting "Girls can't do that; girls can't play ball" like nasty schoolboys, men should help women by encouragement and example. The rare woman of genius, like Mary Wollstonecraft or George Sand, could survive in even a hostile atmosphere (but at what cost only later biographies have told us), but a more congenial climate would bring out the abilities even of the timid, and enrich the world. Men can keep their money, fame, and status symbols, what women need and demand is "the birthright of every being capable of receiving it,—the freedom, the intelligent freedom of the universe to use its means, to learn its secret, as far as Nature has enabled them, with God alone for their guide and their judge."

There is a brief passage on the social value of Old Maids as "saints and sibyls," necessary in a society as complex as nine-teenth-century society was becoming. Unencumbered by a hus-band, the "wise virgin" could spend her time contemplating the mysteries of truth and love, and use her knowledge "for the good of all" instead of only for her family. In an Indian tribe a woman who wished to remain celibate was allowed to do so after she dreamed she was betrothed to the Sun. "She built her wigwam apart, filled it with emblems of her alliance, and means of an in-dependent life." With such a "room of her own" a woman could make her contribution to society, as well as to her own goals. Following this passage, and connected to it by the thread of Mar-garet's own life—for here, as always, she extrapolated the general from her particular experience—is a discussion of the problems of the woman of special gifts, who "sees too much" to conform to the general standards, and is condemned by people who cannot understand her vision. Such women are likely "to be enslaved by an impassioned sensibility" and have weaker bodies as a result of their consuming fires of genius. Women of this sort might have their intellect trained to match the power of their sensibilities. Mysticism was the natural outlet of these women, for it gave an "oracular promise" to them with prototypes of Eve and the Virgin-Mother.

Women had been taught to believe that men had stronger pas-sions than they, "of a sort that it would be shameful for them to share or even to understand." They must submit to their husband's will because "the least appearance of coldness or withdrawal" is wicked, and might "turn her husband's thoughts to illicit indul-gence; for a man is so constituted that he must indulge his pas-sions or die!" Yet women's passions were expected to be checked and curbed, not only physically, but in terms of their ambitions. Margaret's solution in 1845 was for men to attain "if not asceticism" at least some "degree of power over the lower self." Women must assert their will in order to save man from his lower nature, and he then would help her in achieving the liberation of her higher nature. The tendency of our time is to reject this advice as so much Victorian prudishness, but until better means of birth control were devised, the ability of a woman to achieve her goals was at least partially dependent on her ability to limit the size of her family. To do this it was necessary either to be celibate or to live with a man who accepted the principle of self-control. Perhaps it was a choice between two evils, but it was the only choice Margaret and most of these early feminists could devise, given the realities of early marriage, and increasing life-spans. Margaret here accepted the prevailing nineteenth-century scientific and ethical notion that women were able to call a halt to passion more easily than man, partly because of their physiology and partly because of their moral superiority. "If women have any power, it is a moral power," she said, in urging her readers to boycott the war in Texas.

In her conclusions she stressed the importance of an independence arrived at through any legitimate means. "Let them be sea-captains," she flung at the world, or anything else that would pay the rent and remove their child-woman status, and restore the dignity that had been eroded through generations of degraded marriage and unworthy devotion. For her sanctions she invoked "the law of right, the law of growth, that speaks in us, and demands the perfection of each being in its kind—apple as apple, Woman as Woman." Growth to perfection, by the force of the freed will, in the favorable latitude of this new country—the hyperbole of transcendentalism, patriotism, and the do-it-yourself manual which admits to no such obstacles as limited time, energy, or ability, and assumes that serendipity, not disaster, follows the exertion of the sincere seeker.

The force of Margaret's language shocked some of her reviewers, when the book was published by Greeley in 1845. They attacked her for writing about prostitution and passion, and challenged her right to advise women at all, when she was neither a wife nor mother. There were also good reviews, many of them from friends, and a degree of fame which was new and pleasant. (Perhaps more typical of the time than either the favorable or unfavorable reviews, were the posthumous reviews of Margaret's *Memoirs*, which forgave her the excesses of *Woman in the Nineteenth Century* since her last years as wife and mother had proved her a true woman after all.) By the time it was published she was living in New York and had entered a new phase of her career.

Margaret's decision to leave New England and her family was received with noticeable coldness by her friends; if they did not, for the most part, criticize her choice, they did not offer encouragement either. New England represented more than home to Margaret and the literary and cultural life of Boston was permeated with values and assumptions, many of them admirable, even noble, which were assumed to be so sacred that they ought not to be challenged. When Emily Dickinson said she "saw New Englandly" it was a proud admission, but an admission, nonetheless, that other perspectives existed and were not explored. To go to New York was to accept a wider field of vision, in which there was much not exalted, much merely fashionable or flashy, but then as now, much of great color and human activity. "New York is the focus," wrote Miss Fuller, the *Tribune's* first female correspondent, when she was preparing to leave the city two years later, " . . . twenty months have presented me with a richer and more varied exercise for thought and life, than twenty years could in any other part of these United States."

Away from the fond but encompassing gaze of people she had known all her life, she could explore new paths in literature and thought; she could be the person she still wanted to become, not the Margaret they all thought they knew so well. New York also had the pleasurable stigma of the city of sin. If not yet Babylon on the Hudson, it was in the process of building its reputation, and the young woman who ventured there without the guardianship of father or husband was, as Margaret so fervently wished to do, taking her life in her hands. Margaret came to know parts of New York which her New England friends only direly suspected were there, and she felt her own life of scrupulous correctness was enriched for the knowledge. She did not accept the Calvinist dictum that in knowing evil the soul loses its innocence and strength. To her, knowledge was power and compassion, particularly when women were involved. In New York she met women she could never have known in Boston, and herself had the opportunity to try out different aspects of her own womanhood.

She had written about many states of life and emotion common to woman's lot which she had known only vicariously. The quality of empathy so strongly marked in her nature made it possible for her to understand and identify with the problems of the women who sought her confidence, and to imagine the heartbreak of those about whom she read or heard. She had, however, done rather little living. Her few romantic interests had merged, not without pain, into another epistolary relationship or brotherly companionship. Her friends were deep, but in some ways they were narrow, at least insofar as permutations in life styles was concerned. It was hard for them, and remained hard for them, to accept even the reality, much less the necessity or goodness of a woman making a choice other than spinsterhood or domesticity. The liberalism of the Cambridge group extended to aesthetics, politics, and religion; it did not go so far as to liberate the body of woman, although it was concerned with freeing her mind.

Woman in the Nineteenth Century has a kind of certitude and confidence that its author's life, at least to this point, noticeably lacked. It is necessary for the how-to manual to ignore the untidy ends of human life and assume that, with proper guidance from a firm hand, the future will march in straight lines. Theory and fact merge only rarely in the life of the initiator, who knows the weakness of his own argument in the face of the moment's caprice or urgency. Thomas Jefferson abandoned his theories on strict construction to buy Louisiana; Wilson paid no attention to his own treatise on *Constitutional Government* (although perhaps he ought to have re-read it) when he lobbied for the League of Nations; Franklin ignored his own advice regularly in search of more robust pleasures than health, wealth, or wisdom; and Mary Wollstonecraft's life was often a repetition of all the pitfalls and mistakes against which she warned.

There was a side of Margaret's quest which could not be satisfied by all the jobs for women sea-captains in the world. John Stuart Mill, raised like Margaret in sober pedantry to do good for mankind, had a real identity crisis when he read Wordsworth, visited Paris, and realized that all the votes and wage reforms in the world would not make him personally happy. Margaret had a similar crisis in New York and later in Paris. In 1841 she had written, "Once I was almost all intellect; now I am almost all feeling. Nature vindicates her rights, and I feel all Italy glowing beneath the Saxon crust. This cannot last long. I shall burn to ashes if all this smoulders here much longer. I must die if I do not burst forth in genius or heroism." This sense of the unachieved self, the woman with the right to be vindicated in all her nature, not merely in her intellectual life, still smoldered in Margaret during her New York years. Goethe was her Wordsworth; New York her Paris; as she gathered her courage and her determination to make one journey more, before she gave up the struggle to reconcile her opposing forces.

Woman in the Nineteenth Century is a call to arms, urging woman to deny her emotional side until she had satisfied her intellectual side and achieved some parity in the world. Margaret had gone beyond this beginner's book; now she wanted to know the life, in its sweetness, as she had known the intellect. Her timing was always off. She spoke to women who, for the most part, would marry young and find themselves undeveloped in mind and skills. She herself had put off, consciously and unconsciously, emotional fulfillment in order to make herself "the most learned and gifted woman of her day," in Greeley's words. The fear of time, the enemy of youth and women, impelled her to New York and to new experiences, before she settled down, if that was to be necessary, as Miss Sarah Fuller, full of years and wisdom.

At first she lived with the Greeleys in their Turtle Bay home. She could benefit from the presence in their home of much of literary and political New York, and be under her editor's eye when he felt she was falling behind on her deadlines. She also had the mixed blessings of being with the Greeley children, whom she loved, and seeing the often fiery explosions of their marriage. Practically everything about Margaret annoyed Greeley at one time or another, her incessant coffee-drinking, moodiness, migraines, and insistence on gentlemanly courtesies. After all, she'd written a book urging equality between the sexes, so he felt fully justified when she waited for him to hold a door for her in muttering "Let them be sea-captains," as he stalked in front of her. She found his heart "noble," his habits—not surprisingly, in view of the sea-captain routine—"plebeian." Despite her aches and pains she managed to get three articles a week done for him, one on social and two on literary topics.

For the first time she visited the asylums and prisons of the city, spending much time with the woman inmates and increasing her real, as opposed to her vicarious, knowledge of women. She spoke to them as she had spoken to their more fortunate sisters at her Conversations or in her classroom, urging them to exert their will in the face of cruel men and unfair society, and promising them that God, to whom all souls were equal, would help them in their work. He, unlike the hypocrites who had made them what they were, would understand the difficulties under which they labored and appreciate their efforts to improve. She was amazed at the self-knowledge and compassion that these women showed when she won their confidence. She was impressed at their humor and their vitality, perhaps even a little envious. They knew a reality, however hard and unpleasant, that she had never known and might never know, and Margaret craved all female experience. As she developed her skills as a reporter, and learned to accurately relate the conditions and the lives of these women, her critical mind resisted judgments and the imposition of standards, at least not those she had been conditioned to assume were hers, and which certainly belonged to the New England she knew. She was developing new values as she listened and reported, without comment, on what American society had done to its citizens.

The literary articles were more opinionated, according to the standards she had worked out for her critical essays. She angered Edgar Allan Poe, who changed from a benevolent reader of her prose, to a critic and afterwards referred to her as "that old maid." Her relationship with Poe was further jeopardized when, for reasons she never explained, she accompanied the saloniste and minor poet, Anne Lynch Botta, to Poe's house to recover the letters of an indiscreet lady. Presumably she acted under some sense of female solidarity, for the ladies in question were not close friends. Perhaps she was very much aware of the remorse and fear which can come when a love affair is terminated and written testimony remains to provoke laughter or blackmail. Her own friendship with James Nathan ended in such a recrimination, and with his refusal to give her letters back; he eventually sold them for publication.

Nathan, a German Jew living in New York and trying to establish himself in commerce, had been attracted to Margaret because of her "high intellectuality, purity of sentiment and winning conversation." But, whatever the source of his interest, he treated her like a woman and for the first time in many years she enjoyed the idyll of long spring days spent in the woods, love songs from his guitar, and earnest discussions of life and love. It was very much like being a teen-ager in Cambridge again. Her friends, especially the Greeleys, were not pleased at the relationship, and predicted an unhappy end. They took to meeting in secret, which added an even more thrilling note to the progress of the affair. One summer day Margaret wrote, after an intense discussion, "I wish, I long to be human but divinely human. Are you my guardian to domesticate me in the body, and attach it more firmly to the earth?" What exactly she meant by this question, whether it was rhetorical or not, we cannot know. Interestingly enough it is almost exactly the vocabulary used by two of Hawthorne's heroines (Ellen in *Fanshawe* and Phoebe in *House of the Seven Gables*) in stating the role they, as women, hope to be able to fill in the lives of their creative men. Women, according to this definition, stood for the more earth-bound reality in contrast to the soaring spirit of the male intellect. To Nathan it was apparently an invitation to press his suit with ardor. Margaret, frightened and unhappy, regretted his giving in to his "lower" self. She was not that kind of a woman, those were not her intentions at all. He apologized and gave her a puppy to love, but from then on things were cooler.

Perhaps what the travelers said about American women was true, they were frigid. In any case Nathan began to make plans to return to Europe in June. Margaret tried to hold on to the remnants of what had been so beautiful, but his letters were infrequent and they always asked for something, an introduction or help in getting a job. When, in the course of the year following his departure, she was given the chance to go to Europe herself with Marcus and Rebecca Spring, she saw it, not only as the opportunity for growth and information she had looked forward to for so long, but as the last possibility of reunion with Nathan, in the hopes of a happier ending. She had written to him of his attraction to her "weary woman's heart," a place where she could "furl her wings" and rest; he had been to her "as sunshine and green woods," and then he had taken his heart "and cruelly hung it up quite out of my reach, and declare: I never shall have it. Oh *das ist hart.*" (Even in moments of passion, perhaps particularly in moments of passion, Margaret enjoined the pun.) Long after her mind told her the affair was ended, her will refused to accept it, and she moved towards the European journey partly in an effort to exert her will on a situation which had passed beyond her control, as well as in an effort to find something new in which her "woman's heart" could find happiness.

The Springs were a wealthy New York Quaker couple, interested in reform and literature, and supporting both by their philanthropy. Rebecca Spring had read *Woman in the Nineteenth Century*, and wanted to write its author to tell her how "it strengthened and enlightened me, and moved me to a higher and holier effort." Margaret was engaged as a kind of companion-governess for their son, but it was understood that they would benefit from her company as much as the boy. Their salary and her savings enabled her to make the trip, along with the loan of $500 from her old friend Sam Ward, who had accompanied the Farrars on the European tour which Timothy Fuller's death had prevented. She told him that this trip was her last chance and even now it might be too late for Europe to instruct her, since her character was developed, partly by adversity and partly by chance. The most she could hope for was that her new trade of journalism would be improved by her trip, and she could look forward to having a better-paying job on her return, even if the old higher hopes, which they had spent so many happy hours pondering, had faded. With this help, promptly given, she sailed for Europe at last in August, 1846.

Almost as soon as she landed in England she sent letters and articles back home noting the difference between the old world and the new, and, of course, the difference between European and American women. Although she felt that any sojourn in Europe was bound to make a traveller "even more American" she quickly developed the vocabulary and the perspective of the expatriate. The distance between the continents was the vantage point she had been seeking to sharpen her vision on American literature, life, and politics. She had the advantage, which few Americans at that time possessed, of a thorough knowledge of European literature and history, as well as letters of introduction to important thinkers. She renewed her acquaintance with Harriet Martineau, which Margaret's critical candor had strained, and found that they had at least one topic on which they could converse without argument, the advantages of mesmerism. Shortly before leaving for Scotland she received a letter telling of Nathan's engagement to a German girl. While climbing Ben Lomand, she became separated from Marcus Spring, and spent a night alone in the mists, thinking through what was past and what might be to come. When the search party found her at dawn she had, in her own terms, accepted the universe with all its unfairness and treachery, and was willing to see "the other side of the mountain," even knowing the landscape was likely to be just as cruel. She continued her trip, meeting literary and political figures, and drawing conclusions about them. Carlyle was amusing, although long-winded; on the whole (like so many others) she preferred Jane. At the Carlyles she met Joseph Mazzini and heard of the Italian struggle for independence from one of its most romantic and articulate leaders.

In November she and her friends arrived in Paris and here Margaret felt the pangs of so many who have visited the city of lovers alone. She did all the things that she thought ought to be done, met important men and women, saw the originals of paintings which she had seen only in bad reproductions, even went to balls. In George Sand she found a woman who lived up to her high standards, for she had "bravely acted out her nature," that to which, above all else, the individual must be true. Had one man been heroic enough to satisfy her, she would not have needed the series of men who passed through her life. She saw Rachel in classic French tragedy and was moved to tears and further loneliness by the grandeur of passion and the French ability to display it. When, in February, she was preparing to leave for Italy, she met the man for whom she had been searching, who would tell her what she wanted to know and give her the same personal advice in matters of the heart that she had been dispensing to others for years. Adam Mickiewicz was a Polish revolutionary and a poet, interested in the reconstruction of society and the role of women within a new world. He found Margaret's ideas fascinating and Margaret herself sympathetic. "She knows Greek, Latin, and most European languages. She has presentiments and sees apparitions. She believes that in her next incarnation she will be a man and that the present is the era of the liberation of women. Her ideas on marriage and many of her notions about life and the destiny of mankind are quite identical with the Cause, and seem to be taken therefrom . . . She made a vow never to marry. She is certain that the man or woman charged with the realization of the new era has already come to earth and her aim in coming to Europe was to find this messenger of God." (This testimony was from Alexander Chodzko, who had received it from his friend Mickiewicz and recorded it in his memoirs, along with the suspect report that Margaret had been so impressed with Mickiewicz that on being introduced she "fainted on the sofa.")

Margaret wrote to Emerson that here at last was a man "with the intellect and passions in due proportion for a full and healthy being." Perhaps she intended to sound a little cruel, for in Adam Mickiewicz she found a friend who did not respond to her requests for help with passages from "Self-Reliance" and other worthy essays, but with straightforward, even brutal analysis. Mickiewicz found nothing absurd in the sense of destiny, or in the daemons that tried to prevent it. (His own wife was insane, broken down by the conflict between her bourgeois upbringing and his sermons on change.) He accepted very seriously Margaret's mysticism, as he did her feminism, and was concerned with the way in which she could fulfill the destiny for which she was marked. He even discussed the old concept of whether celibacy was necessary for a priestess. After her departure for Italy he wrote her that she was "a true person," which was a high praise. She was illustrative of a time to come when woman would not exert influence unless she had "inner beauty, inner spiritual life." She should learn to appreciate her own beauty, so much higher and nobler than physical beauty, and glory in it. She must also consider whether or not she should remain a virgin, in order to effect her holy mission. In Mickiewicz, as in Mazzini, and in the other patriots she was to meet, Margaret found a group of people convinced that they were in the middle of the best of times, the worst of times—that they were changing the world by their ideas, and the most they could do for their friend was to ask her to join them. This sense of destiny was a part of almost every revolutionary; it was his mainspring to action which could mean death or exile; and it was precisely what Margaret had found lacking in "tame" New England, with so many words and so little action. Here was reality of which George Ripley's little group at Brook Farm had never even dared to dream; here was political change, in which women were an important part, which chose the barricades rather than ballots.

A great many novels, many of them bad, have told of the American spinster finding love and liberation among the fountains and ruins of Italy. Chronologically Margaret stood between the Americans of whom James Fenimore Cooper wrote who made the "hegeira" to Europe, their cultural mecca, and the later generation, chronicled by Henry James, who found in the old world a complexity and richness which they admired yet feared. Margaret was a little old for Daisy Miller, a little dry for Isabel Archer, but she could in some ways have been cast for a James' heroine. She knew a great deal about the culture of the land she had left and the land she visited, but, while she rejected many of the stereotypes about American literature and character, she was willing, even anxious, to accept them about Italy. The group of "fortunate pilgrims" who found personal and artistic sanctuary in Italy came from all the Anglo-Saxon countries, seeking the warmth of life as well as of climate which presumably was forbidden by some hidden clause in the constitution. Corinna, Madame De Staël's heroine, had found Italy the proper haven for her particular genius, for people there had the leisure and the courage to listen to her. In Italy, Margaret wrote, the body was "a thing alive with beauty," while to the Saxon it was merely a "convenience." The Italians were able to "sympathize with my character and understand my organization as no other people ever did," and Italy herself "receives me as a long-lost child." The ripeness of the country, the season, the artistic and political climate, coincided with her own growth. She was ripe for what she believed Italy could offer her.

Saint Peter's Basilica has long colonnades, like welcoming arms. Margaret went to Vespers there on Easter Sunday when, after forty days without incense or flowers, they return to the altars. She became separated from her friends and stood at a chapel peering into the vast church, as the acolytes extinguished all the candles but the vast Paschal candle, and women in shawls brushed by her to kiss the burnished toe of the first Pope. A young man, the Marchese Giovanni Angelo Ossoli, asked if he could help her and, after a moment's hesitation, she accepted his offer to show her to her lodgings. It was nothing so startling as love at first sight. Margaret went on with her plans to visit Venice and Switzerland, and left Ossoli behind in Rome, with his difficult ailing father and his revolution. But she found the young nobleman a disturbing and attractive part of her life during her travels and when she returned to Rome, to live in penny-pinching economy while doing research for a book about Italy. Ossoli was ten years her junior, attractive but uneducated, with that combination of feminine sensitivity and masculine passion which she had always found so attractive in men. They became lovers and, very soon, she was pregnant.

Her letters during this period show both her happiness and her fears. She did not tell her friends about her condition, although she hinted at it broadly in telling Caroline Sturgis that she saw herself as "a poor magnet, with power to be wounded by the bodies I attract . . . with this year I enter upon a sphere of my destiny so difficult, that I, at present, see no way out, except through the gates of death." In the language of the ladies' magazines, and of the popular novel that could mean only one thing. Childbirth, for the nineteenth-century woman, was a kind of highwater mark in her life, her one opportunity to test her heroism within most contexts of true womanhood. Margaret had friends who had died in childbirth, she had been the recipient of many confidences of bungled births, and she was aware of the fact that the older the mother, the harder a first birth was likely to be. But with the fear was the sense of exaltation, heightened in Margaret's case by the quickened pace of the revolution. If she had asked for reality, she was getting it in large doses.

She had made the decision to relinquish her virginity, and with it possibly her chance to be herself the saviour of her sex. Mickiewicz had written her to be as bold in her life as she had been in her book, to be free in the flesh as she was in the spirit: "The relationships which suit you are those which develop and free your spirit responding to the legitimate needs of your organism and leaving you free at all times." This was a call to love, but not a call to marriage, which the revolutionary mind rejected as too tainted with the hypocrisy of unworthy institutions. She did marry Ossoli eventually—whether in December 1847 as she told Emmeline Story (which is unlikely) or in the summer of 1849, just before her baby's birth, or even in the weeks after he was born in September, in order to obtain a baptismal certificate, making the child an heir to heaven and to whatever ancestral estates might remain, there is no accurate record. The date of marriage was not important, except perhaps to her friends at home, who were very busy counting to nine when the news of the birth of a son reached them. Margaret had merged her own ambitions with the ambition of one man and with the cause for which he fought.

In the Italian Republic, rather than in any feminist movement, she found the "high object" which she had advised women to pursue. The Republic was proclaimed in February, 1849 and the siege of Rome by the French began in April and lasted until the collapse of the patriots in July. During most of this time Margaret left her baby in the country with a nurse while she worked herself in the hospitals and on her *Tribune* articles. She was determined that her country should admire the Italians as she did and see in them an example to awaken them from their lethargy. The evils which oppressed the Italians and for which they were prepared to die were not nearly so great as those under which the United States passively endured; the corruption of the state and church in Rome

was as nothing compared to the incomparable moral wrong which
slavery represented. "My country is at present spoiled by prosperity, stupid with the lust of gain, soiled by crime in its willing per-
petuation of slavery, shamed by an unjust war, noble sentiment
much forgotten even by individuals, the aims of politicians selfish
or petty, the literature frivolous and venal." In contrast the Italians,
true to their nature and to their revolution, fought for what was
right.

John Quincy Adams, her father's hero, believed that war was
sometimes necessary in order to jar the too complaisant, too lazy
nation into action. Margaret's dispatches from the besieged city
show a similar belief that this war at least—as well as any war
fought in the name of liberty against tyranny—was a just war, and
one which the United States might well imitate. She found in the
revolution a kind of woman she admired, and she felt that revolution, in its ideology and its reality, produced strength and courage,
as well as devotion, in women like the Princess Belgiojoso, who
appointed Margaret regolatrice of the Hospital of the Fate Bene
Fratelli. There is no doubt that her time spent consoling the dying,
talking with the wounded, writing letters home for them and bringing them small luxuries when she could find them, was the happiest and most fulfilling she had yet known. For the first time she
felt consistently competently alive, even knowing her husband's
life was in danger and that her child was being cared for by others.
On the Fourth of July Garibaldi retreated and the bid for independence was over, along with this period of growth in her own life.

She and Ossoli hurried from the sacked city and found their child
near death from lack of food and care. The fates again, ones that
every nineteenth-century woman knew well, for the death of young
children was a constant factor in the forming of a female character.
Margaret's own young brother had died as a child, and she had seen
Emerson, with all his intellect, and Greeley, with all his influence,
lose infants they loved. She wrote that in her fear for the life of her
child she knew a terror greater than anything she had experienced,
and, when he survived, greater gratitude than she had ever known.
Angelo recovered, and the three of them moved to Florence, where
the Anglo-American colony received them as refugees and expatri-
ates.

The reality of revolution was replaced by a gentler reality, the
development of her child, an experience of such "perfect beauty

and truth" that all her eloquence seemed wasted and she admitted only "hyperbole" could do justice to her emotions. Those who met her during this period found her a gentler person, her will curbed, and her intellect only a part of her life, as it was a part of her, and that not the most important part. "What a difference it makes to come home to a child!—how it fills up all the gaps of life, just in the way that is most consoling, most refreshing! Formerly, I used to feel sad at that hour; the day had not been nobly spent, I had not done my duty to myself and others, and I felt so lonely! Now I never feel lonely." She did not, it is only fair to say, have the sole care of the child, even in her poverty; but the idea that Margaret Fuller was changing even an occasional diaper provided much amusement, some of it malicious, back in Boston.

Even in Florence, with its congenial social and cultural life, there were constant reminders that the position of the little family was precarious. The police occasionally harrassed them, there were bewildered letters from her family who could not understand what she had done and the manner in which she had done it, and the continued hostility of Ossoli's brother. The marriage itself, however, seemed to be a success. Margaret did not mind assuming the male role, insofar as earning a living was concerned. To write was part of her nature and she must follow it, as she had followed that other part of her nature in her love affair. She discussed her husband's personality in a letter to her sister, in which she said she knew that Emerson and others found her choice peculiar. But what they failed to understand was that Ossoli didn't care about literary Boston, or anything else; he had no self-love or ambition; what he cared about was making Margaret happy. He nursed her when she was sick, as devotedly as a mother, and he safeguarded her time and energy for her work. To Caroline Sturgis she said that Ossoli "diffuses such a power and sweetness over every day" that she could not bear to think of the future.

And yet the future in the form of unpaid bills and the obvious impossibility of Ossoli finding a job, was staring her in the face. In choosing this simple honest young man, Margaret made the choice which genius in a woman frequently dictates—the choice of Virginia Woolf and Colette. She needed the services frequently performed by a wife, to have her physical needs provided for and her time kept free from encroachment. Ossoli handled these details to perfection, and was a gay and amusing companion as well. He looked up to her, and wanted to please her. Their child made the circle of relationships complete. Yet the child would need, eventually, to be sent to school and that required money. Reluctantly Margaret moved to the position of returning home, taking Ossoli with her for she felt he would suffer as much as she if separated from their child. In the United States she could use her fame, and even her notoriety, to make money.

Inexorably, as the fates always move, she prepared for the voyage home. Forebodings and presentiments surrounded her, but she had to ignore them because there were no alternatives. At last life as well as the intellect was sweet. Her only regret was that she had not spent more time buying toys for children. In May the family sailed for home on the *Elizabeth*. On July 19, 1850, the ship was wrecked on a sandbar off Fire Island. Only the child's body and a small trunk containing a few love letters were washed ashore; the great work, *History of the Roman Republic*, and the bodies of Margaret and Ossoli were never found.

Her legacy to her sex and her country was her book on women and the example of her own life. Margaret Fuller began her book with two quotations: "Frailty, Thy name is Woman," and "The Earth waits for her Queen." The book is an attempt to bridge the gap between the two by the exercise of the will, the mind and the heart. Her life attempted the same task. Of the two, perhaps her life is the more believable, since it was in the context of a society which the book was expected to change.

NOTES

1. COMING OF AGE IN AMERICA

The American Girl in the Nineteenth Century

1. I am deeply indebted to Dr. Margaret Mead, not only for her books on adolescence in other cultures, which have been very useful to a parochial American historian, but also for the insights into historical womanhood which she has given me in conversations.

2. The vast literature on adolescence in both psychology and sociology could only be sampled, however, I found the following books particularly useful for my purposes: *Adolescent Girls: A Nation-Wide Study of Girls Between 11 and 18 Years of Age made for the Girl Scouts of the U.S.A.* (Ann Arbor: 1957); Ausubel, D. P., *Theory and Problems of Adolescence* (New York: 1954); Bernard, H., *Adolescent Development in American Culture* (Yonkers-on-Hudson, New York: 1957); Blos, P., *Adolescence: A Psychoanalytic Interpretation*; Bier, W., *The Adolescent: His Search for Understanding* (New York: 1964); Chadwick, M., *Adolescent Girlhood* (New York: 1933); Coleman, J., *The Adolescent Society* (New York: 1961); Davan, Eland J. Adelson, *The Adolescent Experience* (New York, London, Sydney: 1966); Duvall, E., *Today's Teen-Agers* (New York: 1966); Fleming, C., *Adolescence: Its Social Psychology* (London: 1963); Freud, A., *The Ego and the Mechanism of Defense* (New York, 1948); Friedenberg, E., *The Vanishing Adolescent* (Boston: 1959); Gesell, A. and Amer, L., *Youth: The Years from 10 to 16* (New York: 1956); Ginzberg, E., *Values and Ideals of American Youth* (New York: 1961); Gottlieb, D., *The American Adolescent* (Homewood, Ill.: 1964); Grossman, Jean, *Do You Know Your Daughter* (New York and London: 1944); Hall, G. S., *Adolescence*, 2 vols. (New York: 1916); Havighurst, R. J., *Developmental Tasks and Education* (New York: 1951); Hollingsworth, Leta, *The Psychology of the Adolescent* (New York: 1928); Hollingshead, A., *Elmtown's Youth* (New York: 1949); Mead, M., *Coming of Age in Samoa* (New York: 1928); *From the South Seas* (New York: 1930); *Growing Up in New Guinea* (New York: 1930); Malinowski, B., *Sex and Repression in Savage Society* (New York: 1927); McClelland, D., *Personality* (New York: 1955), Mauss, R., *Theories of Adolescence* (New York: 1962); and Stone, L. and Church, J., *Childhood and Adolescence* (New York: 1957). I found the volume of readings edited by M. B. Sussman, *Sources in Marriage and the Family* (Boston: 1959) helpful.

3. It is virtually impossible to quantify the data obtained by reading manuscripts and contemporary autobiography, fiction, and periodicals. The existence of data itself is on a random basis. I can only state impressions received from the reading and the saturation in the material, which are, of necessity, partly subjective, and undoubtedly reflect my own middle-class, white, and particularly, female, outlook. I have consulted approximately 400 manuscript diaries in

201

historical societies and libraries, as well as private collections, from Massachusetts to California. The principal collections consulted were: The Library of Congress; the Elizabeth and Arthur Schlesinger Collection at Radcliffe College; the Sophia Smith Woman's Library at Smith College; the Massachusetts Historical Society; the Boston Public Library; the Pennsylvania Historical Society; the New York Public Library, and 408 published autobiographies of women who lived primarily in the nineteenth century.

The best-sellers written by women between 1790 and 1900, according to the rather sketchy lists available; plus, other popular fiction by the same or similar authors, totals approximately 600 books of stories, novels, or poems.

I have read through all the magazines for women with more than a three-year life-span available in the above-listed libraries for the period 1790-1865, and sampled some of the less long-lived ones. I read through the nineteenth century in such popular magazines as: *The Atlantic Monthly, Harper's, The North American Review, The Galaxy* and *Scribner's*, and the post-1865 period of *Cosmopolitan, The Delineator, Good Housekeeping, Frank Leslie's Magazine*, and *The Ladies' Home Journal*. I also read *Do Bow's Monthly, The Southern Literary Messenger*, and *The Southern Journal* for the pre-Civil War period.

For medical literature, the New York Academy of Medicine has a remarkable collection of texts and notes of nineteenth-century obstetricians and gynecologists in manuscript form.

The religious literature of the period is widely available in printed sermons, in the periodicals published by various religious groups, and in the narratives and letters of missionaries and evangelists.

For the most part this material concentrates on the middle-class white American female, who is usually Protestant. I did not consult travel accounts, partly because Frank F. Femstenberg, Jr., uses them in "Industrialization and the American Family: A Look Backward," printed in *Sourcebook in Marriage and the Family* (pp. 95-105) and partly because I think the degree of insight of these people has been vastly over-rated and over-used. I refuse to believe that John Gunther can get "Inside Africa" in six months, and I am nearly as skeptical that Alexis de Tocqueville, however gifted, could learn all there was to know about America in nine months. I am much more interested in the travel accounts by Americans, in which they contrasted other societies with what they felt to be true of their own, 204 of such accounts have been read.

4. Robert Riegel, *American Feminists* (Lawrence, Kansas, 1963) was the first to point this out. It needs qualification and explanation, like so many "statistics."

5. Richard Chase, *Emily Dickinson* (New York, 1955) discusses her preoccupation with status, although not in relation to her society. Besides the wife-status poems, there are many Dickinson poems which reflect unwillingness to leave childhood and girlhood.

6. Edward N. Clarke, *Sex in Education: or, A Fair Chance for the Girls* 5th ed. (Boston, 1873). A spirited answer to Dr. Clarke was given by Mrs. G. B. Duffey, in *No Sex in Education; or, An Equal Chance for Both Girls and Boys* (Philadelphia, 1874[?]). A sample of Mrs. Duffey's approach, when answering Dr. Clarke's strictures on this "critical" monthly period, is: "Critical: fudge!

Let Nature have fair play, and she is perfectly capable of managing the child without repressing physical manifestations of activity or checking mental ones." (p. 67)

7. Dio Lewis, *The New Gymnastics for Men, Women and Children* (3d ed. Boston: 1863) and *Our Girls* (New York: 1871). Sarah Margaret Fuller Ossoli, *Woman in the Nineteenth Century* (Boston, 1855).

8. Some well-known women who expressed such fears were Emily Dickinson, Louisa Mae Alcott, Susan Warner, and Frances Willard. The assumption of the female role, with its accompanying physical manifestations and changes in dress, is sometimes discussed in terms of "breaking the will" of the wayward tomboy, and making her more docile and passive, becomingly female. This calming down process was widely believed to happen with the coming of the menses, and the period just preceding their arrival was commonly believed to be one of agitation, irritability, and potential waywardness for the pre-adolescent girl.

9. Edith Wharton has a passage in *The Age of Innocence*, where the hero, Newland Archer, suddenly sees his fiancé clearly, and concludes her to be, The terrifying product of the social system he belonged to and believed in, the young girl who knew nothing and expected everything. . . . In reality they all lived in a kind of hieroglyphic world, where the real thing was never said or done or even thought, but only represented by a set of arbitrary signs. . . . The result, of course, was that the young girl who was the centre of this elaborate system of mystification remained the more inscrutable for her very frankness and assurance. . . . But when he had gone the full round of her he returned discouraged by the thought that all this frankness and innocence were only an artificial product. Untrained human nature was not frank and innocent; it was full of the twists and defences of an instinctive guile. And he felt himself oppressed by this creation of factitious purity, so cunningly manufactured by a conspiracy of mothers and aunts and grandmothers and long-dead ancestresses, because it was supposed to be what he wanted, what he had a right to, in order that he might exercise his lordly pleasure in smashing it like an image made of snow.

10. There is a whole genre of this "deviate" literature, mostly involving the woman in battle from the Revolution through the Spanish-American War. There are also contemporary accounts of women in remote areas who operate trading posts, dress as a man, smoking cigars and swearing like troopers. There are women who assumed male occupations, like Lucy Ann Lobdell, "The Female Hunter of Delaware County." There are also the group of women involved in murder cases, most of whom are featured by the press and in their autobiographical accounts as completely true to the prevailing image of womanhood, having sinned only through an excess of affection or through ignorance. Prostitutes, in the reform literature of the period, are treated with increasing tolerance because of the feeling that they, too, sinned by being only too womanly and affectionate.

11. This quotation is from Mrs. John Sherwood, *Etiquette* (New York, 1881), p. 133.

12. The psychology of nineteenth century female relationships is perhaps beyond the historian to judge. Woman friendship had a certain distinct mystique connected to it as did the playing fields of Eton camaraderie of male friend-

ships, and the degree to which latent or overt homosexuality played a role in either is hard to say. There were some American women who went rather farther in women friendships than most, for example, the actress Charlotte Cushman.

13.　Sherwood, *The Amenities of Home* (New York, 1884), p. 192.

2.　THE CULT OF TRUE WOMANHOOD
1820–1860

1.　Authors who addressed themselves to the subject of women in the mid-nineteenth century used this phrase as frequently as writers on religion mentioned God. Neither group felt it necessary to define their favorite terms; they simply assumed—with some justification—that readers would intuitively understand exactly what they meant. Frequently what people of one era take for granted is most striking and revealing to the student from another. In a sense this analysis of the ideal woman of the mid-nineteenth century is an examination of what writers of that period actually meant when they used so confidently the vague phrase True Womanhood.

2.　The conclusions reached in this article are based on a survey of almost all of the women's magazines published for more than three years during the period 1820-60 and a sampling of those published for less than three years; all the gift books cited in Ralph Thompson, *American Literary Annuals and Gift Books, 1825-1865* (New York, 1936) deposited in the Library of Congress, the New York Public Library, the New-York Historical Society, Columbia University Special Collections, Library of the City College of the University of New York, Pennslyvania Historical Society, Massachusetts Historical Society, Boston Public Library, Fruitlands Museum Library, the Smithsonian Institution and the Wisconsin Historical Society; hundreds of religious tracts and sermons in the American Unitarian Society and the Galatea Collection of the Boston Public Library; and the large collection of nineteenth-century cookbooks in the New York Public Library and the Academy of Medicine of New York. Corroborative evidence not cited in this article was found in women's diaries, memoirs, autobiographies and personal papers, as well as in all the novels by women which sold over 75,000 copies during this period, as cited in Frank Luther Mott, *Golden Multitudes: The Story of Best Sellers in the United States* (New York, 1947) and H. R. Brown, *The Sentimental Novel in America, 1789-1860* (Durham, N. C., 1940). This latter information also indicated the effect of the cult of True Womanhood on those most directly concerned.

3.　As in "The Bachelor's Dream," in *The Lady's Gift: Souvenir for All Seasons (Nashua, N. H., 1849)*, p. 37.

4.　*The Young Ladies' Class Book: A Selection of Lessons for Reading in Prose and Verse*, ed. Ebenezer Bailey, Principal of Young Ladies' High School, Boston (Boston, 1831), p. 168.

5.　A Lady of Philadelphia, *The World Enlightened, Improved, and Harmonized by WOMAN!!!* A lecture, delivered in the City of New York, before the Young Ladies' Society for Mutual Improvement, on the following question, proposed by the society, with the offer of $100 for the best lecture that should be read before them on the subject proposed;—What is the power and influence of woman in moulding the manners, morals and habits of civil society? (Philadelphia, 1840), p. 1.

6. *The Young Lady's Book: A Manual of Elegant Recreations, Exercises, and Pursuits* (Boston, 1830), p. 29.

7. *Woman As She Was, Is, and Should Be* (New York, 1849), p. 206.

8. "The Triumph of the Spiritual Over the Sensual: An Allegory," in *Ladies' Companion: A Monthly Magazine Embracing Every Department of Literature, Embellished With Original Engravings and Music*, XVII (New York) (1842), 67.

9. *Lecture on Some of the Distinctive Characteristics of the Female*, delivered before the class of the Jefferson Medical College, Jan. 1847 (Philadelphia, 1847), p. 13.

10. "Female Education," *Ladies' Repository and Gatherings of the West: A Monthly Periodical Devoted to Literature and Religion*, I (Cincinnati), 12.

11. *Woman, in Her Social and Domestic Character* (Boston, 1842), pp. 41-42.

12. *Second Annual Report of the Young Ladies' Literary and Missionary Association of the Philadelphia Collegiate Institution* (Philadelphia, 1840), pp. 20, 26.

13. *Mt. Holyoke Female Seminary: Female Education. Tendencies of the Principles Embraced, and the System Adopted in the Mt. Holyoke Female Seminary* (Boston, 1839), p. 3.

14. *Prospectus of the Young Ladies' Seminary at Bordentown, New Jersey* (Bordentown, 1836), p. 7.

15. *Catalogue of the Young Ladies' Seminary in Keene, New Hampshire* (n.p., 1832), p. 20.

16. "Report to the College of Teachers, Cincinnati, October, 1840" in *Ladies' Repository*, I (1841), 50.

17. *Woman's Record: or Sketches of All Distinguished Women from 'The Beginning' Till A. D. 1850* (New York, 1853), pp. 665, 669.

18. "Female Irreligion," *Ladies' Companion*, XIII (May-Oct. 1840), III.

19. *The Lady's Book of Flowers and Poetry*, ed. Lucy Hooper (New York, 1842), has a "Floral Dictionary" giving the symbolic meaning of floral tributes.

20. See, for example, Nathaniel Hawthorne, *The Blithedale Romance* (Boston, 1852), p. 71, in which Zenobia says: "How can she be happy, after discovering that fate has assigned her but one single event, which she must contrive to make the substance of her whole life? A man has his choice of innumerable events."

21. Mary R. Beard, *Woman As Force in History* (New York, 1946) makes this point at some length. According to common law a woman had no legal existence once she was married and therefore could not manage property, sue in court, etc. In the 1840s and 1850s laws were passed in several states to remedy this condition.

22. *Excellency of the Female Character Vindicated: Being an Investigation Relative to the Cause and Effects on the Encroachments of Men Upon the Rights of Women, and the Too Frequent Degradation and Consequent Misfortunes of The Fair Sex* (New York, 1807), pp. 277, 278.

23. By a Lady (Eliza Ware Rotch Farrar), *The Young Lady's Friend* (Boston, 1837), p. 293.

24. *Girlhood and Womanhood: or, Sketches of My Schoolmates* (Boston, 1844), p. 140.

25. Emily Chubbuck, *Alderbrook* (Boston, 1847), 2nd. ed., II, 121, 127.

26. *Woman and Her Era* (New York, 186), p. 95.

27. "The Two Lovers of Sicily," *The Lady's Amaranth: A Journal of Tales, Essays, Excerpts—Historical and Biographical Sketches, Poetry and Literature in General* (Philadelphia), II (Jan. 1839), 17.

28. *The Young Man's Guide* (Boston, 1833), pp. 229, 231.

29. *Female Influence: and the True Christian Mode of Its Exercise; a Discourse Delivered in the First Presbyterian Church in Newburyport, July 30, 1837* (Newburyport, 1837), p. 18.

30. W. Tolles, "Woman The Creature of God and the Manufacturer of Society," *Ladies' Wreath* (New York), III (1852), 205.

31. Prof. William M. Heim, "The Bloomer Dress," *Ladies' Wreath*, III (1852), 247.

32. *The Young Lady's Offering: or Gems of Prose and Poetry* (Boston, 1853), p. 283. The American girl, whose innocence was often connected with ignorance, was the spiritual ancestress of the Henry James heroine. Daisy Miller, like Lucy Dutton, saw innocence lead to tragedy.

33. *The Mother's Book* (Boston, 1831), pp. 151, 152.

34. Mrs. L. H. Sigourney, *Whisper to a Bride* (Hartford, 1851), in which Mrs. Sigourney's approach is summed up in this quotation: "Home! Blessed bride, thou art about to enter this sanctuary, and to become a priestess at its altar!," p. 44.

35. S. R. R., "Female Charms," *Godey's Magazine and Lady's Book* (Philadelphia), XXXIII (1846), 52.

36. Charles Elliott, "Arguing With Females," *Ladies' Repository*, I (1841), 25.

37. *Ladies' Companion*, VIII (Jan. 1838), 147.

38. *The Young Lady's Book* (New York, 1830), American edition, p. 28. (This is a different book than the one of the same title and date of publication cited in note 6.)

39. *Sphere and Duties of Woman* (5th ed., Baltimore, 1854), p. 47.

40. *Woman*, p. 15.

41. *Letters to Young Ladies* (Hartford, 1835), p. 179.

42. *Lecture*, p. 17.

43. *The Young Lady's Friend*, p. 313.

44. Maria J. McIntosh, *Woman in America: Her Work and Her Reward* (New York, 1850), p. 25.

45. *Poems and a Memoir of the Life of Mrs. Felicia Hemons* (London, 1860), p. 16.

46. Letter "To an Unrecognized Poetess, June, 1846" (Sara Jane Clarke), *Greenwood Leaves* (2nd ed.; Boston, 1850), p. 311.

47. "The Sculptor's Assistant: Ann Flaxman," in *Women of Worth: A Book for Girls* (New York, 1860), p. 263.

48. Mrs. Clarissa Packard (Mrs. Caroline Howard Gilman), *Recollections of a Housekeeper* (New York, 1834), p. 122.

49. *Recollections of a Southern Matron* (New York, 1838), pp. 256, 257.

50. *The Lady's Token: or Gift of Friendship*, ed. Colesworth Pinckney (Nashua, N. H., 1848), p. 119.

51. Harvey Newcomb, *Young Lady's Guide to the Harmonious Development of Christian Character* (Boston, 1846), p. 10.

52. "Rules for Conjugal and Domestic Happiness," *Mother's Assistant and Young Lady's Friend*, III (Boston), (April 1843), 115.

53. *Letters to Mothers* (Hartford, 1838), p. 199. In the diaries and letters of women who lived during this period the death of a child seemed consistently to be the hardest thing for them to bear and to occasion more anguish and rebellion, as well as eventual submission, than any other event in their lives.

54. "A Submissive Mother," *The Ladies' Parlor Companion: A Collection of Scattered Fragments and Literary Gems* (New York, 1852), p. 358.

55. "Woman," *Godey's Lady's Book*, II (Aug. 1831), 110.

56. *Sphere and Duties of Woman*, p. 172.

57. Ralph Waldo Emerson, "Woman," *Complete Writings of Ralph Waldo Emerson* (New York, 1875), p. 1180.

58. As in Donald Fraser, *The Mental Flower Garden* (New York, 1857). Perhaps the most famous exponent of this theory is Edgar Allan Poe who affirms in "The Philosophy of Composition" that "the death of a beautiful woman is unquestionably the most poetical topic in the world. . . ."

59. "Domestic and Social Claims on Woman," *Mother's Magazine*, VI (1846), 21.

60. *Woman*, p. 173.

61. *The Young Ladies' Class Book*, p. 166.

62. T. S. Arthur, *The Lady at Home: or, Leaves from the Every-Day Book of an American Woman* (Philadelphia, 1847), pp. 177, 178.

63. Caspar Morris, *Margaret Mercer* (Boston, 1840), quoted in *Woman's Record*, p. 425.

64. These particular titles come from: *The Young Ladies' Oasis: or Gems of Prose and Poetry*, ed. N. L. Ferguson (Lowell, 1851), pp. 14, 16; *The Genteel School Reader* (Philadelphia, 1849), p. 271; and *Magnolia*, I (1842), 4. A popular poem in book form, published in England, expressed very fully this concept of woman as comforter: Coventry Patmore, *The Angel in the Home* (Boston, 1856 and 1857). Patmore expressed his devotion to True Womanhood in such lines as:

> The gentle wife, who decks his board
> And makes his day to have no night,
> Whose wishes wait upon her Lord,
> Who finds her own in his delight. (p. 94)

65. The women's magazines carried on a crusade against tight lacing and regretted, rather than encouraged, the prevalent ill health of the American wom-

an. See, for example, *An American Mother, Hints and Sketches* (New York, 1839), pp. 28 ff. for an eassy on the need for a healthy mind in a healthy body in order to better be a good example for children.

66.   The best single collection of nineteenth-century cookbooks is in the Academy of Medicine of New York Library, although some of the most interesting cures were in hand-written cookbooks found amng the papers of women who lived during the period.

67.   Sarah Josepha Hale, *The Ladies' New Book of Cookery: A Practical System for Private Families in Town and Country* (5th ed.; New York, 1852), p. 409. Similar evidence on the importance of nursing skills to every female is found in such books of advice as William A. Alcott, *The Young Housekeeper* (Boston, 1838), in which, along with a plea for apples and cold baths. Alcott says "Every female should be trained to the angelic art of managing properly the sick," p. 47.

68.   *The Young Lady's Friend*, pp. 75-77, 79.

69.   "A Tender Wife," *Godey's*, II (July 1831), 28.

70.   "MY WIFE! A Whisper," *Godey's*, II (Oct. 1831), 231.

71.   *Letters to Young Ladies*, p. 27. The greatest exponent of the mental and moral joys of housekeeping was the *Lady's Annual Register and Housewife's Memorandum Book* (Boston, 1838), which gave practical advice on ironing, hair curling, budgeting and marketing, and turning cuffs—all activities which contributed to the "beauty of usefulness" and "joy of accomplishment" which a woman desired (I, 23).

72.   *The Young Lady's Friend*, p. 230.

73.   "Learning vs. Housewifery," *Godey's*, X (Aug. 1839), 95.

74.   *Letters to Young Ladies*, p. 25. W. Thayer, *Life at the Fireside* (Boston, 1857), has an idyllic picture of the woman of the house mending her children's garments, the grandmother knitting and the little girl taking her first stitches, all in the light of the domestic hearth.

75.   "The Mirror's Advice," *Young Maiden's Mirror* (Boston, 1858), p. 263.

75.   Mrs. L. Maria Child, *The Girl's Own Book* (New York, 1833).

77.   P. 44.

78.   T. S. Arthur, *Advice to Young Ladies* (Boston, 1850), p. 45.

79.   R. C. Waterston, *Thoughts on Moral and Spiritual Culture* (Boston, 1842), p. 101. Newcomb's *Young Lady's Guide* also advised religious biography as the best reading for women (p. 111).

80.   *Godey's*, I (1828), 1. (Repeated often in *Godey's* editorials.)

81.   *The Lily of the Valley*, n. v. (1851), p. 2.

82.   For example, "The Fatalist," *Godey's*, IV (Jan. 1834), 10, in which Sommers Dudley has Catherine reading these dangerous books until life becomes "a bewildered dream. . . . O passion, what a shocking perverter of mason thou art!"

83.   Review of *Society in America* (New York, 1837) in *American Quarterly Review* (Philadelphia), XXII (Sept. 1837), 38.

84.   "A Finished Education," *Ladies' Museum* (Providence), I (1825), 42.

85. Helen Irving, "Literary Women," *Ladies' Wreath*, III (1850), 93.

86. "Women of Genius," *Ladies' Companion*, XI (1839), 89.

87. "Intellect vs. Affection in Woman," *Godey's*, XVI (1846), 86.

88. "The Only Daughter," *Godey's*, X (Mar. 1839), 122.

89. *The Annual Catalogue of the Officers and Pupils of the Young Ladies' Seminary and Collegiate Institute* (Monroe City, 1855), pp. 18, 19.

90. *Chronicles of a Pioneer School* from 1792 to 1833: Being the History of Miss Sarah Pierce and Her Litchfield School, Compiled by Emily Noyes Vanderpoel; ed. Elizabeth C. Barney Buel (Cambridge, 1903), p. 74.

91. *Mt. Holyoke Female Seminary*, p. 13.

92. *The American Frugal Housewife* (New York, 1838), p. 111.

93. "Female Influence," in *The Ladies' Pearl and Literary Gleaner: A Collection of Tales, Sketches, Essays, Anecdotes, and Historical Incidents* (Lowell), I (1841), 10.

94. Mrs. S. T. Martyn, "The Wife," *Ladies' Wreath*, II (1848-49), 171.

95. *The Young Ladies' Oasis*, p. 26.

96. "On Marriage," *Ladies' Repository*, I (1841), 133; "Old Maids," *Ladies' Literary Cabinet* (Newburyport), II (1822) (Microfilm), 141; "Matrimony," *Godey's*, II (Sept. 1831), 174; and "Married or Single," *Peterson's Magazine* (Philadelphia) IX (1859), 36, all express the belief that while marriage is desirable for a woman it is not essential. This attempt to reclaim the status of the unmarried woman is an example of the kind of mild crusade which the women's magazines sometimes carried on. Other examples were their strictures against an overly-genteel education and against the affection and aggravation of ill health. In this sense the magazines were truly conservative, for they did not oppose all change but only that which did violence to some cherished tradition. The reforms they advocated would, if put into effect, make woman even more the perfect female, and enhance the ideal of True Womanhood.

97. *Girlhood and Womanhood*, p. 100. Mrs. Graves tells the stories in the book in the person of an "Old Maid" and her conclusions are that "single life has its happiness too" for the single woman "can enjoy all the pleasures of maternity without its pains and trials" (p. 140). In another one of her books, *Woman in America* (New York, 1843), Mrs. Graves speaks out even more strongly in favor of "single blessedness" rather than "a loveless or unhappy marriage" (p. 130).

98. A very unusual story is Lela Linwood, "A Chapter in the History of a Free Heart," *Ladies' Wreath*, III (1853), 349. The heroine, Grace Arland, is "sublime" and dwells "in perfect light while we others struggle yet with the shadows." She refuses marriage and her friends regret this but are told her heart "is rejoicing in its *freedom*." The story ends with the plaintive refrain:

> But is it not a happy thing,
> All fetterless and free,
> Like any wild bird, on the wing,
> To carol merrily?

But even in this tale the unusual, almost unearthly rarity of Grace's genius is stressed; she is not offered as an example to more mortal beings.

99. Horace Greeley even went so far as to apply this remedy to the "dissatis-

factions" of Margaret Fuller. In his autobiography, *Recollections of a Busy Life* (New York, 1868) he says that "noble and great as she was, a good husband and two or three bouncing babies would have emancipated her from a deal of cant and nonesense" (p. 178).

100. *Sphere and Duties of Woman*, p. 64.

101. *A Sermon: Preached March 13, 1808, for the Benefit of the Society Instituted in the City of New-York, For the Relief of Poor Widows with Small Children* (New York, 1808), pp. 13, 14.

102. *Lady's Magazine and Museum: A Family Journal* (London) IV (Jan. 1831), 6. This magazine is included partly because its editorials proclaimed it "of interest to the English speaking lady at home and abroad" and partly because it shows that the preoccupation with True Womanhood was by no means confined to the United States.

103. *Sphere and Duties of Woman*, p. 102.

104. "Matrimony," *Lady's Amaranth*, II (Dec. 1839), 271.

105. Elizabeth Doten, "Marrying for Money," *The Lily of the Valley*, n. v. (1857), p. 112.

106. *Letters to Mothers*, p. 9.

107. "Maternal Relation," *Ladies' Casket* (New York, 1850?), p. 85. The importance of the mother's role was emphasized abroad as well as in America. *Godey's* recommended the book by the French author Aimee-Martin on the education of others to "be read five times," in the original if possible (XIII, Dec. 1842, 201). In this book the highest ideals of True Womanhood are upheld. For example: "Jeunes filles, jeunes epouses, tendres meres, c'est dans votre ame bien plus que dans les lois du legislateur que reposent aujourd'hui l'avenir de l'Europe et les destinees du genre humain," L. Aimee-Martin, *De l'Education des Meres de famille ou De la civilisation du genre humain par les femmes* (Bruxelles, 1857), II, 527.

108. *Maternal Association of the Amity Baptist Church*: Annual Report (New York, 1847), p. 2: "Suffer the little children to come unto me and forbid them not, is and must ever be a sacred commandment to the Christian woman."

109. For example, Daniel Webster, "The Influence of Woman," in *The Young Ladies' Reader* (Philadelphia, 1851), p. 310.

110. Mrs. Emma C. Embury, "Female Education," *Ladies' Companion*, VIII (Jan. 1838), 18. Mrs. Embury stressed the fact that the American woman was not the "mere plaything of passion" but was in strict training to be "the mother of statesmen."

111. "How May An American Woman Best Show Her Patriotism?" *Ladies Wreath*, III (1851), 313. Elizabeth Wetherell was the pen name of Susan Warner, author of *The Wide Wide World and Queechy*.

112. Henry F. Harrington, "Female Education," *Ladies' Companion*, IX (1838), 293, and "Influence of Woman—Past and Present," *Ladies Companion*, XIII (1840), 245.

113. Mrs. E. Little, "What Are the Rights of Women?" *Ladies Wreath*, II (1848-49), 133.

114. *Female Influence*, p. 18.

115. *Ibid.*, p. 23.

116. Even the women reformers were prone to use domestic images, i.e. "sweep Uncle Sam's kitchen clean," and "tidy up our country's house."

117. The "Animus and Anima" of Jung amounts almost to a catalogue of the nineteenth-century masculine and female traits, and the female hysterics whom Freud saw had much of the same training as the nineteenth-century American woman. Betty Friedan, *The Feminine Mystique* (New York, 1963), challenges the whole concept of True Womanhood as it hampers the "fulfill-ment" of the twentieth-century woman.

3. THE MERCHANT'S DAUGHTER
A Tale From Life

1. Barbara Welter, "The Cult of True Womanhood: 1820-1860," *American Quarterly*, XVIII, 151-174 (Summer 1966).

2. Caroline Healey Dall who had, as Robert Riegel notes, "the instincts of a magpie," prepared her papers for a future biographer by systematically going over them with a scissors and a heavy pen, cutting or blotting out those passages which she did not judge necessary to present "the truth" to posterity. In her lifetime, 1822-1912, Mrs. Dall outlived most of her contemporaries and judged them as harshly as they judged her. Most of the papers concerning her early years are in the Massachusetts Historical Society; some are in the Radcliffe Women's Archives. Manuscripts will be hereafter identified as either MHS or RWA.

3. Caroline, with her customary passion for setting the record straight, pre-pared *Genealogical Notes and Errata to Savage's Genealogical Dictionary* (Lowell, 1900). Her concern with her own heritage is also shown in a poem she wrote for her daughter's birthday, RWA; Letter of 1840, Dall Papers, MHS; Caroline H. Dall, *Alongside: Being Notes Suggested by A New England Boyhood* of Dr. E. E. Hale (Boston, 1906), 30.

4. *The Boston Annual Advertiser* and *Boston Directory* list Mark Healey as a merchant from 1836 to 1841. In 1844 Healey is listed as President of Atlantic Mutual Insurance Company. He is also listed in *The Boston Almanac* for the same years, although he is absent from *The Merchant's and Trader's Guide* (Boston, 1836). Thomas W. Higginson remembered the golden days of Boston's maritime empire as characterized by "Mark Healey & Son," *Cheerful Yesterdays* (Boston and New York, 1901), 59, but many other memoirs of contemporaries ignore him.

5. CH to CAD, Feb. 22, 1843, Dall Papers, MHS. Although there are some letters of Caroline to Charles which she left reasonably intact, others are mere "Fragments' in which small pieces cut out of the letters of the courtship period flutter from envelopes to frustrate the historian. No letter written by Charles survives. The only treatment of Caroline Healey Dall by a modern historian is by Robert Riegel, *American Feminists* (Lawrence, Kansas, 1963), 156-163. Rie-gel's last·chapter attempts to find some pattern in the lives of these women.

6. *Alongside*, 96 ff.

7. She dedicated her first book, *Essays and Sketches* (Boston, 1849), "To My Father, Who first nurtured in me the love of truth and of God."

8. CH to CAD, Feb. 22, 1843, Dall Papers, MHS.

9. CH to Theodore Parker, Nov. 30, 1841, Dall Papers, MHS. Augusta Evans Wilson specialized in this genre in *Beulah* and *St. Elmo*.

10. TP to CH, Dec. 3, 1841, Dall Papers, MHS. Daniel T. McColgan, *Joseph Tuckerman: Pioneer in American Social Work* (Washington, D. C., 1940); "Mr. Tuckerman's First Quarterly Report" (Boston, 1827). Tuckerman's case history approach makes his work of special interest to the social historian for he gives rare insight into the lives of the illiterate nineteenth century poor; *Alongside*, 82; Biographical information on Charles Henry Appleton Dall is taken from the *Memorial* (Boston, 1887), Dall was born in Baltimore in 1816 and educated at the Boston Latin School, Harvard, and the Cambridge Divinity School from which he graduated in 1840. He worked in St. Louis for a few months but, his health failing, returned to Baltimore to work at a "Tuckerman mission," in 1842; Caroline's own ministry was discussed in her *In Memoriam, Alexander Wadsworth* (n.p., c. 1898), 9.

11. Charles Lowell, *A Discourse Delivered in the West Church in Boston*, Aug. 3, 1845 (Cambridge, 1845), 7, 8; *"Gospel Preaching"*: A Sermon Preached at the Ordination of Dr. Thomas B. Fox as Pastor of the First Church and Religious Association, Newburyport, on Wednesday, Aug. 3, 1831, by Charles Lowell (Cambridge, 1831), 12.

12. *Nazareth* (Washington, D. C., 1903?) and *Fog Bells:* A Sequel to *Nazareth* (Washington, D.C.?, 1905), 28; *Patty Gray's Journey to the Cotton Islands:* A Series of Books for Children; Vol. 1, "From Boston to Baltimore"; Vol. 2, "From Baltimore to Washington"; Vol. 3. "On the Way: or, Patty at Mount Vernon" (Boston, 1869-1870). Caroline's publisher promised "others in preparation" but apparently no others were written. Vol. 3, 9: Vol. 1, 12; Vol. 3, 12.

13. CH to CAD, March, 1843. Dall Papers, MHS.

14. "Transcendentalism in New England": A Lecture Given Before the Society for Philosophical Inquiry (Washington, D. C.: 1895), 6.

15. "Transcendentalism in New England," 35 ff.; Caroline W. Healey, *Margaret and Her Friends*: Or, Ten Conversations with Margaret Fuller upon the Mythology of the Greeks and Its Expression in Art, Held at the House of the Rev. George Ripley in Bedford Place, Boston, beginning March 1, 1841 (Boston, 1897).

16. "Margaret Fuller," MS notes written at Conway, Massachusetts, Aug. 7, 1859, Dall Papers, RWA.

17. Biographies of Parker invariably mention the number and intensity of his female friendships, cf. Octavius Brooks Frothingham, *Theodore Parker:* A Biography (Boston, 1874); John White Chadwick, *Theodore Parker*: Preacher and Reformer (Boston and New York, 1900); Henry Steele Commager, *Theodore Parker* (Boston, 1936). Parker's ideas on women are from "A Sermon on the Public Function of Woman," Preached at the Music Hall, March 27, 1853 (Boston, 1853).

18. "Remarks at the Funeral of Elizabeth Howard Bartol" (Boston, 1883), 20.

19. *Principles and Portraits* (Boston, 1880), 52, 53.

20. C. A. Bartol, "Address in Occasion of the Death of Charles Greely Loring," Delivered in the West Church, Oct. 20, 1867 (Boston, 1867), 6; Charles G. Loring, "Account of the Sunday School of the West-Boston Society" in *The West Church and Its Ministers*: Fiftieth Anniversary of the Ordination of Charles Lowell (Boston, 1856); Caroline's book was *Women's Right to Labor* (Boston, 1860).

21. "Reforms," *Essays and Sketches*, 83, 94; CH to CAD, March 2, 1843, Dall Papers, MHS; CH to CAD, March, 1843, Dall Papers, MHS; Fredrika Bremer, *The Neighbors*: A Story of Every-Day Life (New-York, 1850), x.

22. "The Great Lawsuit: Men and Women *vs.* Custom and Tradition," *Historical Pictures Retouched* (Boston, 1860), 260; CD to CHA, Feb. 27, 1844. Dall Papers, MHS; CD to CHD, March 8, 1843, Dall Papers, MHS.

23. Joseph Tuckerman, "An Essay on The Wages Paid to Females for Their Labor" (Philadelphia, 1830).

24. *Essays and Sketches*, 62, 64, 68. *Women's Rights Under the Law* (Boston, 1862).

25. (Cambridge, 1875), 111.

26. *Alongside*, 51; CH to CAD, Feb. 22, 1843, Dall Papers, MHS.

27. *Alongside*, 51.

28. EH to CH, March 21, 1841, Dall Papers, MHS; *Essays and Sketches*, 17.

29. CH to TP, June 25, 1842 and TP to CH, July 21, 1842, Dall Papers, MHS; "A Sermon on Merchants," Nov. 22, 1846; "A Sermon on the Moral Dangers Inherent to Prosperity," Nov. 5, 1854.

30. Hannah F. Lace, *Three Experiments of Living* (Philadelphia, 21st edition, 1846) and *Elinor Fulton*: Sequel to *Three Experiments of Living* (Boston, 1837); HFL to CD, no date (probably July, 1842), Dall Papers, MHS.

31. Horace Mann, *A Few Thoughts on the Powers and Duties of Women* (Syracuse, 1853), 24, 135; *Annual Reports of the Secretary of the Board of Education for the Years 1839-44.* (Boston, 1891), Fifth Report for 1841, 128; HM to CH, July 1, 1842, Dall Papers, MHS.

32. R. C. Waterston, *George B. Emerson, His Life and Times* (Cambridge, 1884); Alonzo Potter and George B. Emerson, *The School and the Schoolmaster* (New York, 1842), 204, 205, Part I; 287; Part II; GBE to CH, July 30, 1842, Dall Papers, MHS.

33. AH to CH, Aug. 13, 1842, Dall Papers, MHS.

34. Francis Lynde Stetson, *Joseph Hodges Choate* (New York, 1917); Joseph Hodges Choate, *The Boyhood and Early Youth of Joseph Hodges Choate* (New York, 1917); GC to CH, Aug. 1, 1842, Dall Papers, MHS.

35. Prof. Charles Cleveland to CH, Aug. 13, 1842; Henry Doane to CH, July 23, 1842; Tracy Howe to CH, Sept. 3, 1842; Dall Papers, MHS.

36. Rev. T. B. Balch, "Reminiscences of Georgetown, D. C.: A Lecture" (Washington, D. C., 1854); Grace Dunlop Eckes, *A Portrait of Old Georgetown* (Richmond, 1933). Mrs. Eckes passes along some unpleasant gossip about Caro-

line as a crotchety old woman. Caroline describes the school in the Preface to the first *Patty Gray* book.

37. *Patty Gray's Journey*: From Boston to Baltimore, ix.

38. The so-called "Women's Rights" movement was not monolithic. As Martin Duberman and others have pointed out about the Abolitionists, "feminists" possessed widely varying motivations and goals. Although Mrs. Dall became active in a movement she once scorned, she never changed her definition of woman's nature nor her own personality set. She died only a few years before the Nineteenth Amendment was passed, but from all that went before one wonders if, on the threshold of victory, Caroline would not have been like Phyllis McGinley's "Old Feminist," taking ". . . no pleasure in her Rights, | Who so enjoyed her Wrongs."

4. FEMALE COMPLAINTS

Medical Views of American Women (1790-1865)

1. See, for example, Harriet Martineau, *Society in America*, 2 vols. (New York, 1837), p. 258; Frances Trollope, *Domestic manners of the Americans*, 2 vols. (London, 1832), p. 93; Basil Hall, *The modern traveller* (London, 1830), pp. 39-40.

2. Most of the nineteenth-century medical texts and manuscript notes of obstetricians and gynecologists are found in the archives of the New York Academy of Medicine (hereafter referred to as NYAM), to whose research staff I am indebted.

3. John Van Pelt Quackenbush, "An address delivered before the students of the Albany Medical College: Introductory to the course on obstetrics (Albany, 1857), p. 14. Dr. Quackenbush was Professor of Midwifery and the Diseases of Women and Children.

4. Charles D. Meigs, "Lecture on some of the distinctive characteristics of the female: Delivered before the class of the Jefferson Medical College, January 5, 1847" (Philadelphia, 1847), p. 19. Dr. Meigs was Professor of Obstetrics and the Diseases of Women and Children.

5. O. S. Fowler, *Love and parentage applied to the improvement of offspring* (n.p., n.d.), p. 35. Fowler styled himself a "Practical Phrenologist."

6. T. Gaillard Thomas, MS Notes on lectures in obstetrics (c. 1874), NYAM. Prof. Thomas was affiliated with the College of Physicians and Surgeons, New York.

7. Gunning Bedford, *Clinical lectures on the diseases of women and children*, 2nd ed. (New York, 1855), p. 101. Dr. Bedford was Professor of Obstetrics, University of New York.

8. William P. Dewees, *Treatise on the diseases of females*, 2nd ed. (Philadelphia, 1828), p. 19. Dr. Dewees was Adjunct Professor of Midwifery, University of Pennsylvania.

9. W. A. Beach, *An improved system of midwifery* (New York, 1847), p. 45.

10. Hugh L. Hodge, *On diseases peculiar to women* (Philadelphia, 1860),

pp. 147-48. Dr. Hodge was Professor of Obstetrics and the Diseases of Women and Children, University of Pennsylvania.

11. Alexander Walker, *Beauty: Illustrated chiefly by an analysis and Classification of Woman*, edited by An American Physician (New York, 1844), pp. 224-25.

12. C. Morrill, *The physiology of woman and her diseases from infancy to old age* (Boston, 1847), p. 19.

13. Fleetwood Churchill, *The diseases of females: Including those of pregnancy and childbed*, 3rd. Amer. ed. (Philadelphia, 1844), p. 397. Dr. Churchill was Professor of Obstetrics, Queen's College, Ireland.

14. Charles D. Meigs, *Females and their diseases: A series of letters to his class* (Philadelphia, 1848), p. 36.

15. Morrill (n. 12), p. 407.

16. Hugh Smith, *Letters to married ladies* (New York and Boston, 1832), p. 174.

17. John Rodgers, *MS Notes on a course of lectures* on obstetrics (New York, 1802-03), NYAM.

18. Charles H. Goodwin, *Treatment of diseases of women, puerperal and non-puerperal*, 2nd ed. (New York, 1884), pp. 355-80; Dewees, (n. 8); *The Improved American Family Physician: or Sick Man's Guide to Health* (New York, 1833), pp. 25ff.; Henry N. Guernsey, *The application of the principles and practice of homoeopathy to obstetrics* (Philadelphia, 1867); Dr. Guernsey was Prof. of Obstetrics and Diseases of Women and Children, Homoeopathic Medical College of Pennsylvania.

19. Walter Johnson, *An Essay on the diseases of young women* (London, 1849), pp. 55, 248-56. Dr. Johnson was Medical Tutor, Guy's Hospital, London.

20. Cotton Mather's discussion of his techniques in approaching the young girls who claimed to have seen witches is very reminiscent of Freud's early case histories. Rush is called "The father of modern psychiatry" for his pioneering work in mental illness; see Carl Binger, *Revolutionary doctor: Benjamin Rush, 1746-1813* (New York, 1966), chs. 13, 14.

21. Morrill (n. 12), p. 413.

22. Harriot K. Hunt, *Glances and glimpses: or fifty years social, including twenty years professional life* (Boston, 1856), pp. 139, 397-401.

23. Quackenbush (n. 3), p. 9.

24. John King, *Woman: Her diseases and their treatment* (Cincinnati, 1858), p. 10. King was Professor of Obstetrics at the Eclectic Medical Institute, Cincinnati.

25. Johnson (n. 19), p. 4.

26. John C. Peters, *A treatise on the diseases of married females* (New York, 1854), p. 17.

27. Joseph Warrington, *The obstetric catechism* (Philadelphia, 1842), p. 41.

28. Ibid., p. 40.

29. Samuel Bard, *A compendium of the theory and practice of midwifery* (New York, 1807), pp. 65-67; Morrill (n. 21), p. 46.

30. Edward H. Clarke, *Sex in Education: or, A fair chance for the girls*, 5th ed. (Boston, 1873), pp. 23, 83, 104. Dr. Clarke's conclusions were challenged by Mrs. E. B. Duffey, *No Sex in Education: or, An equal chance for both girls and boys* (Philadelphia, 1874?), Mrs. Duffey refuses to accept Clarke's arguments about "an element of imagined feminine weakness and invalidism to which it is necessary to yield. . . ." p. 7.

31. Morrill (n. 12), p. 8.

32. Ibid., p. 150.

33. Samuel Ashwell, *A practical treatise on the diseases peculiar to women* (London, 1843), p. 19.

34. Warrington (n. 26), p. 50; Goodwin (n. 18), p. 421.

35. Morrill (n. 12), pp. 45-46; Beach (n. 9), p. 270.

36. An Old Physician [William Alexander Alcott], *The physiology of marriage* (Boston, 1856), ch. 5, pp. 67-79.

37. Mary S. Gove [Nichols], *Lectures to ladies on anatomy and physiology* (Boston, 1842), p. 284. Mrs. Nichols was surprised at the widespread incidence of this vice among American women who were so untutored in marital pleasure that they were unaware of what they were doing.

38. Morrill (n. 12), p. 176.

39. Guernsey (n. 18), p. 54.

40. Beach (n. 9), p. 270.

41. Morrill (n. 12), p. 180.

42. [Alcott] (n. 36), p. 170.

43. Gunning Bedford, *The principles and practice of obstetrics* (New York, 1861), p. 97.

44. Edward H. Dixon, *Scenes in the practice of a New York surgeon* (New York, 1856), p. 59.

45. Practically every medical treatise takes up this fad in order to denounce it; one of the most extensive treatments is the Appendix to Smith (n. 16), entitled "Letters on corsets by the American editor."

46. Joseph Brevitt, *The female medical repository* (Baltimore, 1810), p. 94.

47. Joseph S. Longshore, *The practical importance of female medical education: an introductory lecture delivered September 6, 1853, in the Pennsylvania Medical College of Philadelphia* (Philadelphia, 1853), pp. 19-20. Dr. Longshore was Professor of Obstetrics and the Diseases of Women and Children.

48. William H. Byford, *The practice of medicine and surgery applied to the diseases and accidents incident to women* (Philadelphia, 1865), p. 152.

49. Dixon (n. 44), p. 62. According to the New York physician "indigestion was an almost necessary concomitant of fashionable life" (p. 57).

50. Johnson (n. 19), p. 26.

51. *New family manual: and ladies' indispensable assistant* (New York, 1852), p. 33.

52. O S. Fowler (n. 5), p. 23.

53. Quoted in O. S. Fowler, *Amativeness: or, evils and remedies of excessive and perverted sensuality* (n.d., n.p.), p. 19.

54. Ibid., p. 20.

55. [Alcott] (n. 36), pp. 199, 122.

56. Byford (n. 48), p. 213.

57. Beach (n. 9), p. 269.

58. Francis H. Ramsbotham (Philadelphia, 1842), pp. 437ff., *The principles and practice of obstetric, medicine and surgery*; Hodge (n. 10), p. 301; [Alcott] (n. 36), p. 153.

59. T. C. Nichols and Mary S. Gove Nichols, *Marriage: Its history, character and results; Its sanctities, and its profanities; Its science and its facts. Demonstrating its influence, as a civilized institution, on the happiness of the individual and the progress of the race* (Cincinnati, 1854), pp. 202, 207. Mrs. Nichols replaced the "Law of Marriage" with the principle of "Fidelity to the law of one's own life," a radical departure into female free-thinking: "The day that I was able to say, I owe no fealty to a husband, or any human being, I will be faithful to myself, was my first day of freedom" (p. 268).

60. King (n. 23), p. 15.

61. Churchill (n. 13), John Rogers (n. 17); Bedford (n. 43).

62. Chandler Gilman, MS Notes on his lectures on obstetrics (New York, c.1846), NYAM; Bedford, (n. 7), pp. 520ff.

63. Gilman (n. 62).

64. MS Diary of Anna Mercer La Roche Francis (December, 1865), Special Collections, Columbia University Library.

65. Quackenbush (n. 3), p. 14.

66. Meigs (n. 14), p. 18.

67. Peters (n. 25), pp. 19-20. Peters quotes "Ticknor's rules for pregnancy," which are quoted in several other contemporary sources.

68. MS Reports of midwifery cases attended by students of New York University Medical College and New York Asylum for Lying-In Women (1842-43), NYAM; A. Curtis, *Lectures on midwifery and the forms of disease peculiar to women and children*: Delivered to the members of the Botanico-Medical College of Ohio (Columbus, Ohio, 1841) p. 11. Dr. Curtis was president of the college.

69. Bard (n. 28), p. 182.

70. Bedford (n. 43), p. 708.

71. Ann Preston, *Introductory lectures to the course of instruction in the Female Medical College of Pennsylvania for the session 1855-56* (Philadelphia, 1855), p. 12. Dr. Preston, who received her degree in 1850, was Professor of Physiology at the College. America's "First Woman Doctor," Elizabeth Blackwell, wrote several pamphlets on the same question.

5. ANTI-INTELLECTUALISM AND THE AMERICAN WOMAN
(1800–1860)

1. Intellectual, in this paper, is used as Richard Hofstadter defines it in contradistinction to intelligence: "Intellect . . . is the critical, creative, and contemplative side of man. Whereas intelligence seeks to grasp, manipulate, re-order, adjust, intellect examines, theorizes, criticizes, imagines." *Anti-Intellectualism in American Life*, New York, 1963, 25. Although this paper discusses the anti-intellectualism of American women it is understood that many of the generalizations might apply to men as well. However, even if creative intelligence was denigrated in a romantic age, it was a faculty of man; he might not value it, but he possessed it, while women did not.

2. One summary of woman's total lack of intellectual abilities was by Friedrich Nietzsche: "Man thinks woman profound, because he cannot fathom her depths. Woman is not even shallow." *The Twilight of the Idols, Maxims and Missiles*, trans. Anthony M. Ludovici, New York, 1941, 27. No nineteenth-century American male made so ungallant a remark, although some of Orestes Brownson's grumblings came close. In general, woman's anti-intellectualism was approved by society, since it contributed to the division of labor on which the order of that society rested.

3. William P. Dewees, *Treatise on the Diseases of Females*, 2nd ed., Philadelphia, 1828, 19.

4. Hugh L. Hodge, *On Diseases Peculiar to Women*, Philadelphia, 1860, 149, 150.

5. John King, *Woman: Her Diseases and Their Treatment*, 3rd ed., Cincinnati, 1867, 14; and Charles D. Meigs, *Females and Their Diseases*, Philadelphia, 1894, 66.

6. Alexander Walker, *Beauty*, ed. by an American Physician, New York, 1844, 229.

7. See, for example, George Combe, *Lectures on Phrenology*, with notes, an introductory essay, and an historical sketch by Andrew Boardman, New York, 1839; Jessie A. Fowler, *A Manual of Mental Science*, London and New York, 1897; G. Spurzheim, *Outlines of Phrenology*, Boston, 1832; and Joseph A. Warne, *Phrenology in the Family*, Philadelphia, 1839, *passim*.

8. Lorenzo N. Fowler, *Marriage*, New York, 1847, 202.

9. "The Social Position and Culture Due to Women," a Sermon Delivered Before the Maternal Association of the Amity Street Baptist Church, New York, 1847, 26.

10. A. B. Muzzey, *The Young Maiden*, Boston, 1840, 13, 7-8.

11. Jane Kinderly Stanford, *A Lady's Gift: Woman As She Ought to Be*, Philadelphia, 1836, 40.

12. "Maria," *Godey's Lady's Book*, II (October, 1831), 206.

13. "Hints to Young Ladies," *The Mother's Magazine*, VI (1838), 25.

14. Mrs. John Sandford, *Woman, in Her Social and Domestic Character*, 6th American ed., Boston, 1843, 106.

15. Ella Herbert, "Florence Lee: or, the Model Wife," *The Ladies' Wreath*, VII (1853), 389-98.

16. An excellent discussion of text-books in the nineteenth century as inculcators of values and indicators of society is given in Ruth Miller Elson, *Guardians of Tradition*, Lincoln, Nebraska, 1964. Woman's status is discussed 301-12.

17. Charles Butler, *An American Lady*, Philadelphia, 1839, 156-7.

18. George Wood, "Address to the Graduating Class," the 1st Annual Commencement of the Brooklyn Female Academy, July 21, 1847, New York, 1847, 37.

19. "Education of Women," *Peterson's Magazine*, II (1842), 156.

20. D. Fraser, *The Mental Flower Garden*, New York, 1807, 158.

21. John Greenleaf Whittier, "In School Days," *The Complete Poetical Works of Whittier*, Cambridge Edition, Boston, 1894, 407-8. Margaret Mead in *Male and Female*, New York, 1949, also quotes this poem to make her point about modern woman's problems in co-education, and finds it significant that the poet "very deftly and definitely kills the lady off" in the concluding stanza, 317-18.

22. Mrs. S. M. Perkins, "Woman and Fame," *The Lily of the Valley* (1852), 75. A widely-quoted and much anthologized poem by Felicia Hemans, "Woman's Fame," had a similar theme.

23. *The Young Lady's Companion*, ed. by A Lady, Philadelphia, 1851, 9.

24. "Female Orators," *The Mother's Magazine*, VI (1838), 27.

25. John S. C. Abbott, *Letters to Young Women*, New York, 1844, 20.

26. T. S. Arthur, *Advice to Young Men*, Philadelphia, 1860, 150.

27. Horace Mann, *A Few Thoughts on the Powers and Duties of Woman*, Syracuse, 1853, 25.

28. "Woman," *The Present*, I (December, 1843), 165.

29. Leon Edel suggests that this was one of the reasons Henry James never married, in *Henry James*, Vol. 1, "The Untried Years," New York and Philadelphia, 1951, Ch. V. "Venus and Diana."

30. Nathaniel Hawthorne, *Fanshawe*, Modern Library Edition, New York, 1937, 79-80. Fanshawe rejects this offer and goes back to his books to die young, burned-out by the consuming intellectual fires.

31. Madame de Stael, *Corinne in Italy*, 2 vols., London and Philadelphia, 1894, II, 182.

32. Emma C. Embury, "Corinna," *Selected Prose Writings of Mrs. Emma C. Embury*, New York, 1893, 86-99.

33. MS copy of "Guido, a Tale and Other Poems," Emma C. Embury Papers, Manuscripts Division, New York Public Library.

34. John S. Hart, *Female Prose Writers of America*, Philadelphia, 1866, 139-40.

35. Margaret Fuller Ossoli, *Women in the Nineteenth Century*, Boston, 1874, 174, 176.

36. J. Christopher Herold, *Mistress to an Age*, New York, 1958.

37. Margaret Fuller Ossoli, *Memoirs*, edited by James Freeman Clarke *et al.*, Boston, 1854, 118.

38. Ossoli, *Woman in the Nineteenth Century*, vi.

39. Hawthorne's passage in his *Italian Note-Books* is quoted in full in Mason Wade, *Margaret Fuller*, New York, 1940, 280-2. Wade sees no sympathy in this diatribe, but calls it "an amazingly malign passage."

40. Sarah Josepha Hale, *Woman's Record*, New York, 1853, 669.

41. "Margaret Fuller's Memoirs," *Westminster Review*, LVII (April, 1852), 212.

42. Harriot K. Hunt, *Glances and Glimpses*, Boston, 1856, 409.

6. THE FEMINIZATION OF AMERICAN RELIGION
(1800-1860)

1. Martin Duberman has done this very effectively in his introduction to *The Anti-Slavery Vanguard: New Essays on the Abolitionists* (Princeton, 1965) and his biography of James Russell Lowell (Boston, 1966). Alice Felt Tyler, *Freedom's Ferment: Phases of American Social History to 1860* (Minneapolis, 1944) and Arthur M. Schlesinger, Sr., *The American as Reformer* (Cambridge, 1951) attempt a synthesis of the reform movements of the nineteenth century. A contemporary account of the nature of the reformer by Ralph Waldo Emerson. "Man the Reformer," in Ralph Waldo Emerson, *Nature, Addresses, and Lectures*, ed. Edward Waldo Emerson (Boston, 1903) is the first and perhaps the best attempt at this kind of social history.

2. For example, Max Weber, *The Theory of Social and Economic Organization*, translated by A. M. Henderson (Glencoe, Ill., 1957); Robert Merton, *Social Theory and Social Structure*, Rev. Ed. (Glencoe, Ill., 1960); Talcott Parsons, *Structure and Process in Modern Society* (Glencoe, Illinois, 1960); Richard H. Tawney, *Religion and the Rise of Capitalism* (New York, 1922); W. Seward Salisbury, *Religion in American Culture* (Homewood, Ill., 1964); Hadley Cantril, *The Psychology of Social Movements* (New York, 1941); Cyclone Covey, *The American Pilgrimage*, (Stillwater, Oklahoma, 1960); and David O. Moberg, *The Church As a Social Institution: The Sociology of American Religion* (Englewood Cliffs, N.J., 1962).

3. See especially Robert Briffault, *The Mothers: The Matriarchal Theory of Social Origins* (New York, 1931) and Johann Jakob Bachsfen, *Myth, Religion and Mother Right*, translated by Ralph Manheim (Princeton, New Jersey, 1967).

4. For basic histories of American religion see Winthrop Hudson, *American Protestantism* (Chicago, 1961); W. W. Sweet, *The Story of Religions in America* (New York, 1930); W. L. Sperry, *Religion in America* (New York, 1946); T. C. Hall, *The Religious Background of American Culture* (Boston, 1930); J. W. Smith and A. L. Jamison, eds., *Religion in American Life* (Princeton, 1961); and E. S. Bates, *American Faith: Political and Economic Foundations* (New York, 1940).

5. For example, Eliza W. Farnham, *Woman and Her Era*, 2 vols. (New York, 1964), and Charlotte Perkins Stetson Gilman, *His Religion and Hers: A Study of*

*the Faith of Our Fathers*and* the *Work of Our Mothers* (New York and London, 1923).

6. A classic account is in Thorstein Veblen, *The Theory of the Leisure Class* (New York, 1919). In nineteenth-century tariff policy, women are urged to consume only goods manufactured at home. In his report on manufactures in 1790, Alexander Hamilton urged the adoption of manufacturing as a means of providing employment for women, an argument approved of by the nineteenth-century economist Matthew Carey. However, the use of women as cheap labor paid scarcely any lip service to these rhetorical rationalizations, and Veblen's theory of women as consumers and symbols of prosperity increasingly applied only to the middle classes.

7. Henry Adams, *Democracy: An American Novel* (New York, 1882).

8. The best brief sketch of Antoinette Brown Blackwell is by Barbara M. Solomon in *Notable American Women: 1607-1950*, 3 vols., Vol. I, 158-60 (Cambridge, Mass., 1970), hereafter referred to as NAW. Other biographies are Laura Kerr, *Lady in the Pulpit* (New York, 1951) and Elinor Rice Hays, *Those Extraordinary Blackwells* (New York, 1967). Mrs. Blackwell became increasingly dissatisfied with pastoral work and the Congregational Church and by 1854, after one year's service, resigned her pulpit to do volunteer work among the poor and mentally disturbed. In later life, after her family was raised, she returned to the ministry, where she campaigned for woman suffrage. Mrs. Blackwell was a philosopher rather than a theologian and, like her sister-in-law Elizabeth, was more concerned with the application of her profession to women's life than in achieving distinction in her own field.

9. *The Works of Orestes A. Brownson, Collected and Arranged by Henry F. Brownson*, 20 vols. (New York, 1966) give a complete picture of Brownson's views of women. Briefly, he was opposed to the "woman worship" of his age, and horrified at the woman's movement because it preached interference with marriage and procreation. "Of course we hold that the woman was made for the man, not the man for the woman, and the husband is the head of the wife, even as Christ is the head of the Church. . . ." (Vol. XVIII, p. 386) He saw the weakening of American family life as the greatest crisis of the age, and the women's movement, in its stress on individual rights, hastened the dissolution of the family as a social unit and contributed to the disastrous trend of isolation. (Vol. XVIII, 388.) Moreover, the woman's movement was yet another indication of the increasing "spirit of insubordination" in society and like other such movements required "no self-sacrifice or submission of one's will." (Vol. XVIII, 416.) He was convinced that its leaders were not only opposed to the Christian family, "but to Christianity itself." (Vol. XVIII, 414.)

10. Quoted in Henry Steele Commager, *Theodore Parker* (Boston, 1936), 150 and in Theodore Parker, *A Discourse of Matters Pertaining to Religion* (Boston, 1842), 201. The issue of infant damnation led several Congregational ministers into the more permissive theology of Unitarianism, including Sheba Smith and Antoinette Brown Blackwell. Barbara M. Cross, *Horace Bushnell: Minister to a Changing America* (Chicago, 1958) deals with one minister's solution to the tensions of change. Unitarian theology is covered fully in E. M. Wilbur, *History of Unitarianism*, 2 vols., (Cambridge, Mass., 1945-1952.)

11. E. Digby Baltzell, *The Protestant Establishment: Aristocracy and Caste in America* (New York, 1964); Henry F. May, *Protestant Churches and Industrial America* (New York, 1949); Louis Wright, *Culture on the Moving Frontier* (Bloomington, Indiana, 1955), and David O. Moberg, *Church As a Social Institution* (Englewood Cliffs, N.J., 1962).

12. *Testimony of the Life, Character, Revelations and Doctrines of Our Ever Blessed Mother, Ann Lee and the Elders With Her; Through whom the word of eternal life was opened on this day of Christ's Second Appearing; Collected from living witnesses, by order of the ministry, in union with the Church* (Hancock, Massachusetts, 1816). A basic history of the Shakers is Marguerite Melcher, *The Shaker Adventure* (Princeton, 1941).

13. Theodore Parker, "A Sermon of the Public Function of Woman," Preached at the Music Hall, March 27, 1953 (Boston, 1853) and in many other sermons.

14. Susa Young Gates, *History of the Young Ladies' Mutual Improvement Association of the Church of Jesus Christ of Latter Day Saints* (Salt Lake City, 1911), 16ff. Eliza R. Snow Smith, wife of both Joseph Smith and Brigham Young, wrote a hymn on this theme, "O My Father," in *Poems, Religious, Historical and Political* (Salt Lake City, 1877), 173.

15. Nathaniel Hawthorne, *The Scarlet Letter* (Boston, 1850), "Earlier in life, Hester had vainly imagined that she herself might be the destined prophetess, but had long since recognized the impossibility that any mission of divine and mysterious truth should be confided to a woman stained with sin, bowed down with shame, or even burdened with a life-long sorrow. The angel and apostle of the coming revelation must be a woman indeed, but lofty, pure, and beautiful; and wise, moreover, not through dusky grief, but the ethereal medium of joy; and showing how sacred love should make us happy, by the truest test of a life successful to such an end." (240) This new saviour will reveal "a new Truth" to re-order the relations between men and women.

16. This idea is set out most clearly in Eliza W. Farnham, *Woman and Her Era*, 2 vols. (New York, 1964).

17. A history of the major theological and social changes in Christianity could be written in which the primary sources were biographies of Christ. A perceptive treatment of this subject is Edith Hamilton, *Witness to the Truth: Christ and His Interpreters* (New York, 1948). Another sort of survey is *Christ In Poetry*, an anthology compiled and edited by Thomas Curtis Clark and Hazel Davis Clark (New York, 1952). Two popular nineteenth-century biographies were Lyman Abbott, *Jesus of Nazareth: His Life and Teachings* (New York, 1869) and Frederic William Farrar, *The Life of Christ* (New York, 1874). A sample of the "Sunday School" biography is Caroline Wells Dall, *Nazareth* (Washington, D.C., 1903). Mrs. Dall saw the mission of the Saviour as the revelation of "the universal Fatherhood of God, the common brotherhood of man" and the repudiation of the "old dogma of a corrupt nature by showing how Godlike a human life could be," 24.

18. C.A. Bartol, "The Image Passing Before Us: A Sermon After the Decease of Elizabeth Howard Bartol" (Boston, 1883).

19. Theodore Parker had several sermons on this subject, including "A Sermon of Merchants" (November 22, 1846); "A Sermon on the Moral Condition of Bos-

ton" (February 11, 1849); "A Sermon on the Spiritual Condition of Boston" (February 18, 1849); and "A Sermon of the Moral Dangers Incident to Prosperity" (November 5, 1854).

20. Frances Trollope, *Domestic Manners of the Americans* (New York, 1949; original edition 1832), 75. This American phenomenon (which has parallels in most Western countries) of women forming the majorities of church congregations, has been explained in various ways. The way most favored by the nineteenth century involved the natural predilection of women for good and therefore for religion. One twentieth-century writer believes that church-going is accounted for largely by a "psychology of Bereavement." The Puritans were bereft of England, the nineteenth-century woman was bereft of her children (or her personhood), and so forth. Therefore insofar as the individual American was pleased with himself, self-confident, and victorious over nature or property he had, presumably, increasingly less need for church—Cyclone Covey, *The American Pilgrimage*, 44-69. Another sociological explanation believes that women are "conditioned to react in terms of altruism and cooperation rather than of egocentrism and competition," and therefore are prime candidates for submission to external authority in both worlds—W. Seward Salisbury, *Religion in American Culture*, 88. Other explanations stress the supposed attraction of children to authority figures of the opposite sex. God is the father, ergo Oedipus aeternus. Woman's supposed innate masochism might, it could be argued, produce more guilt feelings than are produced in males, and religion is supposed to remove feelings of guilt. In any case, whether psychological or cultural, the historic fact of female-dominated churches and male-dominated clergy remains.

21. Hymn books consulted were: Baron Stow and S.F. Smith, *The Psalmist: a new collection of hymns for the use of the Baptist Church* (Boston, 1843); *Psalms and Hymns Adapted to Social, Private and Public Worship in the Presbyterian Church in the United States of America: Approved and authorized by the General Assembly* (Philadelphia, 1843); *Hymns of the Protestant Episcopal Church in the United States of America: Set Forth in the General Convention of Said Church in the Year of Our Lord, 1789, 1808, 1826* (Philadelphia, 1827); *Collection of Hymns for Public and Private Worship: Approved by the General Synod of the Evangelical Lutheran Church* (Columbus, Ohio, second edition, 1855); Abiel A. Livermore, ed., *Christian Hymns for Public and Private Worship* (Boston, 1846); Samuel Longfellow and Samuel Johnson. *A Book of Hymns for Public and Private Devotion* (Cambridge, 1846) (Unitarian); *Plymouth Collection of Hymns and Tunes; for the use of Christian Congregations* (New York, 1855); *Hymnal of the Presbyterian Church: Ordered by the General Assembly* (Philadelphia, 1866); *The Hymnal: Published by the Authority of the General Assembly of the Presbyterian Church in the United States of America* (Philadelphia, 1895); *Hymns of the Faith with Psalms* (Boston, 1887) (Congregational); *The Baptist Hymn and Tune Book* (Philadelphia, 1871); *Hymns: Approved by the General Synod of the Lutheran Church in the United States* (Philadelphia, 1871), revised from the edition of 1852; *Hymns for Church and Home* (New York, 1860) (Episcopal); and *Hymnal: According to the Use of the Protestant Episcopal Church in the United States of America printed under the authority of the General Convention* (Oxford, 1892; original edition 1872).

22. "O Perfect Love" was written by Charlotte Elliott, a pious English invalid, who also wrote the popular revival hymn "Just As I Am"—Harvey B. Marks, *The*

Rise and Growth of English Hymnody (New York, London and Edinburgh, 1937), 127. Sarah Adams, perhaps the most famous of the nineteenth-century hymn writers, had the dubious distinction of seeing her most popular hymn, "Nearer, My God to Thee," identified with imperialism and patriotism. It was reputedly quoted by McKinley on his deathbed, was Theodore Roosevelt's favorite hymn, and was sung by the gallant men on the sinking *Titanic*—Louis F. Benson, *The English Hymn: Its Development and Use in Worship* (1962, Richmond, Virginia; original edition, 1915), 272.

23. Mary Clemmet, ed. *The Poetical Works of Alice and Phoebe Cary: With a Memorial of Their Lives* (New York, 1876), 172; Alice Cary, *Ballads, Lyrics and Poems* (New York, 1866), 276.

24. "I Need Thee Every Hour" was written by Mrs. Annie S. Hawks, and was considered a particularly appropriate hymn for Women's Circles and Mothers' Meetings—Edward S. Ninde, *The Story of the American Hymn* (New York, 1921), 150.

25. Charlotte Elliott in Marks, *Rise and Growth of English Hymnody*, 128.

26. The Christianizing of the West is seen as a central theme in virtually all standard accounts of the American religious experience. T. Scott Miyakawa, *Protestants and Pioneers: Individualism and Conformity on the American Frontier* (Chicago and London, 1944) applies Frederick Jackson Turner's frontier thesis to the religious life of the West, and agrees with Turner that in this, as in other areas, the frontier "either drastically altered or rejected the older cultural traditions." 226. Nineteenth-century witnesses to the propagation of the faith included the travel accounts of Robert Baird, *Religion in America: or, an Account of the Origins, Progress, Relation to the State and Present Condition of the Evangelical Churches in the United States* (New York, 1844): Caroline Kirkland, *The Evening Book: Or, Fireside Talk on Morals and Manners, with Sketches of Western Life* (New York, 1852); Harriet Martineau, *Retrospect of Western Travel*, 3 volumes (London, 1838); and *Society in America*, 3 volumes (London, 1837), as well as the critical Mrs. Trollope.

27. Robert F. Berkhofer, Jr., *Salvation and the Savage: An Analysis of Protestant Missions and American Indian Response, 1787-1862* (Lexington, Kentucky, 1965) and R. Pierce Beaver, *Church, State, and the American Indians: Two and a Half Centuries of Partnership in Missions Between Protestant Churches and Government* (St. Louis, 1966).

28. Mrs. Owens, ed., "Diaries of Pioneer Women of Clatsop County," *Oregon Pioneers Association*, Vol. XXIV (1896), 89-94.

29. Adoniram Judson, a baptist missionary, brought three wives to join him in his labors in Burma: Ann Hasseltine (1789-1826), followed by Sarah Hall Boardman (1803-1845) and Emily Chubbuck (1817)1854) who returned to the United States after her husband's death in 1850. The combined trials of these three women culminating in their early deaths were considered excellent propaganda for the Mission Boards—James D. Knowles, *Memoir of Mrs. Ann H. Judson, Late Missionary to Burma* (New York, 1829); Arabella W. Stuart, *The Lives of Mrs. Ann H. Judson and Mrs. Sarah B. Judson, with a Biographical Sketch of Mrs. Emily C. Judson* (New York, 1851); Gordon L. Hall, *Golden Boats from Burma* (New York, 1961); Emily Forester [Judson], *Memoir of Sarah B. Judson* (New York, 1848); Walter N.

Wyeth, *Sarah B. Judson* (Boston, 1889); Asahel Clark Kendrick, *The Life and Letters of Mrs. Emily C. Judson* (New York, 1860). Another popular missionary heroine was Harriet Atwood Newell (1793-1812), who was the first American to die on a foreign mission—NAW, Vol. II, Mary Sumner Benson, "Harriet Atwood Newell," 619-620; Harriet Newell, *The Life and Writings of Mrs. Harriet Newell* (Boston, 1831).

30.   The Whitmans were married in 1836 and almost immediately embarked for Oregon. Narcissa survived the hazards of frontier life, the loss of her daughter by drowning, increasing blindness and constant harassment by Indians and rival religious groups only to die with her husband in a massacre at Waiilatpu in 1847— Clifford M. Drury, *First White Women over the Rockies*, 3 volumes (New York, 1963-66); Jeanette Eaton, *Narcissa Whitman* (New York, 1941); Opal Sweazea Allen, *Narcissa Whitman* (New York, 1959); and the *Proceedings* of the Oregon Pioneers Association, *passim*.

31.   Eliza Spalding, whose health continued to decline with each year in the West, died of tuberculosis in 1851 at the age of forty-three—Clifford M. Drury, *The First White Women ove the Rockies*, I, 173-233; "Diary of Mrs. E.H. Spalding," Oregon Pioneers Association, Vol. XXIV (1896), 106-110.

32.   T.E. Elliott, ed., Narcissa Prentiss Whitman; *The Coming of the White Woman*, 1836, as Told in the Letters and Journals of Narcissa Prentiss Whitman (Portland, 1937), 108.

33.   Histories of revivalism in the United States are numerous. One of the best is Timothy L. Smith, *Revivalism and Social Reform in Mid-Nineteenth Century America* (New York and Nashville, 1957). An interesting psychological study is Sidney George Dimond, *The Psychology of the Methodist Revival: An Empirical and Descriptive Study* (London, 1926). Other sources are Paulus Scharpff, *History of Evangelism: Three Hundred Years of Evangelism in Germany, Great Britain, and the United States of America*, translated by Helga Bender Henry (Grand Rapids, Michigan, 1966); F.G. Beardsley, *A History of American Revivals* (The Tract Society, n.p., 1912); Bernard A Weisberger, *They Gathered At the River: The Story of the Great Revivals and Their Impact Upon Religion in America* (Boston and Toronto, 1958); C.A. Johnson, *The Frontier Camp Meeting* (Dallas, Texas, 1955); and Whitney R. Cross, *The Burned-over District: The Social and Intellectual History of Enthusiastic Religion in Western New York, 1800-1850* (Ithaca, New York, 1950). The most famous nineteenth century account of revivals was by the man who made them, Charles G. Finney, *Lectures on Revival* (Boston, 1836).

34.   Mrs. Maggie N. Van Cott, *The Harvest and the Reaper: Reminiscences of Revival Work* (New York, c.1883), 49, 67-9.

35.   Ellen G. White, *Life Sketches* (Mountain View, California, 1915; first edition, 1860), 32-34.

36.   MS Diary of Myra S. Smith, June 19, 1859, Elizabeth and Arthur Schlesinger Library, Radcliffe College, Cambridge, Massachusetts.

37.   Richard Hofstadter, *Anti-Intellectualism in America* (New York, 1963).

38.   Barbara Welter, "Anti-Intellectualism and the American Woman: 1800-1860," *Mid-America*, Vol. 48 (October, 1966), 258-70.

39.   Caroline Dall, "Transcendentalism in New England: A Lecture Given

before the Society for Philosophical Enquiry, Washington, D.C., May 7, 1895, in *The Journal of Speculative Philosophy*, Vol. XXIII, No. 1 (1897), 1-38. C. Gregg Singer, *A Theological Interpretation of American History* (Nutley, New Jersey, 1964) saw Transcendentalism as a direct repudiation of Puritanism, because it glorified man instead of God.

40. Octavius Brooks Frothingham, *Recollections and Impressions, 1822-1890* (New York and London, 1891), 136. Ralph Waldo Emerson, *The Complete Writings of Ralph Waldo Emerson* (New York, 1929, 1st edition 1875), "Woman," 1178-84.

41. Caroline Dall, in her voluminous diaries and notes, recorded many impressions of these conversations besides the ones she published—Caroline Healy Dall MSS, Massachusetts Historical Society and Radcliffe Women's Archives.

42. Octavius Brooks Frothingham, *Memoir of William Henry Channing* (Boston and New York, 1886), 296.

43. David Riesman, Introduction to Jessie Bernard, *Academic Women* (New York, 1966). The late David Potter also reconsidered his assessment of the American character in his essay, "American Women and the American Character" in John A. Hague, ed., *American Character and Culture* (De Land, Florida, 1964), 65-84.

44. See in particular Margaret Fuller (Ossoli). *Women in the Nineteenth Century* (New York, 1845), *Life Without and Life Within*, edited by A.B. Fuller (Boston, 1859) and Caroline W. Healey (Dall), *Margaret and Her Friends: Or, the Conversations with Margaret Fuller Upon the Mythology of the Greeks and Its Expression in Art* (Boston, 1896).

45. Donald Meyer, *The Positive Thinkers* (Garden City, New York, 1965).

46. John Van Der Zee Sears, *My Friends at Brook Farm* (New York, 1918), 89.

47. Charles Nordhoff, *The Communist Societies of the United States* (New York, 1912; original edition 1875), 412.

48. New Harmony (Indiana), Yellow Springs Community (Ohio), Brook Farm (Massachusetts), North American Phalanx (New Jersey), Ceresco (Wisconsin), Northampton Association (Massachusetts), Fruitlands (Massachusetts), Oneida (New York) and Modern Times (New York).

49. John Thomas Codman, *Brook Farm:Historic and Personal Memoirs* (Boston, 1894), 111, and articles in *The Dial* and *The Harbinger*, throughout their publication, translating and commenting on Fourier. Fourier's ideas on the role of women in the new society can be found in Francois Marie Charles Fourier, *Theory of Social Organization* (New York, 1876).

50. Amelia Russell, "Home Life of the Brook Farm Association," *The Atlantic Monthly*, Vol. 42 (October, 1878, pp. 457-66) and (November, 1878, pp 556-63), 561.

51. Robert Allerton Parker, *A Yankee Saint: John Humphrey Noyes and the Oneida Community* (New York, 1935), is an excellent biography with many quotations from Noyes' writings.

52. *Ibid.*, 67.

53. *Ibid.*, 182-3.

54. *Ibid.*, 183.

55. Phrenology was a nineteenth-century mixture of science, religion, and cultural reinforcement; both conservatives and liberals used its terminology, sometimes seriously, sometimes with tongue in cheek. Among the most popular phrenological manuals were Jessie A. Fowler, *A Manual of Mental Science* (London and New York, 1897); G. Spurzheim, *Outlines of Phrenology* (Boston, 1832), and Lorenzo N. Fowler, *Marriage* (New York, 1847).

56. Susa Young Gates, *History of the Young Ladies' Mutual Improvement Association,*

57. *History of the Relief Society of the Church of Jesus Christ of Latter Day Saints* (Salt Lake City, 1966), 18.

58. For example, see the testimony of Joseph Smith's wives in Don Cecil Corbett, *Mary Fielding Smith: Daughter of Britain: Portrait of Courage* (Salt Lake City, 1966), and the women in Edward W. Tullidge, *The Women of Mormonism* (New York, 1877). Tullidge quotes Eliza Snow Smith as saying that the Mormon Church "is the oracle of the greatest emancipation of womanhood and motherhood," 194. Mrs. Hannah T. King, in 1870, proposed a resolution opposing the federal bill outlawing polygamy which ended with an acknowledgment of the Church of the Latter Day Saints "as the only reliable safeguard of female virtue and innocence; and the only sure protection against the fearful sin of prostitution . . .", 385. There is also a considerable literature of anti-Mormonism, in which the Mormons are portrayed as despoilers of female virtue and degenerates of the worst sort, very much in the Maria Monk tradition.

59. Octavius Brooks Frothingham, *George Ripley* (Boston, 1882), 236-7.

40. MSS Letters of Sophia Dana Ripley and Charlotte Dana, Dana Papers, Massachusetts Historical Society, Boston, Massachusetts; March, 1848.

61. For example, Ellen in *Fanshawe*, Phoebe in *The House of the Seven Gables*, and Annie in "The Artist of the Beautiful" all represent the principle of the common humanity of the ordinary man rather than the singular arrogance of the individual.

62. Louis Auchincloss, *Pioneers and Caretakers: A Study of Nine American Women Novelists* (Minneapolis, 1965).

63. Sylvester Judd, *Margaret: A Tale of the Real and Ideal* (Boston, 1882; first edition, 1851),378-9.

64. Morris Raphael Cohen, *American Thought: A Critical Sketch* (New York, 1962; original edition, 1954), 41.

65. Orestes Brownson, *Works*, "Literature, Love and Marriage," Vol. XIV, 421.

7. DEFENDERS OF THE FAITH

Women Novelists of Religious Controversy in the Nineteenth Century

1. The list of best-sellers is taken from Frank Luther Mott, *Golden Multitudes*: The Story of Best Sellers in the United States, (New York, 1947); James D. Hart, The Popular Book: A History of America's Literary Taste, New York, 1950); and Jacob Blanck, *Peter Parley to Penrod*: A Bibliographical Description of the

Best-Loved American Juvenile Books, (New York, 1956). The accuracy of the lists in these references, as well as the exclusion of certain titles, is certainly subject to question. Nonetheless they are the best available research tool.

2. There are a number of very interesting books written explicitly on reform topics and feminism by, among others, Abigail Duniway, Lillie Devereaux Blake, Octave Thanet (Alice French), Ursula Gestefeld, Gertrude Atherton and Helen Gardiner. However, they did not achieve "best" or even "better" seller status. An English best-seller of 1893, *The Heavenly Twins* by Sarah Grand, dealt with the issue of social disease and, somewhat ambivalently, with the "New Woman."

3. David O. Moberg, *The Church as a Social Institution*: The Sociology of American Religion (Englewood Cliffs, N.J., 1962), and W. Seward Salisbury, *Religion in American Culture* (Homewood, Ill., 1964).

4. Neither the religious manual nor the religious novel was the exclusive property of women. Among the best-selling works by men in the same period were Parson Brownlow, *Parson Brownlow's Book* (1862), Edward Roe, *Barriers Burned Away* (1872) and *Opening a Chestnut Burr* (1874), Thomas Hughes, *Manliness of Christ* (1880), Lew Wallace, *Ben-Hur* (1880), William Stead, *If Christ Came to Chicago* (1894), Hanryk Sienkiewicz, *Quo Vadis?* (1896), James Allen, *The Choir Invisible* (1897), Hall Caine, *The Christian* (1897), and John Fox, *The Little Shepherd of Kingdom Come* (1903). Best-sellers by English women, especially Marie Corelli, also defended religion.

5. William Perry Fidler, *Augusta Evans Wilson: 1835-1909* (University, Alabama, 1951).

6. David Brion Davis, "Some Themes of Counter-Subversion: An Analysis of Anti-Masonic, Anti-Catholic, and Anti-Mormon Literature," *The Mississippi Valley Historical Review*, XLVII (September, 1960), 205-224.

7. Fidler, 64.

8. *Ibid.*, 54.

9. Mary Angela Bennett, *Elizabeth Stuart Phelps* (Philadelphia, 1939). The anonymous *Confessions of a Wife* (1902) is attributed to Mrs. Ward by the Library of Congress Catalogue and certainly is written according to her themes and idiom.

10. Elizabeth Stuart Phelps Ward, *Chapters from a Life* (Boston and New York, 1896), 107-8.

11. *Ibid.*, 251-2.

12. Elizabeth Stuart Phelps Ward and Herbert D. Ward, *The Master of the Magicians* (Boston and New York, 1890).

13. J.S.W., *Antidote to 'The Gates Ajar'* (New York, 1872).

14. Elizabeth Stuart Phelps Ward, *The Struggle for Immortality* (Boston and New York, 1889), 104.

15. Elizabeth Stuart Phelps Ward, *Austin Phelps:* A Memoir (New York, 1891), 57. Later novels by Mrs. Phelps also discussed the changing roles of women.

16. Ward, *Chapters from a Life*, 11.

17. [Monroe Stephens], *The 'A Singular Life' Reviewed and Gloucester Vindicated* (n.p., 1897).

18. Lorin Deland was the author of *Imagination in Business* (New York, 1909), and *At the Sign of the Dollar and Other Essays* (New York, 1917). Mrs. Deland published thirty-six volumes, but several of them were de-luxe editions of short stories included in other volumes. Her letters to Lilian Whiting, which discuss her spiritual ideas, are in the Manuscript and Rare Book Division of the Boston Public Library. Mrs. Deland, in her later novels, often dealt with the strong-minded business woman and with the question of more social and economic freedom for women.

19. Mrs. Humphry Ward, *A Writer's Recollections* (New York and London), 1918, 2 vol., I, 120.

20. Margaret Deland, *Golden Yesterdays* (New York, 1940), 224. Mrs. Deland wrote another autobiography, *If This Be I: As I Suppose It Be* (New York, 1935).

21. *Harper's Magazine*, 77 (November, 1888), 964-5.

22. This ideology owes much to the prevalence of "higher thought" religions, such as Theosophy, Unified Christianity, and New Thought, as well as to Christian Science.

23. William O'Neill, *Divorce in the Progressive Era* (New Haven, 1967).

8. MURDER MOST GENTEEL
The Mystery Novels of Anna Katharine Green

1. Edgar Allen Poe, writing in the 1840s, even when he used an American crime as his source, had it solved by a French detective working in Paris.

2. An account of *The Experiences of a Lady Detective* was published by "Anonyma" in 1862 in London. However the authorship is not known and Mrs. Paschall, the heroine, did not return. Wilkie Collins had a species of woman detective in Valeria Woodville, the heroine of *The Law and the Lady* published in 1875, but Mrs. Woodville appears in only one case, the effort to remove the "Not Proven" verdict in the trial of her husband for his first wife's murder. Nora Van Snoop, the "Lady Detective from New York" appears in the pages of Harmsworth's *London Magazine* in 1898, and Hagar Stanley, the Gypsy girl created by Fergus Hume, solves a series of cases in 1898 before marrying and going forth in a caravan stocked with books. Basic bibliographies in the history of novels of detection are Jacques Barzun and Wendell Hertig Taylor, *A Catalogue of Crime* (Harper & Row, New York: 1971); Ordean A. Hagen, *Who Done It*: A Guide to Detective, Mystery and Suspense Fiction (R.R. Bowker Co., New York and London: 1969); and Eric Osborne, *Victorian Detective Fiction Catalogue* (The Bodley Head, London, Sydney and Toronto: 1966).

3. Howard Haycraft, *Murder For Pleasure*: The Life and Times of the Detective Story (D. Appleton-Century, New York: 1941), 83, and Joseph Wood Crutch, "Only a Detective Story," (April, 1944), 181.

4. Julian Symons, *Bloody Murders*: from the detective story to the crime novel: a history (Faber & Faber, London: 1972), 46.

5. Erik Routley, *The Puritan Pleasures of the Detective Story*: a personal monograph (Victor Gollancz, London: 1972), 22.

6.	William O. Aydelette, "The Detective Story as a Historical Source," in Francis M. Nevins, Jr., *The Mystery Writer's Art* (Bowling Green University Popular Press, Bowling Green, Ohio: 1970), 325.

7.	Wilkie Collins, *The Woman in White* (1860) is more a suspense than an actual crime story, although a criminal action takes place. *The Moonstone* (1868), *No Name* (1874) and *The Law and the Lady* (1875) all have detection as part of their plot and all have interesting and strong-minded women doing at least part of the detecting.

8.	See Barzun and Taylor, *Catalogue of Crime, passim.*

9.	Grant M. Overton, *The Women Who Make Our Novels* (Moffat, Yard, and Co., New York: 1918), 204-14.

10.	Haycraft, *Murder for Pleasure*, 83-84.

11.	Willard Huntingdon Wright, "The Great Detective Stories" (1927) in Haycraft, *Murder for Pleasure*, 41.

12.	Dorothy L. Sayers, "Introduction to the Omnibus of Crime" (1929) in Haycraft, *Murder for Pleasure*, 79, and 92.

13.	Ralph Harper, *World of the Thriller* (Press of Case Western Reserve University, Cleveland, Ohio: 1967); A.A. Allinson and F.E. Hotchin, *Mystery and Crime* (F.W. Cheshire, Melbourne, Canberra, Sydney: 1968); A.E. Murch, *The Development of the Detective Novel* (Philosophical Library, New York: 1958) and Sutherland Scott, *Blood in Their Ink:* The Modern Detective Novel (Stanley, Paul and Co., London, New York, Toronto: 1953) all treat Green as a purely historical figure, chiefly remembered for the creation of Gryce.

14.	Serge Radine, *Quelques Aspects du roman policier psychologique* (Editions des Mont-Blanc, Geneve: 196), 145-147.

15.	John Dickson Carr, "The Locked-Room Lecture," in Howard Haycraft, ed., *The Art of the Mystery Story* (Simon & Schuster, New York: 1946), 279.

16.	Edward Wagenknecht, ed., *Murder By Gaslight*: Victorian Tales (Prentice-Hall, New York: 1949).

17.	Symons, *Bloody Murders*, 64. Some historians of the genre refuse to consider her work except as a historical foot-note. Ellery Queen takes this position in *The Female of the Species*: The great women detectives and criminals (Little, Brown and Co., Boston: 1943) and so does H. Douglas Thomson, *Masters of Mystery*: a study of the detective story (Williams Collins Sons and Co., London: 1931).

18.	H. Meriam Allen, "Anna Katharine Green—Weaver of Mysteries," *The Book News Monthly*, 35 (September 1916), 51-52; "Anna Katharine Green," Carlin T. Kindilian, *Dictionary of Notable American Women* (Cambridge, Massachusetts, The Belknap Press of Harvard University: 1971), II, 79-80. Her later life as Mrs. Charles Rohlfs, wife of the Buffalo designer of ornamental iron and furniture, (they were married in 1884), saw little financial pressure but a gracious life-style to be maintained.